Gun Digest Book of

FOLDING KNIVES

By Jack Lewis and B.R. Hughes

DBI BOOKS, INC., NORTHFIELD, ILLINOIS

ON THE COVER: Clockwise, from upper left: Camillus, Gutmann, Schrade, A.G. Russell, and Gerber folding knives. Photos courtesy of manufacturers, except Schrade and Gerber folders by Dean A. Grennell.

EDITORIAL DIRECTOR
BOB SPRINGER

CONTRIBUTING EDITORS
ROGER COMBS
DEAN A. GRENNELL

ART DIRECTOR
FELICITY WHITER

ASSOCIATE ARTIST
JOHN VITALE

COPY EDITORS
DEBORAH PAYNE
RUSTY SPRINGER

PRODUCTION COORDINATOR
BETTY BURRIS

ASSOCIATE PUBLISHER
SHELDON L. FACTOR

Produced by

Charger Productions

ISBN 0-695-80839-7   Library of Congress Catalog Card Number 77-82700

CONTENTS

THE AUTHORS

B.R. "BILL" HUGHES, a native of Arkansas who now resides in the Lone Star State, has written extensively on the subject of handmade knives in recent years, with articles published in more than a dozen different magazines. He is currently on the staffs of two outdoor-orientated monthly publications. He launched his outdoor writing career in the early 1960s after having worked for a number of daily newspapers in various capacities.

Hughes holds two college degrees, has taught journalism at the college level and is currently public relations director for a Texas community college.

JACK LEWIS, editor and publisher of GUN WORLD Magazine for the past eighteen years, has pursued a wide and varied career, ranging from ranch hand and farm worker to Hollywood stuntman. He deserted the last calling after suffering a broken back; the author of a number of novels, many of them dealing with the Marine Corps, he has been laborer, pea picker, structural steel worker, newspaper reporter, private detective, process server, horse wrangler and screen and television writer.

A veteran of World War II and Korean actions, he is a Lieutenant Colonel in the Marine Corps Reserve and was on active duty in 1970 to pursue a special study in Vietnam. As a knife collector, he favors those that can be put to practical use in the field. He also is publisher of BOW & ARROW and HORSE and HORSEMAN Magazines.

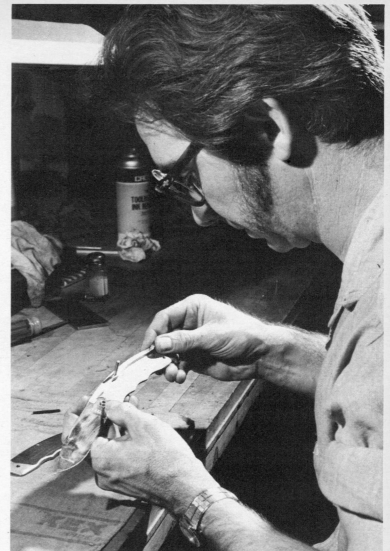

Ron Lake, inspecting innards of his distinctive folder, is credited with starting current boom in handmade folding knives when he displayed his first creation at 1971 Knifemakers Guild show held in Houston, Texas.

Chapter I

FOLDING KNIVES & TERMINOLOGY

In This Growing Field Of Cutlery There Are Some Terms That The Fixed-Blade Buff May Not Find Familiar!

THERE ARE knives, then there are folding knives.

There is nothing new about folders, and the history of this style will be discussed at considerable length in the following chapter. However, it must be pointed out that there seemingly is greater interest in folders today than at any previous time.

In terms of custom cutlery, even a decade ago there was little interest in folding models. It was just a tool that a lot of us carried around like car keys and a cigarette lighter. To be sure, Bill Scagel, the first great crafter of handmade knives in the Twentieth Century, was offering a few as early as 1910, but in truth there was little of a select nature available, nor did anyone seem to care.

It would be difficult to prove, but it seems likely that the current boom in handmade folding knives dates back to the 1971 Houston Gun Show. This also was the site of the

Large, skillfully decorated pivot pin is clearly evident on this knife made by A.J. Freiling. Large pin does much to make possible a blade with little or no sideplay when open, even after many years of continuous use.

second annual meeting of the Knifemakers Guild and an impressive number of makers descended upon this Texas city to set up displays. Virtually all of the big names of custom cutlery were there, but an unknown maker from Illinois stole the spotlight from the stars. Ron Lake, whose name is now revered by aficionados of the custom blade, appeared with a single folding knife he had made; it is not an exaggeration to state that Lake could have sold that one knife at least fifty times for a staggering price! Unbelievable as it may seem, that was the first such knife that this talented lad had made, but, today, Ron Lake is acknowledged by many as the pick of the pack when it comes to handmade folders.

Today, the number of cutlers who offer similar knives are legion. There now are, in fact, more makers who offer folders than do not! One maker recently commented, "I had quite a few reservations before I worked up enough courage to try my first folding model. I had been making

W.F. Moran, left, has exhibited a keen interest in the development of superior knife steels down through the years. During 1973 Knifemakers Guild show in Kansas City, Moran unveiled his line using Damascus steel, a major breakthrough.

sheath knives for several years, and I thought I was pretty good, but that first folder almost convinced me otherwise. I kept telling myself, 'So-and-so can make 'em, and I'm as good a knifemaker as he is!' Since then, I've made maybe five hundred folders, and I'd much rather make them. To me, they are much more challenging and thus more satisfying."

This may illustrate current trends: at the 1976 guild show in Dallas, most makers who offered folding models enjoyed an excellent trade, but those with only fixed blade knives on their tables were almost overlooked. Several good knivemakers sold only one or two knives, while the lads with the folders were selling every specimen on their tables!

As the demand has increased, so have prices. It is easily possible to spend as much as $250 for a more-or-less standard handmade folding knife, but it is just as possible to purchase an excellent custom folder for well under $100. Some of the makers' pricing brings to mind a recently published statement concerning British shotguns: "They make an excellent $3000 shotgun for $8000."

While it is evident that the folding knife market is the hottest thing in handmade knives at this time, it still is possible to find some real bargains, as some of the cutlers who specialize in this area have not yet established themselves on the national level. Accordingly, there are some fantastic $60 and $75 knives available at this writing in mid-1977.

On the other hand, you'll pay a hefty sum for one of

A.G. Russell, one of the nation's leading knife authorities, recently commented that, in his opinion, the future for imaginative and capable cutlers will be even brighter than it has been in the immediate past.

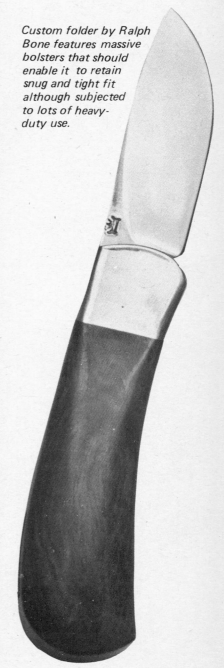

Custom folder by Ralph Bone features massive bolsters that should enable it to retain snug and tight fit although subjected to lots of heavy-duty use.

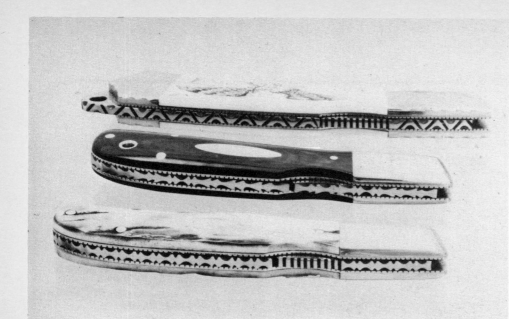

Three exquisite custom folders from shop of Harvey McBurnette. Close examination reveals fine overall fit of various elements.

these knives with a big name on it. But because of the long waiting period for such knives, it generally is possible to turn right around and double your money! The right custom knife is still a good investment.

Naturally, folding knives have been big business with the factories for years, representing the bulk of knives these firms sell. Moreover, there are thousands of collectors who specialize in production folders bearing such names as Case, Western, Ka-Bar, Schrade, etc. Until recently, if you wanted a good folder you purchased a factory model, and there still is no better bargain than a good quality knife bearing the trademark of a large plant.

If one is just venturing into the world of the folding knife, there are a number of terms with which one should become familiar. The illustrations accompanying this chapter are worth thousands of words, but here are a few terms that should be in every buff's vocabulary:

Nail nick — the indentation in the blade that is used to open the blade. There should be an adequate nick in each blade, and it should be placed in an accessible spot.

Pivot pin — the pin that holds the blade in the handle. As the name implies, the blade pivots on this pin, which on

An array of fine factory-produced folding knives offering excellent value to the buyer. From left to right are the products of Browning, Puma, Precise, Gerber, Buck, and Jet-Aer; all fine bargains.

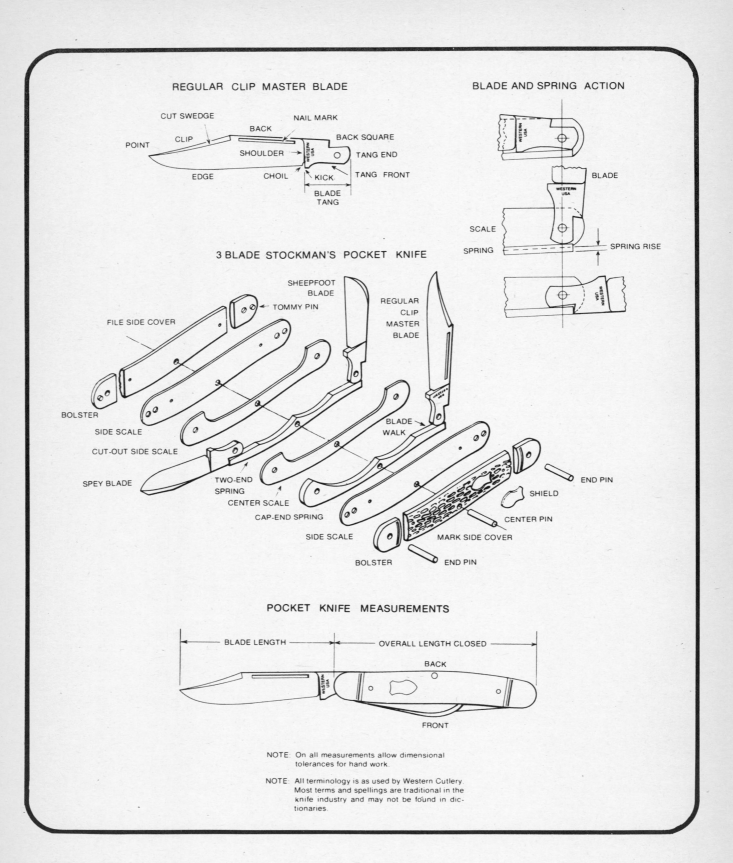

REGULAR CLIP MASTER BLADE

CUT SWEDGE NAIL MARK
BACK
POINT CLIP BACK SQUARE
SHOULDER TANG END
EDGE CHOIL KICK TANG FRONT
BLADE
TANG

BLADE AND SPRING ACTION

BLADE
SCALE
SPRING SPRING RISE

3 BLADE STOCKMAN'S POCKET KNIFE

SHEEPFOOT
BLADE
TOMMY PIN
FILE SIDE COVER
REGULAR
CLIP
MASTER
BLADE
BOLSTER
SIDE SCALE
CUT-OUT SIDE SCALE
SPEY BLADE
BLADE
WALK
TWO-END
SPRING
CENTER SCALE
CAP-END SPRING
SIDE SCALE
BOLSTER
END PIN
SHIELD
CENTER PIN
MARK SIDE COVER
END PIN

POCKET KNIFE MEASUREMENTS

BLADE LENGTH OVERALL LENGTH CLOSED
BACK
FRONT

NOTE: On all measurements allow dimensional
tolerances for hand work.

NOTE: All terminology is as used by Western Cutlery.
Most terms and spellings are traditional in the
knife industry and may not be found in dic-
tionaries.

The maker of these fine folders is custom maker Gary Kelley, a talented newcomer who is well on his way to establishing a national reputation.

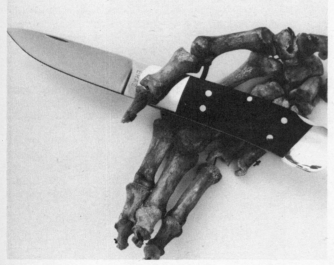

Russ Andrews, who made this handsome folder, became a professional cutler in the early Seventies and today enjoys top ranking among custom folding knifemakers.

many models is made of stainless steel. A small pin is to be avoided, as it obviously will be weak and a loose blade will develop. It sometimes is called an endpin.

Bolster – the metal tips at the blade end of the knife. If there are blades on both ends, there will bolsters also on both ends. The bolsters should be well-fitted and made of tough, durable material.

Liners – the material between the handle slabs and the blades. Generally, these are made of brass, but they may also be made of stainless steel. Liners are sometimes called side scales and the fit of the liners to the handle slabs should be airtight.

There are other specialized terms for folders, but if you know these few you can pretty well speak the lingo.

In subsequent chapters, discussion will be devoted to exactly what to look for when purchasing a folding knife. In a nutshell, a knife should show evident signs of being well-made. There should be no gaps; the blades should open and close with a snap; and once closed they should stay that way until you want them open. A blade that drops or droops from the handle after being closed is a positive sign of a poorly made and/or designed knife! When a blade is opened, it should remain in the open position and show no sideplay.

A.G. Russell, considered one of the nation's leading knife authorities, recently said that, in his opinion, we are going to see an even greater interest in well-made knives in the forthcoming years than has been the case even in the boom years of the 1970s.

This is not to say there will be more custom makers than is currently the case. On the contrary, the actual number of cutlers probably will decline, but the overall quality will go up, and so will demand and prices. In addition, the factories will continue to turn out better and better products.

All of which is simply one way of saying that the person who loves fine cutlery seems to have great years ahead!

Chapter 2

...AND IN THE BEGINNING

Folding Knives Originated Before The Birth Of Christ, But Design Changes Are Relatively New!

THE WHEEL MAY hold some sort of reputation as man's most useful invention and it no doubt is among the oldest, but the folding pocketknife has to have some sort of reputation of its own in this direction. Specimens of pocketknives have been unearthed from the ancient ruins of Rome and Pompeii, suggesting it was a household item long before the birth of Christ.

In America, the folding knife — usually referred to as a jackknife in early written records — came ashore with the early English and French explorers. There are recorded documents referring to its use in Europe as early as 1672, and during the Revolutionary War soldiers on both sides were equipped with some variation of folding knife. In fact, two of the colonies — New Hampshire and New York — required that each of their militiamen be equipped with such a knife.

Regarding its origin, the term "jackknife" has come in for a lot of discussion over the years. But Lord Hale — an Englishman and etymologist of the era — may have come as close as any in tracing the origin in his writings of about 1776, stating that "the etymology of the word remained unknown till, not many years ago, an old knife was found having the inscription 'Jacques de Liege,' the name of the cutler." The only problem with accepting this as the true origin of the term lies in the fact that students of etymology have failed to find any mention of a Belgian cutler who signed his work with such a signature — or, for that matter, any such craftsman in the Belgian city in that period.

From historical examples that have been found in ruins and otherwise unearthed, it appears that the early folding models were rather large — hardly what one would carry in the pocket of his Levi's in the field these days — and invariably had only one blade. When closed, most were five to seven inches in length, although a few Eighteenth Century styles apparently were as short as four inches, folded.

The smaller type of folding knife, classified as a penknife and built with two blades, apparently became popular sometime in the Nineteenth Century.

Our first recollection of mention of the Barlow knife comes from the works of Mark Twain, who made it obvious that such knives were highly valued by lads of the post-Civil War era.

However, the knife seemingly was manufactured under that name — or at least the design came to be known as the Barlow — much earlier in history than the period in which Tom Sawyer and Huck Finn became famous in American literature. There is mention in American writings as early as the late Eighteenth Century, and the indication is that this type of knife had been in use for some decades before that.

There is not even an indication as to how the knife came to be called the Barlow, although it is suspected that the first knives of such design were manufactured by a man named Russell Barlow. But history has revealed no such cutler to date.

In recent years, several manufacturers, including Schrade, have reintroduced replicas of the original Barlow design and have found a ready market. Perhaps part of the renewed popularity is a reflection of the past aside from nostalgia. The popularity of the Barlow was among youngsters and the less-monied classes because it was relatively cheap, yet well made and functional. The original version was kept low in price, with the blade forged from high-carbon steel, while the bone handle was rough, showing little attempt to polish it off. In actuality, the original Barlows were somewhat crude in manufacture, if the early models we have seen are any indication. A feature of the Barlow was the long bolster, extending a full third the length of the knife handle, which was meant to give it added strength. In some of the styles being made today, an additional blade has been introduced, but the long bolster still is retained for cosmetic purposes, if nothing else.

The first known manufacturer of knives in the Barlow pattern was one John Russell, and versions of his style still were appearing as late as the 1920s. These were the same rough-looking models described in the preceding paragraph, but the sturdiness of the knife could not be argued. It was made for using.

The penknife, mentioned earlier, became the going pocketknife for most gentlemen of the Eighteenth Century and before. Small in size and especially sturdy, it was designed specifically for sharpening the heavy goose and turkey quills that were used as writing instruments in those early days prior to the introduction of the steel pen more than a hundred years ago. Most of these knives were less than three inches in length, folded, and were light in construction, limiting their use pretty much to sharpening quills and cleaning fingernails. The original designs were limited to one blade, although models with two, three and even four blades began to appear in America shortly after the Revolutionary War.

Actually, there has been little change in the design of pocketknives since 1600 A.D., although a number of blades have been designed for specific uses along the way. Some of these designs were successful, and continue today in the products of some of the leading companies, while others of limited use and interest died with time.

For a time, farriers, for example, tended to favor folding knives that incorporated hooks for removal of rocks from the frog of a horse's hoof. Some even had hoof files folded into the handles. Today, though, we have yet to see a modern farrier who uses any kind of folding knife for his horseshoeing work. Most use fixed-blade models that have a hook at the end for trimming hard-to-reach crevices around the frog. The farrier of today tends to favor a full-length rasp, making much shorter work of shoeing a horse rather than attempting to trim away the hard hoof material with a short, inefficient rasp, as was the case with the folding knife.

Fishermen then came into consideration, with knives especially designed to aid in the removal of hooks, as well as the incorporation of scalers on the backs of the blades.

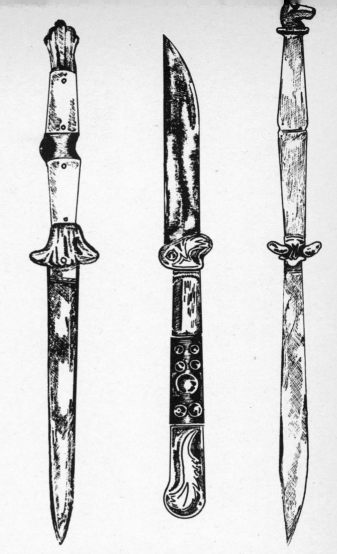

Artist's rendition of these folding knives of the late Sixteenth and early Seventeenth Centuries illustrates that the fixed-blade influence still was in evidence. By standards of a century later they were quite crude.

In time, special knives — still being used extensively today by the average citizen as well as stockmen — were designed for use by cattle ranchers — incorporating castration blades, et al; seamen wanted a special knife and one was designed with a marlin spike to aid in splicing ropes and cables; nurserymen came up with a design for a hooked-blade pruning knife; and there were all sorts of designs for carpet layers, linoleum layers, electricians and plumbers, to name a few of the trades that came to demand specialized treatment by the cutlers of the nation.

The changes over the centuries have been in the blade designs and uses. The basic form has remained pretty much the same, although there have been numerous variations in handle materials down through the ages.

One of the earliest handle materials was ivory, which appears to have been used by the Romans and perhaps the Greeks. For the less affluent, bone became the standard, the porous materials often being dyed in various colors.

According to respected historians, as late as the beginning of the Nineteenth Century, bone still was the most widely used handle material, although mother-of-pearl, tortoise shell, some types of animal antlers and metals such as iron, brass and even gold were incorporated in handle

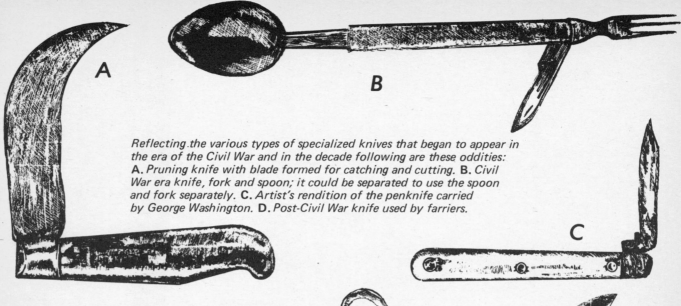

Reflecting the various types of specialized knives that began to appear in the era of the Civil War and in the decade following are these oddities: **A.** Pruning knife with blade formed for catching and cutting. **B.** Civil War era knife, fork and spoon; it could be separated to use the spoon and fork separately. **C.** Artist's rendition of the penknife carried by George Washington. **D.** Post-Civil War knife used by farriers.

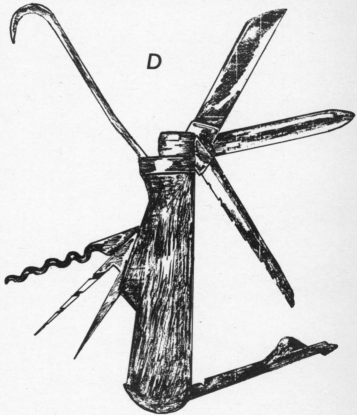

designs. Horn and wood were used, too, in knives favored by the masses. It also should be pointed out that the materials listed were used with most of the fixed-blade knives of the various eras.

To bring knives even more within the realm of possession for the masses, synthetics and plastics of the day began to appear on knife handles in the decade following the Civil War. During that era, the liners began to be made of brass, most of it die-stamped in the beginnings of mass production. Bolsters began to be plated with nickel over the iron bolster, with chrome, and, by the turn of the century, many bolsters were being made of aluminum. The introduction of chrome steel, replacing carbon steel for blades, came about in the early 1920s.

Today's so-called Swiss Army knife — now made by numerous other countries, including Japan — is not as new as one might think. In fact, it might well have been inspired by the gimmick knives of the Civil War period that could have combined between their liners half a dozen or more different tools, ranging from the earlier mentioned hook for removing stones from horse's hooves to a leather awl, corkscrew, file, saw blade, screwdriver, can opener and almost any other type of tool that might be enclosed within the framework of the design. During the Civil War period, although not issued by the government, a popular item with soldiers was a combination knife, fork and spoon that came apart in such a manner that the knife became a separate item from the combination fork and spoon.

The types and styles of pocketknives developed for use by various armed forces around the world is almost endless. It was a common statement among Marines during World War II that "a man without a knife is like a ship without a sail." At that time, the Marine Corps issued huge fixed-blade K-Bar knives to every man and officer, but more often than not, the individual carried that battle blade on his belt, with a more practical type of folding knife in his pocket.

In recent years, the custom knifemakers, as well as the manufacturers have started to move away from the large, bulky folding knives that require a scabbard to carry them on the belt. The trend is toward flatter, more compact handles so that the knife can be carried in the pocket without making an unsightly bulge. Such manufacturers as Gerber Legendary Blades in Oregon have continually designed new concepts, proving that the same blade as that

of the bulky sportsman's knife can be contained in a flat, reasonably unbulky handle and do the same work of skinning out a deer or whatever else might be desired.

Although the folding knife has been with us since before the birth of Christ and it appears that all possible variations have been manufactured, designers now are working in a highly competitive market and continue to try for new designs that will intrigue the potential buyer.

With the recent revival in the interest of turquoise and Navajo Indian jewelry, one Southwestern craftsman is doing quite well by purchasing standard knives from manufacturers, removing the wooden handles, then inlaying the handle area with turquoise, red coral, jet and other materials of the Indian craftsman.

Two-Blade Jack Knives with Cocobolo and Ebony Handles.

No. 6K16831 Wilbert Pocket Knife. Has rosewood handle, steel lining, iron bolster. Length of handle, 3½ inches. Length, with large blade open, 6 inches. Price....................20c
If by mail, postage extra, 4 cents.

No. 6K16835 Wilbert Equal End Pocket Knife. Has cocoa handle, German silver bolsters, caps and shield, brass lined, finished inside and out. Length of handle, 3⅜ inches. Length, with large blade open, 5⅞ inches. Price....................39c
If by mail, postage extra, 5 cents.

Wilbert Easy Opener, 48c.

No. 6K16858 Wilbert Hand Fitting High Grade Easy Opener Knife. Ebony handle, German silver bolsters, caps and shield, brass lined. Length of handle, 3¾ inches. Length, with large blade open, 6½ inches. Price....................48c
If by mail, postage extra, 5 cents.

No. 6K16863 Wilbert Missouri Favorite, has clip point saber blade, made of full 12-gauge steel. Has ebony handle, long German silver bolsters, caps and shield, brass lined, finished inside and out. Length of handle, 3¾ inches. Length, with large blade open, 6⅝ inches. Price....................49c
If by mail, postage extra, 6 cents.

Two-Blade Jack Knives with Stag Handles.

No. 6K16880 Wilbert Pocket Knife, clip point, stag handle, two blades, steel lining, iron bolster. This is a standard size, full weight knife; is durable, and will give splendid satisfaction. Length of handle, 3½ inches. Length, with large blade open, 6⅛ inches. Price....................23c
If by mail, postage extra, 5 cents.

No. 6K16885 Wilbert Razor Blade Jack Knife, stag handle, steel lining, iron bolster. Length of handle, 3½ inches. Length, with large blade open, 6 inches. Price...33c
If by mail, postage extra, 5 cents.

No. 6K16886 Two-Blade Barlow Pattern Jack Knife, steel lined, 1¼-inch iron bolster, bone handle. This is the original Barlow pattern. Length of knife, 3½ inches. Length, with spear blade open, 6 inches. Price....................25c
If by mail, postage extra, 5 cents.

No. 6K16889 Wilbert Stag Handle Chain Knife, clip point, two blades, steel lining, iron bolsters and caps, German silver shield, with chain of suitable length to fasten over button. Length of handle, 3⅜ inches. Length, with large blade open, 6⅛ inches. Price....................38c
If by mail, postage extra, 6 cents.

No. 6K16894 Wilbert Jack Knife, stag handle, swell butt, steel lining, iron bolster, German silver shield. Length of handle, 3⅜ inches. Length with large blade open, 6⅛ inches. Price....................37c
If by mail, postage extra, 5 cents.

No. 6K16902 Wilbert Carpenters' Sensible Knife, having two large blades, one with clip point and one sheep's foot or carpenter's marking blade. The blades of this knife are made of 11-gauge steel; has stag handle, steel lining, iron bolster, German silver shield, finished inside and out. Length of handle, 3½ inches. Length, with large blade open, 6⅛ inches. Price..........43c
If by mail, postage extra, 5 cents.

No. 6K16907 Wilbert Gentlemen's Jack Knife, stag handle, German silver bolsters, caps and shield, brass lining, thoroughly finished in every particular, inside and out. Length of handle, 3⅜ inches. Length with large blade open, 5⅞ inches. Price.....(Postage extra, 5 cents.)....42c

> Wilbert Cutlery is guaranteed, and if found unsatisfactory money and transportation charges will be refunded. Wilbert Cutlery is sold exclusively by us.

Two-Blade Stag Handle Jack Knives, 45 Cents.

No. 6K16913 Wilbert Little Giant Equal End Pocket Knife, with saber clip blade, stag handle, German silver bolsters, caps and shield, brass lined, finished inside and out. The amount of work which this knife will do is something never before attained in a knife of its size. Length of handle, 3⅜ inches. Length with large blade open, 5¾ inches. Price....(Postage extra, 5 cents)...45c

No. 6K16917 Wilbert Easy Opener Pocket Knife, with stag handle, German silver bolsters, caps and shield, brass lining. Finished inside and out. Length of handle, 3½ inches. Length with large blade open, 6¼ inches. Price....................47c
If by mail, postage extra, 5 cents.

No. 6K16921 Wilbert Equal End Knife, has stag handle, brass lining, German silver bolsters, caps and shield. Length of handle, 3⅝ inches. Length with large blade open, 6¼ inches. Price....................46c
If by mail, postage extra, 5 cents.

No. 6K16924 Wilbert Solid Worth Jack Knife, stag knife handle, brass lining, finished inside and out, iron bolsters and caps, German silver shield. Length of handle, 3½ inches. Length with large blade open 6¼ inches. Price..(Postage extra, 5 cents)..42c

No. 6K16934 Wilbert High Grade Easy Opener Jack Knife, stag handle, German silver bolsters, caps and shield, brass lined, finely finished throughout. Length of handle, 3⅝ inches. Length with blade open, 6⅛ inches. Price....(Postage extra, 5 cents.)....50c

No. 6K16939 Wilbert Texas Toothpick, has stag handle, German silver bolster and shield, brass lining, finely finished inside and out. Clip point saber blade. While the blade is long and slim, the peculiar shape makes it very strong and durable as well as an excellent whittler. Length of handle, 3⅞ inches. Length with large blade open, 7 inches.
Price....(Postage extra, 5 cents.)....51c

> **THE SURPRISINGLY LOW REDUCED PRICES prevailing in this catalogue mean greater savings to our customers than ever before.**

67c

No. 6K16944 Wilbert Sensible Cattlemen's Knife with saber clip point blade and spaying blade 3 inches long from bolster. The practical man will readily see the great advantage in the length of spaying blade in this knife. Has stag handle, German silver bolsters and shield, brass lined, highly finished throughout. Length of handle, 4 inches. Length, with clip point blade open, 7 inches. Price....................67c
If by mail, postage extra, 5 cents.

58c

No. 6K16965 Wilbert Hunter's Pride Knife. It has stag handle, long, heavy German silver bolsters, caps and shield, brass lining, highly finished inside and out. The blades open and close freely without wearing. The knife blade is always true in the center, and it is these little points, to which we pay so much attention, that cause our knives to give better satisfaction than those you can procure from any other dealer. Length of handle, 4¼ inches. Length with large blade open, 8 inches. Price....................58c
If by mail, postage extra, 6 cents.

Hunting Knives.

60c

No. 6K16970 Wilbert Daniel Boone Hunting Knife. Cocobolo handle, steel lined, iron bolsters and caps, saber clip point blade. Length of handle, 5¼ inches. Entire length with blade open, 9½ inches. A large, strong, well finished knife, fully warranted. Price....................60c
If by mail, postage extra, 7 cents.

Lock Blade Hunter.

70c

No. 6K16973 Wilbert Arkansas Lock Blade Hunter. A knife in which nearly every cent of the cost is spent in quality and not looks. It has clip point saber blade, flush lock back so blade cannot shut on the fingers, curved stag handle which just fits the hand nicely, fancy iron bolsters, steel lining. Length of handle, 4⅝ inches. Length with blade open, 8½ inches. Price..........70c
If by mail, postage extra, 7 cents.

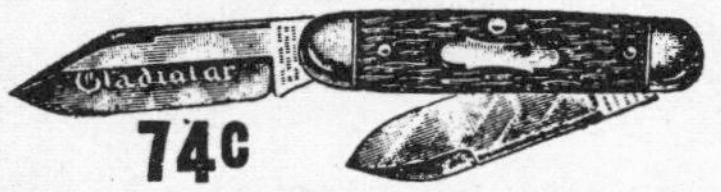

74c

No. 6K16997 Wilbert Gladiator Double Ender, has stag handle, German silver bolsters and shield, brass lined and finely finished throughout. Has saber clip and spear point blades. Length of handle, 4¼ inches. Length with spear blade open, 7½ inches. Price, 74c
If by mail, postage extra, 5 cents.

Pearl Handle Jack Knives.

No. 6K17007 Wilbert Gentlemen's Pearl Handle Jack Knife. Has pearl handle, German silver bolsters, caps, and shield. German silver lining, satin finish. The blades are full crocus polished. The knife is in every way finished as finely as the best penknife you ever saw. Length of handle, 3⅜ inches; length with large blade open, 5⅞ inches. Price....................90c
If by mail, postage extra, 5 cents.

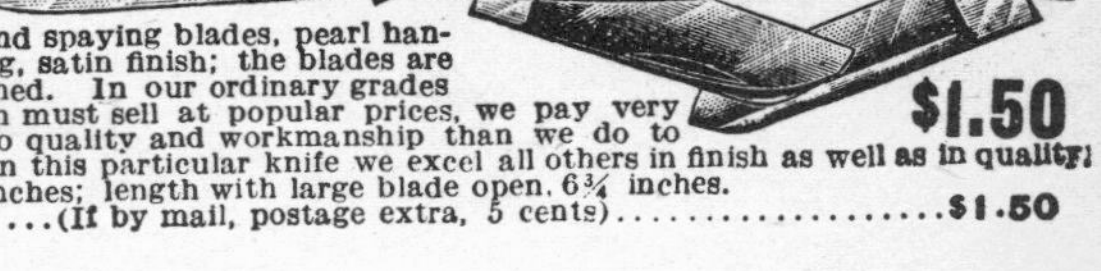

No. 6K17025 Wilbert Montana Beauty Stockmen's Knife. Has clip, sheep's foot and spaying blades, pearl handle, German silver lining, satin finish; the blades are beautifully crocus polished. In our ordinary grades of knives, knives which must sell at popular prices, we pay very much more attention to quality and workmanship than we do to beauty and finish, but in this particular knife we excel all others in finish as well as in quality. Length of handle, 3⅞ inches; length with large blade open, 6¾ inches.
Price..............(If by mail, postage extra, 5 cents)..........$1.50

$1.50

$1.12

No. 6K16976 Wilbert Hudson Bay Hunting Knife. A very nicely finished hunting knife. Clip point saber blade, flush lock back, curved stag handle, fancy German silver bolsters, caps and linings. Length of handle, 5¼ inches. Length with blade open, 9¾ inches. Price....................$1.12
If by mail, postage extra, 7 cents.

For other Hunting Knives and a full line of Hunter's Goods see Sporting Goods Department.

Pruning Knives.

35c

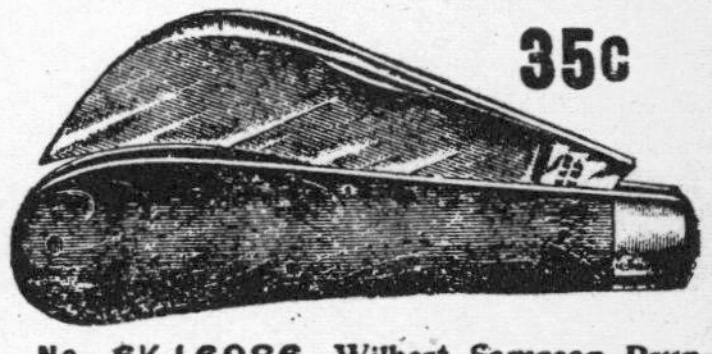

No. 6K16986 Wilbert Sampson Pruning Knife. Blade made of 10-gauge steel. The shape of blade, method of grinding, etc., being according to the ideas of one of the best fruit growers in the country, who had the original made just exactly the way he wanted it regardless of expense. Has cocobolo handle. Length of handle, 4 inches. Length with blade open, 7 inches.
Price....................35c
If by mail, postage extra, each, 6 cents.

Two-Blade Double End Knives with Stag Handles.

No. 6K16991 Wilbert New England Workmen's Knife. A great favorite with carpenters, cabinet makers and other woodworkers. It has stag handle, German silver bolsters and shield, brass lining, finely finished and polished inside and out. Length of handle, 3¾ inches. Length with large blade open, 6⅛ inches.
Price....................52c
If by mail, postage extra, 4 cents.

No. 6K16993 Wilbert Double End Two-Blade Stag Handle Brass Lined Knife, one large clip blade, one pen blade, polished brass bolsters and shield. Length of handle, 3½ inches; length with large blade open, 6 inches. This is a well finished and fitted knife, guaranteed to give satisfaction.
Price....................49c
If by mail, postage extra, 4 cents.

$1.43

No. 6K17017 Wilbert Ranchero Cattle Knife. Has pearl handle, German silver bolsters and shield, German silver lining, satin finish. The blades are full crocus polished. It cannot fail to give satisfaction to those who want a knife of superior cutting qualities, workmanship and beauty. Length of handle, 3⅝ inches; length with large blade open, 6¾ inches. Price....................$1.43
If by mail, postage extra, 5 cents.

The page above is reproduced from a Sears, Roebuck & Co. catalog of 1908 and reflects the materials, quality and price ranges of that particular era. For today's everyday knife carrier, quality has become important.

Chapter 3

LET'S LOOK AT MATERIALS

Knowing Something About What Goes Into A Knife Can Save You Money And Unhappiness

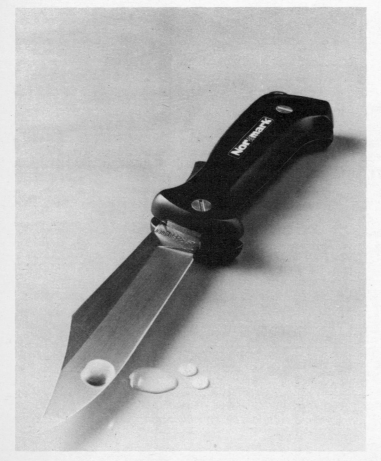

Stainless-steel blades, such as the one on this Normark folder, are better used in folding knives than in most fixed-blade models, as is explained fully in the text.

Skilled maker Lloyd Hale opens his electric heat-treat oven. With more custom cutlers beginning to handle this facet on their own, superior blades are being produced.

BACK WHEN THE world was a simpler place and there was time for pleasant delusions, we all dreamed of a marvelous super-knife steel.

This material would be highly stain resistant, capable of being hardened to Rockwell C 62-64 with good edge-holding capabilities, but with nary a trace of brittleness. This steel also would have exceptional tensile strength and, perhaps most important, it would be extremely easy to sharpen when it finally did get dull from frequent use.

For all practical purposes, you can file this away with stories about the Easter bunny, Santa Claus, the pot of gold at the end of the rainbow, and little green men.

There are, to be sure, some modern steels that have most of the features listed above. It is not difficult to find a steel that can be hardened to Rockwell C 62, hold an edge pretty well, resist staining and be tough. Sad to say, such a knife is difficult to sharpen.

There are other steels that take an edge easily and are extremely tough, but they either stain or lose that nice cutting edge all too rapidly.

If we use the middle 1950s as the actual beginning of the age of the American handmade knife, we also can use that date as the birth of modern cutlers' quest for a superior knife steel. For perhaps a decade, virtually all good quality knives either were forged or ground from 1095 or a similar good, simple steel — such blades were good. But down through the last fifteen years or so a number of cutlers have led the drive for a better knife steel. Men who deserve much credit in this area include R.W. Loveless, T.M. Dowell, Chubby Hueske and W.F. Moran, Jr., plus a few others.

These men came up with a number of steels that have not seen a great deal of use even today. Included among such steels could be listed F8 and M2, both of which have seen only limited use. Some of these steels cut well but leaned towards brittleness; others were both tough and wear-resistant, but when they finally became dull they were virtually impossible to sharpen. Bob Loveless came up with a dandy super steel back in the late 1960s, but it had two flaws; it would rust if you looked at it hard, and it was too expensive for the mills to produce.

A good deal has been written concerning this ongoing search for a superior steel. Gradually, however, it has become evident that there are available a number of excellent cutlery steels: F8 is great, provided the resulting blade is used only for flesh cutting or skinning; for heavy-duty use, it is less than great. Moreover, an F8 blade is difficult to sharpen. For all-around purposes, today's better steels include D2, 154CM, A2 and 01. For all of that, the perfect cutlery steel is not yet with us and perhaps never will be.

The custom makers order steel in small batches by industry standards, and it is not profitable for a steel mill to spend large sums of money developing a cutlery steel that will, at best, find only a small market with restricted application. To put it bluntly, there just isn't any profit.

Available steels meet the needs of the major knife factories. This is not intended as a criticism of factory knives. They use good steel, and it is a miracle that they can offer such high-grade products for the modest prices involved. It does mean that those who desire something better for custom knives must use steels that were de-

T.M. Dowell, who made these attractive and functional folders, was a pioneer in the quest for better steel for knives in the late Sixties. He was among the first to use such steels as D2 and F8 in forming his blades.

veloped primarily for other purposes, such as jet engine turbines.

During the late 1960s, a number of cutlery steels put in their apperance, and while some have faded in popularity, all are still around. As mentioned, D2 is quite popular, and the same can be said for 06, 440C and W2. Loveless first popularized 154CM and it is today's most-used high-chromium blade material.

All of these steel formulations will — properly made and properly heat-treated — produce an excellent knife blade.

Some will be slightly better than others, but we are not talking about twice as good or three times as good. It is rather a matter of only a few separating points on a scale of one to one hundred. The average nimrod who may dress out one deer, a few doves or quail and perhaps half a dozen ducks each season will not be able to see any difference at all between a good D2 blade and a blade from one of the other aforementioned steel variations.

The matter of heat-treatment is a subject that has not received the attention in the past that it so richly deserves.

This stag-handled folder is by Art Wiman. Stag is not difficult to obtain, but when available, still is one of the most-popular handle materials. It does, however, have a tendency to shrink over the years as it dries out.

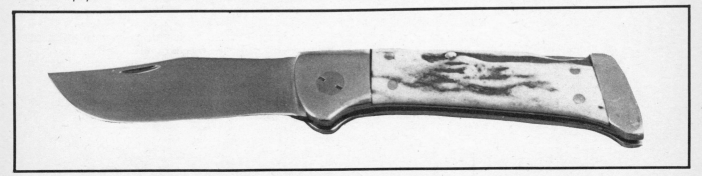

It is a standard answer among makers who have their treating performed by commercial firms that this is an ultra-important step; one that should be entrusted only to professionals.

We agree that it is an important step. If actual performance and not appearance is the thing that you look for in a new knife, it is the most important step in the making of a knife. Sad to say, though, many commercial firms look upon the treatment of knife blades as a piddling chore that is performed as a sort of by-product.

One well-known custom knifemaker reports that he visited the plant at which his blades were being treated and, to his dismay, discovered they were being stuck in with larger items, and the treatment was dependent upon the major item, not upon his specifications. Thus, some of his blades were cooked, while others were undertreated.

This cutler soon purchased his own electric furnace, and since then the quality of his blades has gone up dramatically.

Perhaps even more absurd is the incident related to us by another maker who dropped in on the plant where his blades were treated. In the course of the conversation he discovered that the firm treating his blades was following the recommended procedures for 01 steel. The problem was that the steel actually used was D2 and the maker had specified this to the firm. Not surprisingly, this maker also decided to change heat-treating practices and he, too, bought his own furnace.

Merle Seguine, one of this century's most famous cutlers, has been retired from knifemaking for several years, but he once told us he did not consider a man an accomplished maker unless he performed his own heat-treatment. That's only one man's opinion, but it would appear to have some merit.

There are professional heat-treating firms that do extremely competent jobs even with small orders. The problem is finding out who the firms are and a recommendation of their techniques.

There is no ready, easy answer to this, except if a maker can furnish you with a number of names of satisfied customers who have actually used said maker's knives, then this can be a guide.

It is difficult to discuss forged blades in terms of modern steels, because forging is an ancient art and the smith does in fact actually manufacture his own steel as well as perform his own heat-treating. Let us merely say that, if the smith really knows his business, the resulting blade will be

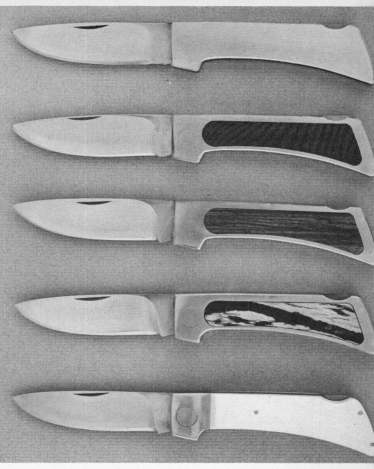

These folders by Jimmy Lile illustrate a wide range of handle materials. From top are stainless steel, wood micarta, rosewood, stag and ivory. Most of this man's blades are fashioned of D2 steel, which he now favors.

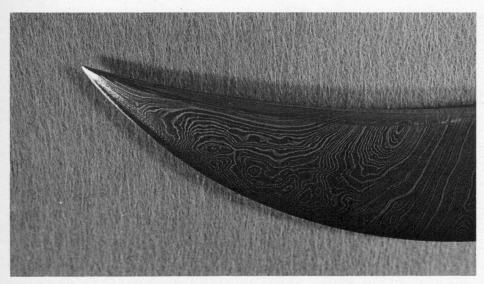

This close-up of Bill Moran's work in Damascus steel illustrates its beauty. Ancient art was renewed in 1973 by Moran. No modern cutlery steel can surpass it for strength, edge holding, flexibility and for ease in sharpening the blade.

as good as any currently available. The problem here is that there are not more than half a dozen or so forge-qualified smiths in America today!

Below is a breakdown on the elements found in some of today's more popular cutlery steels. Iron accounts for most of the content, and listed are the elements added to this iron:

154CM	%		W2	%
Carbon	1.05		Carbon	.06
Manganese	0.60		Manganese	.25
Phosphorus	0.03		Silicon	.25
Sulfur	0.03		Vanadium	.25
Silicon	0.25			
Chromium	14.00			
Molybdenum	4.00			
440C	**%**		**01**	**%**
Carbon	1.00		Carbon	0.90
Manganese	.50		Tungsten	.50
Silicon	.40		Manganese	1.35
Chromium	17.05		Silicon	.35
Molybdenum	.45		Chromium	.50
Nickel	.20			
D2	**%**		**A2**	**%**
Carbon	1.50		Carbon	1.00
Manganese	.25		Tungsten	.50
Silicon	.30		Manganese	1.35
Chromium	11.50		Silicon	.35
Molybdenum	1.00		Chromium	5.00
Vanadium	.90		Molybdenum	1.00

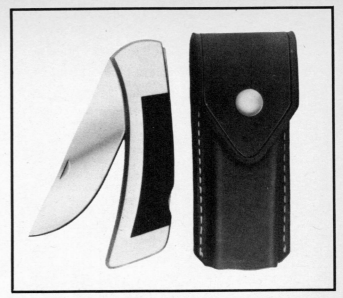

This folding Sportsman III model from Gerber features a blade made from 440C, considered one of today's most-sophisticated steels. Today's quality-made factory knife takes a back seat to none for performance and for value.

Bob Schrimsher of Ennis, Texas, not only makes knives, but operates a supply house for cutlers, offering the materials needed for any type of knife ranging from the smallest type of folder desired to monstrous Bowies.

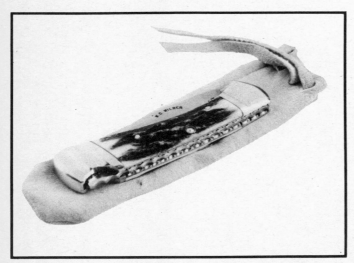

Collector items such as this folding knife made by Bill Wilbur — one that obviously is not likely to see much use — can be kept in a soft buckskin pouch to protect the sharp lines and detail work. Knives such as this, like rare coins, gain value when in mint condition.

There's no magic here. Bob Loveless once told us, "A knife is, after all, only a knife." All of these steels, as well as many others, can be made into superb cutting instruments. The more important factors involve the skill of the maker and the competence of the heat-treater.

When it comes to folding knives, it is possible to make a much better case for the stain-resistant steels than one in reference to sheath knives. Because of the nature of a folding knife, there are more nooks and crannies for blood, mud, dirt and grime to get into than with fixed-blade knives. No question about it: it is tougher to clean a folder. If a man is purchasing a folder to use for his hunting chores, there is a good chance that it will be used on trips covering several days. We would suggest for this, that the blade be made of 154CM, 440C or D2 steel.

While the blade is indeed the heart of the knife, handle materials are important, too.

In handle materials, there are only three that we feel merit serious consideration. For a using knife, one of the various micartas must receive attention. Our favorite is the white or ivory micarta, but many prefer wood-grained micartas. To our eyes, the blue, green and zebra micartas are garish, but if you like them, these materials are as durable as the others. It takes all kinds of tastes, or they wouldn't make such shades.

Nothing is more attractive than good stag slabs, but it is becoming increasingly difficult to obtain good sambar stag, while domestic stag leaves much to be desired. Even if good Indian or sambar stag can be obtained, it does have a tendency to shrink. In a few months, the slab that was an airtight fit may no longer fit so snug.

On a knife that is nothing more than a bona fide collector's item and never will be used in the field, ivory ranks at the head of the class. It has its faults, but its beauty and inherent value make it the number one choice.

Brass and nickel silver are standard bolster materials, but in our opinion, the latter is much preferred. A custom knife generally will cost a few dollars more with nickel silver bolsters, but this feature is worth the slight additional expenditure. A few makers offer stainless steel as an extra-cost item, and this costs quite a bit more than nickel silver. It's a nice touch, but from a practical standpoint, there is little advantage.

A few custom makers are offering ultra-light folders with aluminum bolsters. W.D. Davis comes immediately to mind. These are great for carrying and, although those we have used have not been severely tested, they have stood up well to date.

Brass liners have been standard for centuries, but more and more makers are turning to stainless steel. Much the same holds true for pins.

Theoretically, were a person ordering a custom folder for long, hard service with a minimum of maintenance, a model with 154CM or 440C blade, stainless bolsters, liners and pins, and slabs of micarta would offer the most durable, maintenance-free knife possible. It would also be expensive. G.W. Stone, among others, offers just such a model.

Much of what has been said here primarily applies to handmade folders, although there is considerable application to the better factory models. When ordering a handmade knife, one may request virtually anything within reason, provided this customer has the money. In factory versions, one must take what the plants offer, although there is a tremendous selection from which to choose.

Regardless of the various materials selected for construction, the most important ingredients still are skill, know-how and patience.

Texan G.W. Stone is one of the few modern knifemakers who will use stainless steel for every metal part of a knife. With micarta handle slabs, one has a folder that will last a lifetime with a reasonable amount of care.

One of the neatest and best-designed custom knife shops we have seen is that of W.C. Wilbur in Spartansburg, South Carolina. Note bars of blade stock on the floor.

Chapter 4

BLADE SHAPES & OVERALL DESIGN

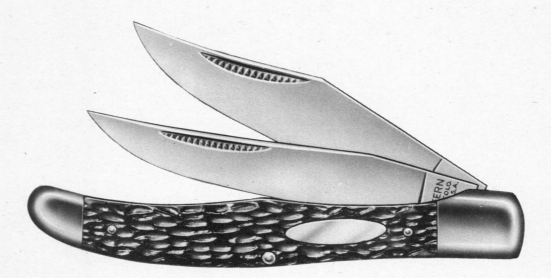

A Knife That Is Comfortable

In The Hand And Does

The Job Is The Ultimate!

SEVERAL YEARS ago, in a West Texas deer camp, a fellow hunter came in at the end of a long day with a touching tale of woe. While stalking around the rimrock, he noted that the guard screw on his bolt-action rifle had worked loose.

Not having a screwdriver handy, he used his $100 custom sheath knife as a tool. The result was a broken blade point.

It could have been worse. Later, the maker reground the blade so that it didn't look too bad. No trophy presented itself during the remainder of the day, so the loose screw had no effect on the accuracy of the rifle.

That evening, the hunter used a ninety-nine-cent screwdriver, which did an admirable job of tightening the screw. While he was engaged at this chore, another nimrod pulled a folding knife out of his pocket and stated, "If you'd have had this, you could have tightened the screw and saved the blade of your knife." The folder was a Western four-bladed camper's model. This model features a punch blade, a cap opener, a standard cutting blade and a screwdriver that can do double-duty as a bottle opener. Camillus and others offer similar models. Such knives are not particularly bulky, although they would hardly do for daily packing in a business suit.

The variety of blades available in modern pocketknives is indeed wide. You can buy folders with nail files, scissors, Phillips-head screwdrivers, fish scalers, leather punches, bone saws, pruning blades, plus a host of blades designed for cutting.

Different knives have different uses. The model above is known as an electrician's or pruner's knife. As such, it has limited value to the hunter/outdoorsman. Case pocketknife (right) features a long clip and a pen blade, ideal for pocket but rather light for most field use.

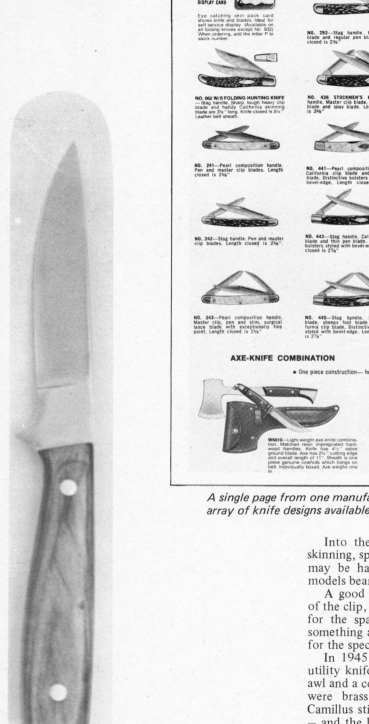

A single page from one manufacturer's catalog gives some idea of the vast array of knife designs available. Compare with small sheath knife at left.

Into the latter category falls such blades as the clip, skinning, spay, saber, sheepfoot, spear and caping. The clip may be had in two forms: short and long. The two clip models bear a strong resemblance to the famous Bowie.

A good working knife should possess at least one blade of the clip, skinner or spear design. There is much to be said for the spay blade as a second design and, if you desire something a bit unusual, the third blade is the place to opt for the special service tool.

In 1945, the Marine Corps adopted an all-metal folding utility knife that featured a master blade, a cap opener, an awl and a combination screwdriver-bottle opener. The liners were brass and the handles were made of aluminum. Camillus still offers a similar knife — perhaps even identical — and the last time we checked, the cost of this knife was less than $5, but that was a couple of years ago and it may have gone up slightly. The man who wants a knock-about utility knife could do no better. The edge-holding qualities of the master blade are nothing to write home about, but it will take a good edge quickly and easily; it is useful and the price is right.

The person looking for a little better quality knife similarly designed might take a long look at the so-called Swiss Army knives that are carried by most good cutlery shops. A.G. Russell generally stocks a good supply of them. These are excellent knives, although a bit bulky, and if you do a lot of traveling in connection with your sporting junkets, they are a good idea. Prices for good-quality Swiss Army knives generally begin at about $12.95 and go up to as much as $40, depending upon the extra features and number of blades. Those with corkscrews, scissors, ad infinitum, may seem novel, but they are of dubious use for the outdoorsman. Stick to the more practical and compact models.

The matter of compactness can be carried too far. Countless so-called gentlemen's pen knives are sold each year. These are slender, almost delicate knives, usually with one or two small blades, that are ideal for cleaning fingernails and opening the daily mail, but good for little else.

It is possible for no more, if indeed as much money, to purchase a small version of a stock knife. This will do an equally good job of paring nails or slitting envelopes, but also can handle a few tougher jobs and be little if any more bulky or heavy.

A knife should have sturdy bolsters if it is to stand up to normal chores over a long period of time. Shun those that

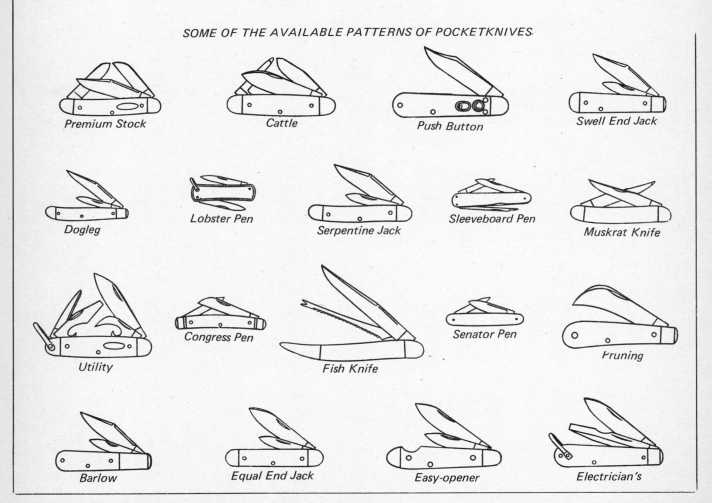

SOME OF THE AVAILABLE PATTERNS OF POCKETKNIVES

Premium Stock — Cattle — Push Button — Swell End Jack

Dogleg — Lobster Pen — Serpentine Jack — Sleeveboard Pen — Muskrat Knife

Utility — Congress Pen — Fish Knife — Senator Pen — Pruning

Barlow — Equal End Jack — Easy-opener — Electrician's

have no bolsters, instead, rely on the liners and handle material to retain the blade pin. Sooner or later — usually sooner — you will find a considerable amount of side play in the blade when it is in the open position.

There are any number of small, slim, well-made knives that will fill this prescription and one or two favorites include the Buck Companion and the Boker Senator.

A little looking in a knife shop will reveal quickly that there are a multitude of good, serviceable knives that can be purchased for virtually any task for well under $20. Just do not expect one of those $2.95 drug store specials to satisfy you — unless you're easily satisfied!

One aspect that must be considered when purchasing a new folder is the type of grind put on the blade. There are three basic styles: saber, hollow and flat. The saber grind features a blade that is left full thickness for perhaps one-half of its width; the flat is ground evenly from the back to the edge, while the hollow-grind has concave sides. Any one of these types, properly executed, will do the job. Personal preference is probably more important here than the actual style.

Try the knife in your hand. Try it in several positions in which the knife will find itself in actual use. It should feel comfortable and the corners of the bolsters should not bite your hand. If the knife doesn't feel good at this stage of the game, consider how it is going to feel after thirty minutes of hard use.

Novelty designs and features are nice in collections, but somewhat less than desirable in the field or when whittling a toy boat for Junior.

Your folding knife should be a partner and a partnership is a two-way street.

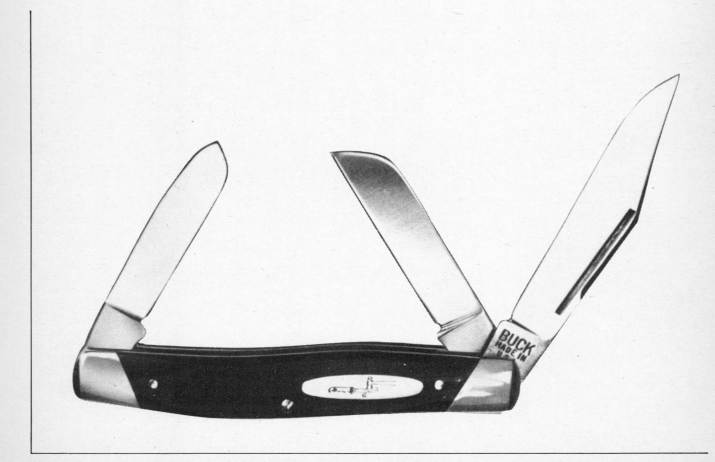

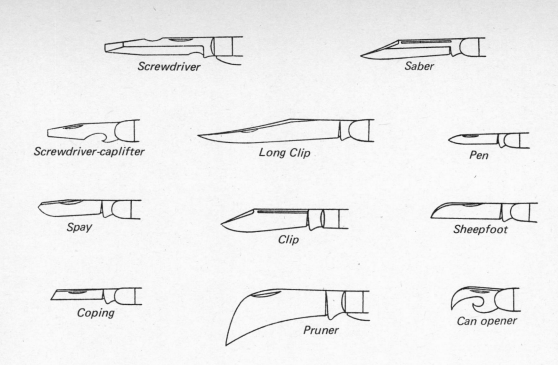

Screwdriver

Saber

Screwdriver-caplifter

Long Clip

Pen

Spay

Clip

Sheepfoot

Coping

Pruner

Can opener

Skinning

Spear

STANDARD POCKETKNIFE BLADES

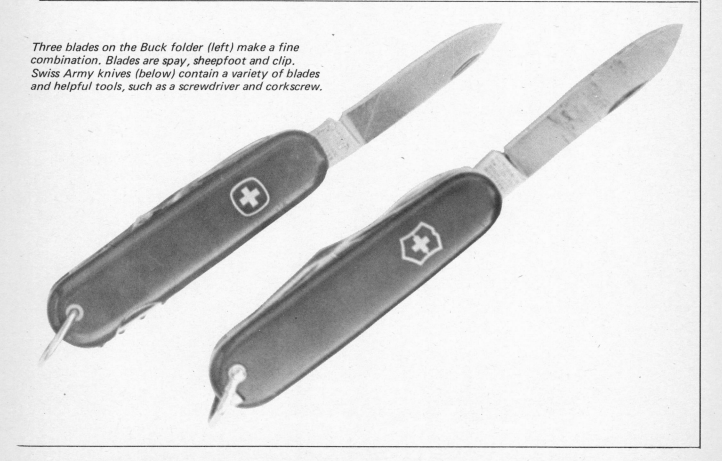

Three blades on the Buck folder (left) make a fine combination. Blades are spay, sheepfoot and clip. Swiss Army knives (below) contain a variety of blades and helpful tools, such as a screwdriver and corkscrew.

SHARPENING THE FOLDER

Chapter 5

The Techniques For Putting An Edge On A Blade Differ Little For Results!

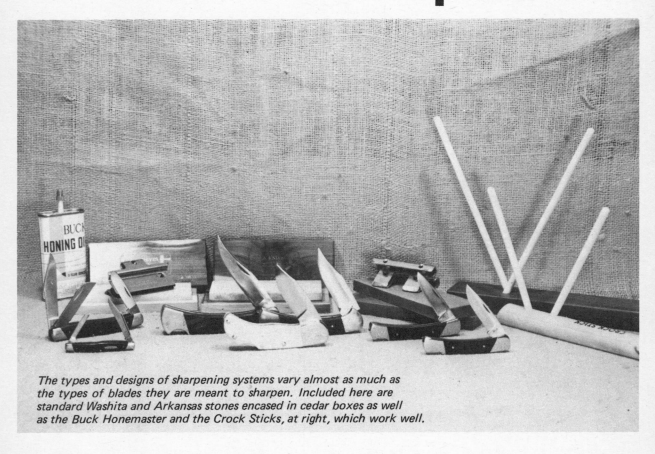

The types and designs of sharpening systems vary almost as much as the types of blades they are meant to sharpen. Included here are standard Washita and Arkansas stones encased in cedar boxes as well as the Buck Honemaster and the Crock Sticks, at right, which work well.

An oil of some type such as the Buck Honing Oil is necessary to coat the stone for a better edge. Washita stone at left is medium, while the Arkansas type is hard.

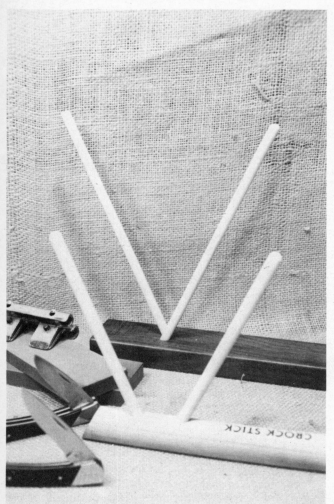

The Crock Stick is a pair of ceramic rods that have been impregnated with sharpening materials. They are inserted into the wooden base at the correct angle for sharpening.

KEEPING YOUR FOLDING knife well edged is just as important as with a fixed-blade sheath knife. Some of the techniques are the same, although the folding action and relatively small size of the blades present some extra problems.

Most folders are made with one of two styles of blade: wedge shape or hollow ground. Most of the smaller pocketknives on the market are available with a wedge blade that presents no real problem in sharpening. A cross section of the wedge blade looks just as it sounds, wedge shaped with a continuous even taper from spine to cutting edge.

The bigger folding blade knives and many of the newer custom folding knives are hollow ground. Viewed in cross section, the blade has a hollow or concave shape from spine to cutting edge. Hollow ground blades move easier through meat or skin when field dressing. Most sheath knives are hollow ground and sharpening the larger hollow folder is done much the same as for fixed blades.

The first step in sharpening any blade is to clean the stone with a paper towel, then coat the surface with a ribbon of light honing oil. Most stones are meant to be worked with water or oil, but never dry.

Blades on most folding knives are relatively small compared to sheath knives, so sharpening systems and gadgets won't always work well with them. The Razor Edge tool works well on sheath blades and the larger folding knives, so does the Buck Honemaster. Neither, however, will work on smaller model knives.

The Razor Edge comes with a two-stone system that should always be used dry without the usual honing oil. Proper use will put an edge on any blade in short order. The edge of the blade, when using the Razor Edge or Honemaster, should be at least a half inch beyond the edge of the device. This gives the proper angle for the edge to work on the stone.

The Buck Honemaster was used on a Buck 110 Folding Hunter recently and in a short time a shaving edge was on the blade. This is one of Buck's larger blades and is big enough to use with the sharpening aid. One must remember to lock the blade open and place the Honemaster one-half inch back from the cutting edge, turn the wheel and lock in onto the blade. Using two stones, one medium grit Washita and one hard Arkansas, you should obtain a cutting edge that will be sharp and lasting with minimum effort.

All knives should be sharpened when you buy them. The edge put on at most factories is done with buffing wheels and will definitely shave the hair on your arm. However, this edge won't last too long in the field as a rule. Sharpen the knife yourself and it will stay sharper longer.

The two stones mentioned, the Washita and Arkansas,

will handle any steel tried so far. Most folding knives are made of 440C stainless steel to resist rust. They hold an excellent edge and with proper care will last for many years. Any knife must be sharpened from time to time, no matter of what quality.

The smaller folding knives won't sharpen with the edge-making devices. You must manually hold the blade at the proper angle to obtain a cutting edge. This is not difficult and with a little practice you can do it each time.

First apply some honing oil to the stone you plan to work with. A simple system with a new stone is to soak it in the honing oil until it is saturated in the oil. Use a drop or two each time a knife is worked on.

To properly sharpen a blade without a sharpening device, place the edge of the blade flat on the stone. Tilt the back edge of the blade until you feel the bevel of the blade flatten on the stone. The trick is to sort of rock it up and down to get the correct angle. Too high and you dull the point or edge and it will never sharpen; too shallow and you never touch the edge and work only on the bevel. The object of using a stone is to cut the steel with the fine grit of the stone and work it to a sharp edge. You remove a bit of steel and a bit of stone with each honing. Most cutlers recommend an angle between blade and stone of about twenty degrees.

Move the blade across the stone, holding it as if you were trying to slice a very thin section off the top of that stone. That in reality is just what you are doing. Cutting the stone hones the steel. Slice on one side, turn the blade over and

The current model of the Buck Honemaster can be operated only with larger blades, in this case the large Buck Folding Hunter. The device holds the proper angle for sharpening, if it is being used properly.

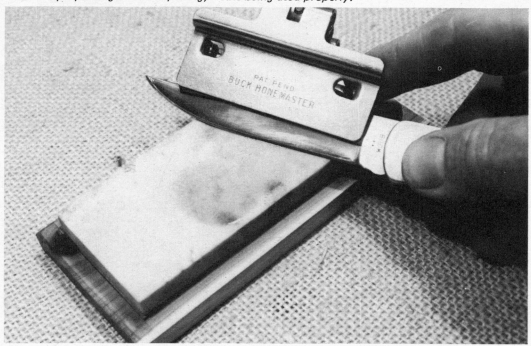

In using the Buck honing device, one must reverse the blade so that both sides are stroked properly on the unit. This works the edges evenly and avoids the possibility of coming up with a burred edge.

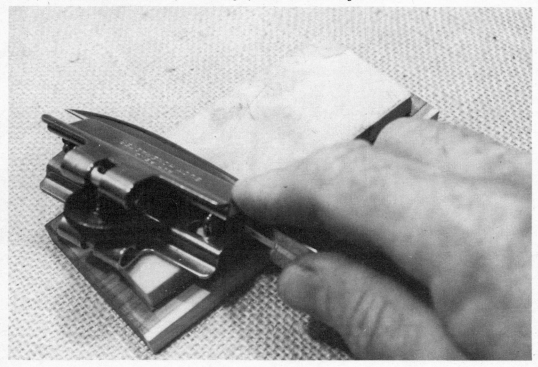

slice back the other way, starting from the base and working to the tip. Hone the tip, too. Repeat this process of slicing first one side of the blade, then reversing and slicing the other side. This puts the edge on your blade.

You may be satisfied with the edge you obtain with the medium grit Washita stone. Most knife users will stop there. You may go further. Using the harder Arkansas stone, you can refine the edge further. Use the honing oil and stone the same as before. This finer stone makes finer cuts on the steel, removing the coarser edge left by the coarser stone. Hone until satisfied.

You may want to stop there but you can go even further. A piece of heavy leather can be impregnated with jeweler's rouge and used to put a shaving edge on your favorite folding blade. This is a much finer grit and you must use a slightly different technique. Move the blade

the Washita stone and it becomes the general purpose blade. A second blade might be honed down with the jeweler's rouge and used for skinning or special purposes. A third blade of special shape might be honed with the Arkansas and left at that stage. Three different shaped blades, each with a different sharpness for different purposes.

How sharp should your blade be? The best answer is another question: what do you plan to use it for? Most of us don't use a knife to shave, so we really don't need a shaving edge.

A butcher doesn't use a razor when he's skinning or slicing. Sharpening steels were used mostly by butchers in the past but in recent years they have become popular as a field method for touching up an edge. They work a bit differently from a stone. Steels align the blade edge in a straight line instead of the toothed edge a stone puts on a blade. Many hunters prefer to carry a steel in the field and

There are many ways to check for sharpness. One can cut paper as a test, but drawing the blade across the thumbnail is another test. If the worked blade seems to slip easily, more sharpening is needed.

away from the edge not slicing into the leather as you did with the stones. Move the blade with the leather, first one side then the other. This makes finer teeth, as they are sometimes called, in the steel of your blade. The finer the teeth, the sharper and finer the cutting edge will be.

Most men who carry a multibladed knife have a blade for each use. The big major blade might be honed only with

use it for folding and sheath knives. Steels are simple and fast to use. Some brands have a wedged edge that can be used as a chisel for opening the pelvis on a deer. It is far better to use this steel than hammering on the back edge of your folder.

Ceramic sharpeners have become more popular as the system has progressed to the point of working well. One

(Top) The Washita and Arkansas stones can be used for sharpening virtually any blade. The flat-edged blade shown is easy to sharpen, but one must maintain the correct angle of metal to stone. Lay it flat, then lift the back edge a trifle and start honing first one side, then (above) turn the blade over to hone the other side. By alternating strokes one should end up with an even edge without any obvious burrs.

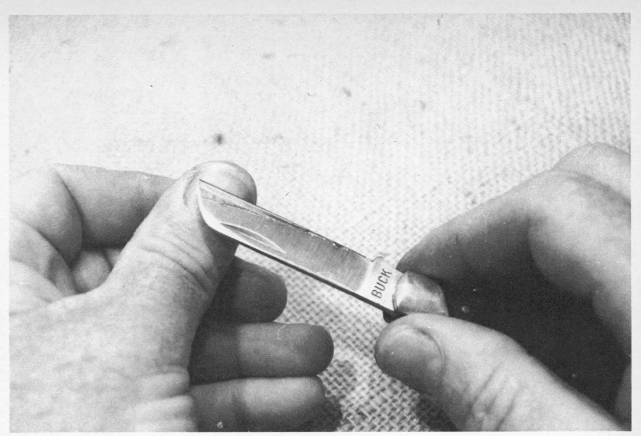

Some oil from the stone still clings to the edge of the blade as
the knife is tested on the thumbnail for sharpness. Test showed
that the tip of the blade required a few more passes on the stone.

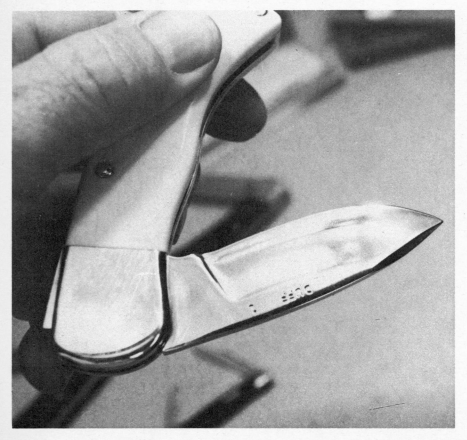

This Duff Custom folder came with a
shaving edge, but even custom knives
can need sharpening. This edge has
been done with buffing wheels and it
doesn't hold the edge made with a hone.
Note hollow grinding in custom blade.

make tried and found satisfactory is the Crock Stick, which is a pair of ceramic rods impregnated with dust to produce a fast, clean knife edge. The company went even further by placing the rods in a base to give the proper angle for sharpening blades. Most systems give best results using about a twenty-degree angle. With the Crock Stick you merely insert the rods into the wooden base, and they are automatically at the proper angle. All you have to do is hold your blade vertically and run it down the ceramic rod to the bottom. Pull the blade back so you work the full length and do one side. Then do the other side. In just a short time you have an excellent cutting edge that will hold. This is one of the simpler systems which works well.

Two styles of the Crock Stick are available. One is large enough for the shop with rods about twelve inches long and a base of hardwood with predrilled, angled holes. The rods store in the end of the base in holes drilled for that purpose.

The smaller model is intended for camp and field use with rods about six inches long. The base has the proper angle holes drilled for the rods. These store in the base in holes for that purpose. People who say they can't sharpen a knife have done so with this system.

Regardless of the system you use — stones, steels or ceramic — keep the blades of your folder sharp. Nearly sharp blades are dangerous. You exert more pressure than needed and tend to cut yourself with a semisharp blade. Also, the extra pressure isn't good for the pivot pins in the handle assembly.

There are certain things you should never do with a folding knife of any type. Never pry. You may pop the rivets on the pivot pins. Never throw a folding knife. Throwing will not only open the rivets but can possibly break blades. Use common sense with a good sharp folding knife and it will last many years.

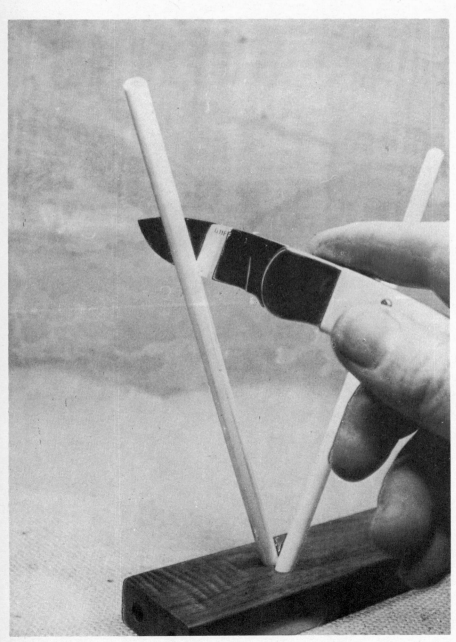

The Duff Custom knife was touched up with Crock Sticks. They're designed to provide the proper angle when the blade is held straight up and down.

Chapter 6

*Here's A Finishing
Technique That Also
Can Be Used To
Clean Up Your
Knives At Home!*

THE BASICS
OF BUFFING

Don't give up if your folding knife looks anything like one of these with dirty, scratched and nicked blades, and tarnished brass or silver bolsters. Using the techniques outlined in text, it may look like new.

Standard buffing pad on left may be used with 400-grit polish for next-to-last finish. At right is the Scotch Brite wheel which spins faster and stays cleaner.

KNIVES GET DIRTY. If good-looking equipment means anything to you, clean yours from time to time. The urge to clean up knives can come upon you at any time, especially on nonhunting weekends. Best bet is to give in and do it. It's just as easy to do six as one.

There are several ways to clean up your knife steel and the handles. The blades can be worked clean with a series of increasingly finer grade steel wool until they shine. You can buy steel wool in any hardware store. It takes more time than other methods, however. Buffing wheels clean fast, are simple to work with and should last for many moons in a home shop. You can make your buffers from new wheels or find some that are no longer needed in a commercial shop and recycle.

You should have four different grits. Start with the red-colored, coarse 120 grit. Next use a finer 240 grit which is gray. Finer grits may include a green stiff wheel of about 600 grit. With these wheels you can take out most nicks and polish up any knife. You may want to go one step further and make a floppy wheel. Cut some of the pads to make the wheel floppy and use the 600 grit for a really fine finish. This works well on steel blades, micarta, phenolic or wood handles and will leave brass and metal bolsters with a high polish.

The buffing wheels can be mounted on the shaft of a washing machine motor if you have an old one around. You will have to change for each grit but that is simply done. It's possible to mount two on an arbor and change half as often. Buffing wheels require a bit of care. You need to dress them occasionally to keep them cutting properly.

The 3M Company makes a series of Scotch-Brite wheels of material in medium, fine and very fine surfaces. These wheels cost about $20 for a 6x1-inch wheel but they will last in the average home shop for a long time. Pick one up of the grit you use the most to try first. These wheels are clean, need little maintenance and do a great job of cleaning and buffing.

Regardless of the method you plan to use, the first step to cleaning a folder is to check the blades and bolsters. They should be tight when the blade is open. Lock blade folders should be solidly locked open before you start cleaning. The home craftsman can't do much about a loose

First step in bringing dirty folders back to life is to clean blade and bolsters with Scotch Brite wheel.

This Buck Folding Hunter needs help. Note deep scratches in blade and bolster from heavy use.

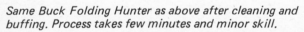

Same Buck Folding Hunter as above after cleaning and buffing. Process takes few minutes and minor skill.

Final buffing may be done with floppy soft muslin wheel and 600-grit polishing compound.

blade but most good knives have a warranty and the manufacturer will usually honor it with replacement or repair.

Recently, a group of knives to be cleaned included a three-blade Buck Stockman and a really messy Yachtsman, complete with marlin spike. Someone had used it to cut tar paper, or worse, and the blade was a total mess. Some blades merely needed buffing to restore the finish. The brass and wood on the Buck folding lock blades needed polishing.

The first wheel used was the fine-grit Scotch-Brite. It cleaned the roughness off the blades in a hurry but left some scratches of its own. But that's the way the buffing system works. Clean with one wheel and remove the lines with a finer one. The folding lock blades were cleaned, and the wood and brass handles buffed. Some owners may leave the bolsters and the blades in this satin finish. Not quite as shiny but not everyone wants a shiny knife.

When using powerful buffing wheels on a knife, proper safety precautions are necessary. Safety glasses or goggles are a must. A piece of the grit could come flying up and zap the operator in the eye. Goggles prevent eye damage and should always be worn around powerful equipment.

When working a buffing wheel, a good plan is to make a leather or rug holder for the handle. Lock blade folders and sheath knives are safer but a folding blade knife may fold on the wheel. If you have your hand in the wrong place, you may end up cut to the bone. A simple wrap of leather around the handle will prevent the blade from closing on the hand. You may also use the wrap to hold the knife by the blade while buffing handles.

Hold onto the knife with force when using power buffers. If the knife slips, hold on and try to prevent the blade from getting away from you. If it does get away, don't grab. You might get the sharp blade. When a blade does get away, let it go and step to the side fast. One experienced buffer had a knife get away from him. It went completely around a shielded, guarded wheel and came back to jab him in the chest. He was more frightened than injured but had a nasty wound. Common sense and simple precautions will prevent accidents.

Clean all blades first on each knife you plan to clean. Do one grit at a time and place the knives aside as you finish them. This might be compared to a mini-production line and is the fastest and easiest method. First, do both sides of the blades. Then the back and liner edges. With lock blades,

This Buck Yachtsman knife was coated with tar or pitch, blade was scored and handle was badly scratched just a short time ago.

Safety is important when using buffing wheel with folding knives. Even a lock-blade knife can be dangerous if not handled properly.

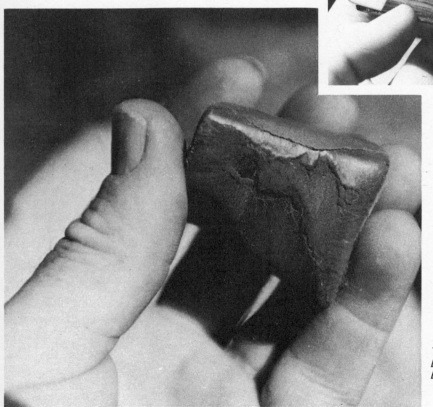

The buffing compound appears to be a hard piece of clay before being applied to spinning wheel.

make certain they are solidly locked and handle them as sheath knives. Polish all the scratches. If there are some deep scores in the blade, it is often best to let them stay rather than go deep enough to remove them.

When all the knives have been buffed on the wheel, the next step is the hard green buffer. This really brings up the shine in the brass, metal bolsters and blades. When you clean with buffers, you may also obtain a shaving edge on the blade if you work it right. It won't last long but it is very sharp.

The final buffer is the floppy green grit: Danger! This is the dude that will grab a knife and pull it from your hands if you relax tension or push too hard. Don't get too low on a wheel or you may lose the knife. Best bet is to stay in the midsection of the buffer surface. The grit on this wheel is the same 600 green as the prior wheel, but the floppy pad really does a job.

When you finish with this wheel, you may have little gobs of polish stuck to the knife. This will easily wipe off. The heat of the wheel and blade in contact will melt the polish and cause some adhesion. A clean soft cloth will remove it.

A few minutes on a set of wheels will take a badly abused knife to almost new condition. You may not remove all the scratches on the blade but it will be highly polished.

You will find you can't get into the liners and do the interior with a buffer. A Q-Tip works great for this. Dip one in some wood alcohol and run it into the interior of the liners where the blades rest when closed. Most of the lint picked up from the pocket will come out and the alcohol won't hurt the metal. Your knife will work and look better for the extra few minutes.

Your knife should now look practically like new. Take as long as you like to restore the finish. A knife factory worker can't take as long as you. With the right wheels you can put a mirror finish on your favorite knives.

As a final step, place a drop of light machine oil on the hinge of each blade. Work the blade several times to get the oil onto all surfaces. The blade will work better and smoother and the bearing surfaces will last longer. Not too much oil or you will get oil stains in your pocket.

Buff 'em or steel wool 'em, but get 'em cleaned up. With a little care, your knives will look like new for years to come.

Compare these refinished knives with same group at beginning of chapter. Proper maintenance will keep your expensive — or your inexpensive — folding knives looking like new for years. Takes but a few minutes.

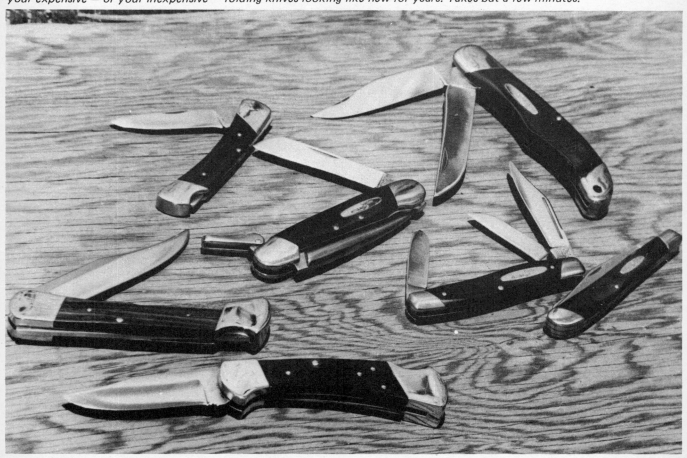

Chapter 7

BIRTH OF A FOLDER

From Drawing Board To Finished Prototype Is A Long, Hard Trail!

Knifemaker Bill Duff sketched and resketched the design for his first folding knife before construction.

BILL DUFF OF El Cajon, California, has joined the ranks of custom cutlers who are producing high-quality folding knives. He calls his the Duff 801 Custom Folder. The 801 features a lock-open blade, and Duff feels it is of a size that may be carried in the user's pocket or in a leather sheath to be ready for use in the field.

Duff, who has worked for a couple of the major commercial knife companies for the past dozen or so years, opened his own custom shop a bit more than a year ago.

Unhardened 440C stainless-steel blade material is dyed before etching (above), so blade outline is plainly visible. Next step (below right) has the cutler band-sawing blade shape from stock.

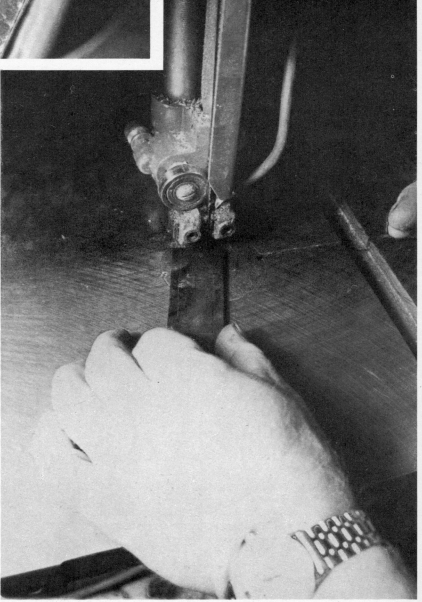

The folder's rocker arm and spring retainer section are etched and formed from steel softer than blade material.

Until now, his line was restricted to fixed-blade sheath knives, a skinning axe, a toothpick model and a Bowie knife. Duff feels the addition of the folder gives him a wider range of knives for his customers.

The design of the 801 didn't come easy or fast. In fact, it took Duff the better part of his first year in business to work out the final set of specifications and drawings before he commenced work on the prototype. He was continually doodling on scratch pads and odd pieces of paper working out the design in his mind. He sketched, rejected and modified many times before arriving at the present model.

Now that Duff has finished his first folding lock-blade custom knife, he is pleased with the results. The folder features a 2½-inch blade which will stay locked open under the toughest conditions. Overall length when open is 6½ inches. The handle doesn't have finger grooves but does

Basic shape of the Duff folding knife blade is compared with original design sketch. At this point, the knifemaker has added locking notch and pivot pin hole to blade blank. Blade will be worked and hollow ground before hardening.

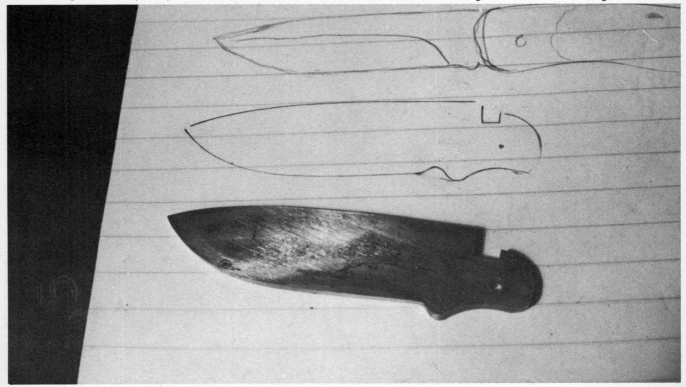

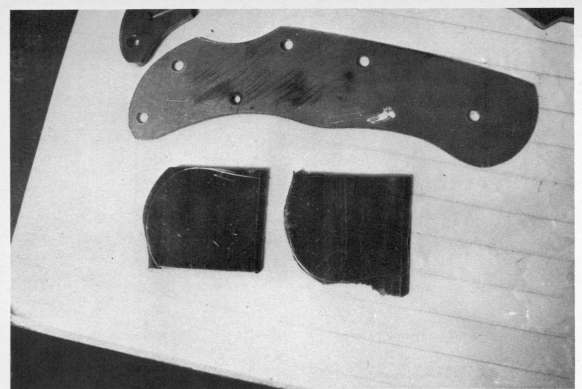

Pair of nickel silver bolsters have been sketched on stock. Above them is light steel liner. Rivet holes are drilled through plate following precision measurements.

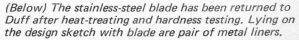

(Below) The stainless-steel blade has been returned to Duff after heat-treating and hardness testing. Lying on the design sketch with blade are pair of metal liners.

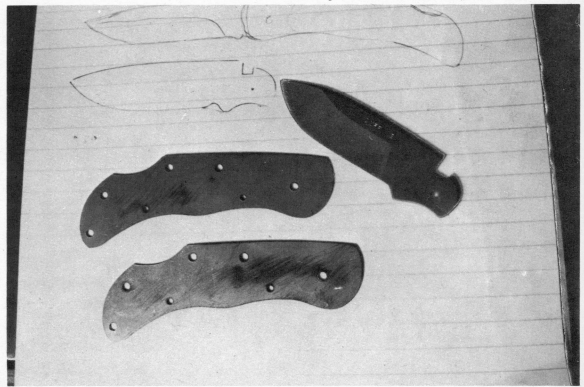

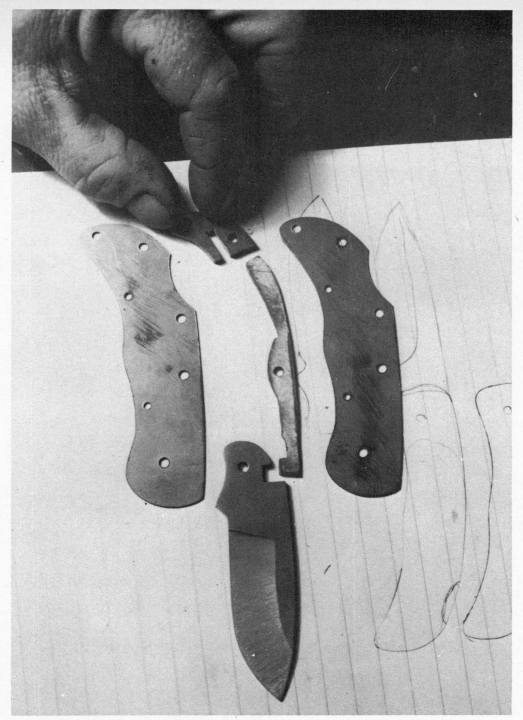

Duff begins to assemble the internal working parts, less the lock spring and external handle materials, prior to assembly. Duff is holding the rocker arm just above the spring keeper. Dimensions and shape of internal parts are critical to folder operation.

have a slight belly to its shape, which gives it a nice solid feel in the hand.

Handle material depends on the customer's preferences, and Duff will make it from various colors of micarta, exotic woods or ivory. The prototype has bolsters of nickel silver, but brass bolsters and rivets may easily be substituted on order.

Duff is offering his folders with blades made of 440C stainless steel or 0-1 oil-hardened tool steel rated at a hardness of Rockwell 58-60 on the C scale. He has been working up some of his sheath knives with blades of 154CM steel that are impressive, although he's made no firm decision as yet on adopting this third blade material. A Duff knife leaves the shop sharp enough to shave the hair off a man's forearm and it's up to the owner to keep it in this condition.

How did the Duff 801 Custom Folder, Serial Number One, get to the velvet-covered display case in El Cajon? It started awhile back, with Duff making the final decision to make his first folder blade in basically the same pattern as his fixed hunter.

According to Duff, a light cardboard template is cut and placed on a plate of soft 440C steel that has been previously dyed for etching. Once etched, the steel is bandsawed to shape with as much care as a dozen years' experience can muster. Duff found cutting a folding blade somewhat more complicated because of the locking system pattern, so cutting the blank takes longer than for a comparable non-folder.

The rocker arm that operates the folder locking system is made of 301 stainless steel, half-hardened. It must be springy, yet tough. It's held in place by a rivet in the middle. By depressing one end of the arm, the notched opposite end raises to release the blade for closing. The system is simple to look at but complicated to produce.

Below and to the rear of the rocker is the spring keeper. The keeper is the same thickness as the blade base and is constructed with rivet holes and a slot which holds the spring that maintains pressure on the rocker arm. The spring is a short rod of 300 series half-hard stainless steel. It

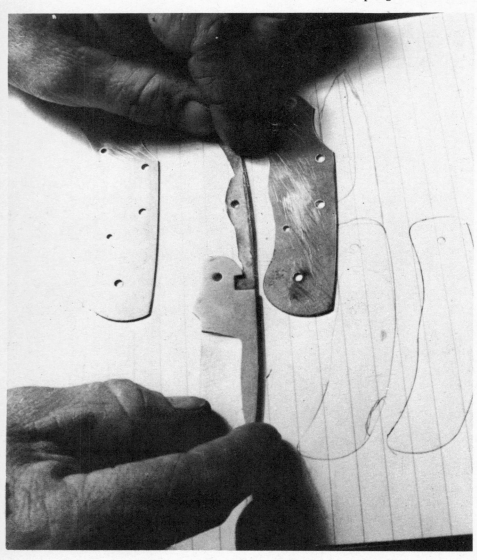

The fit of the blade-lock notch and the rocker arm detent must be precise to ensure no play when blade is locked open. Rocker arm is constructed of 301 stainless steel, half hardened, to produce springy but tough internal control.

The folder blade blank then is hollow ground on a wheel before it is heat-treated. This procedure applies to either type of blade steel.

The next step is to cut the stainless-steel liner. Duff uses steel of 300 series, unhardened. The liner must be absolutely rustproof, of course, and needs to be softer than the blade material but hard enough to take the wearing action of the pivoting blade as the knife is opened and closed. The .040-inch thick liner gives the knife its basic shape when closed and helps form the handle when opened.

After cutting the liner material to primary shape, holes for the pivot pin and rivets are drilled. Duff does this by clamping both sides together before drilling through, as at this point, there is no right or left side to the knife.

should last many years, says Duff, as it is far stronger than required. The spring rests in a spring slot, which, when both liner sides are riveted together, has no place to go. There is a detent on the rocker to keep the spring from moving forward and the keeper holds it in position at the base and midsection.

The last bit of preassembly work Duff has to do is construct the nickel — or brass — bolsters. As with the blade itself, the cutler first outlines the shape of the bolster on a dyed plate of the type metal chosen. The parts are cut out on a bandsaw and cleaned up on belt grinders. Final shaping and buffing await handle assembly.

The bolsters are soldered and riveted in place and Duff is ready to solder the spring keeper to one side of the liner

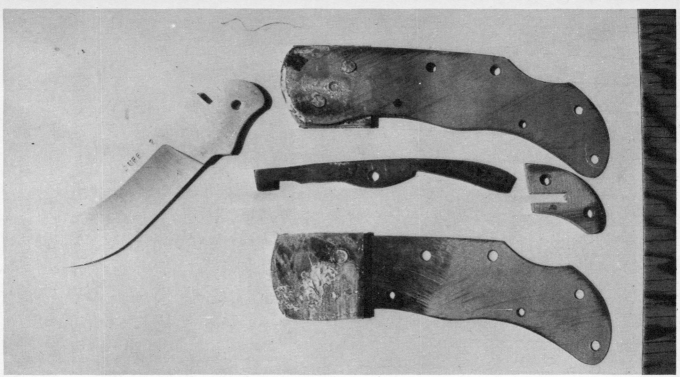

The nickel silver bolsters have been riveted and soldered to the unhardened 300 stainless-steel liner material.

Parts of the Duff folder, except for the handle slabs, are ready for assembly. Note spring retainer with spring inserted. Riveted liners will prevent spring side play.

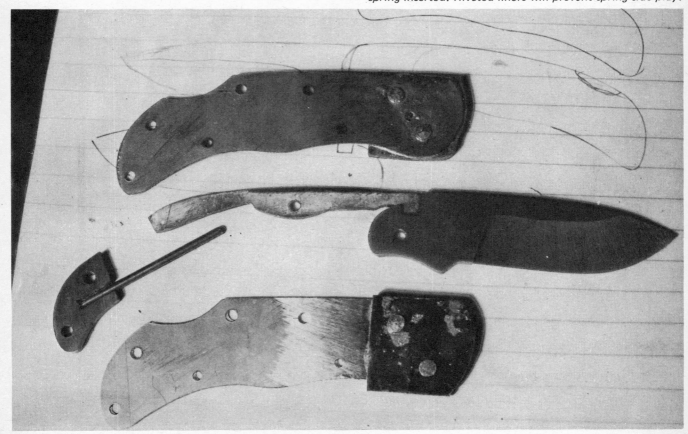

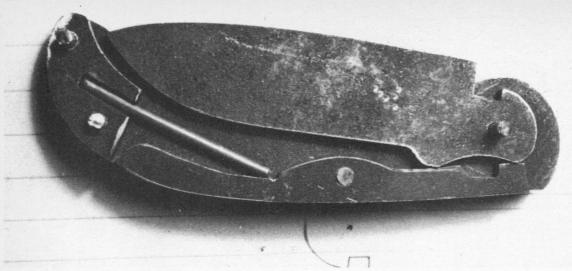

Duff has constructed a working model of soft metal to test the parts fitting and lock mechanism.

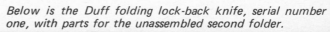

Below is the Duff folding lock-back knife, serial number one, with parts for the unassembled second folder.

Phases of a folding knife (below) include micarta slabs at bottom, soft metal model, finished blade and liner (second from top) and the completed folder. Although Duff works each knife up from same design, each knife will be unique.

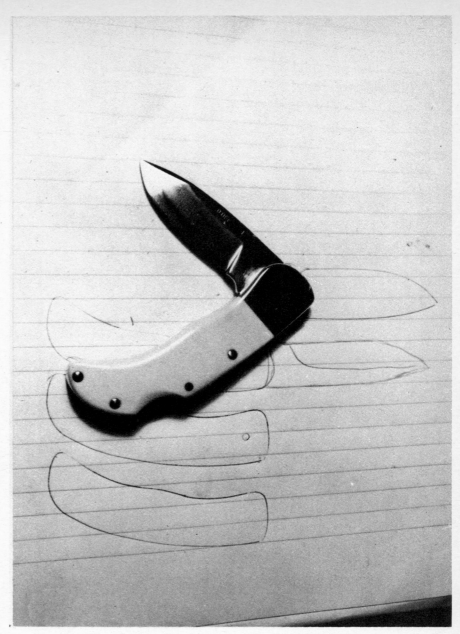

Completed Duff Custom Folder Number One, precursor of new design.

section. This provides him with the area he needs to fine tune the locking system for proper fit and action.

Duff insists on flawless action and fit for his folder. It must have a clean, positive locking action and the rocker arm height must be the same when the blade is closed or open. The rocker spring must be checked and its length adjusted by grinding or cutting where necessary. There are no shortcuts to achieving these goals. It's a matter of fitting, working the action, removing the parts, honing and reworking everything until the maker is satisfied.

The positive locking notch on the rocker arm must be precisely fitted into the honed slot in the upper section of the now-hardened blade. Duff's folder has a solid feel when it clicks open with no play in the blade.

The rivets holding the liners are carefully peened by Duff for proper fit. The rocker arm is a few thousandths of an inch smaller than the blade and spring keeper and when the rivets are peened down, the liner compresses onto the rocker arm, so the blade has absolutely no side play. The blade has no up and down play because of the fine tuning done by Duff so as to achieve a positive match for the locking notch slot and the rocker arm detent. The pivot pins are of stainless steel and Duff feels they will wear for years unless somehow abused by a customer. The blade moves easily in and out of the liner, not touching sides or bottom, and when it reaches its open position there is a satisfying click as it locks.

Final construction steps are shaping and applying the handle material slabs. The slabs — of material selected by the customer — are first rough-cut, then placed on the liners for closer finishing before the liners are riveted together. Slabs are fitted, removed and finely ground to form a smooth transition from handle to bolster. Fit must be perfect for Duff's satisfaction.

Finally, the formed handle slabs are cemented to the liners with epoxy, clamped and allowed to cure. Final cleaning and polishing of the blade is done just before the liners are closed by riveting.

The finishing process of a folder is not unlike that for a regular sheath knife. Duff takes the rough edges down on a series of gradually finer-grit sanding belts. At a point determined by the builder, the knife moves to a series of buffing wheels for a fine polish job.

The number of belts and wheels used and the number of graduations determine the quality of finish on the handle and blade. Duff likes to take his finish down to what he calls a high satin. High satin is somewhat brighter than the average factory-built knife sold in retail stores, but is short of mirror finish. On request of the customer, Duff will do a mirror finish but feels that the high satin looks as good and will last longer as the knife is put to hard use.

Duff is obviously well pleased with his prototype folder, serial number one. Number one of all Duff's knives are never sold, incidentally. The first Duff 801 Custom Folder will remain in the shop along with his other first makes.

Duff will stamp number the next several folders he makes, until such time as he feels the needs of collectors have been satisfied.

The California knifemaker envisions a couple of other folder models and other sizes for the 801. He is thinking of folders similar to his 701 and 702 sheath blades with up-sweep or drop blades. He sees a smaller version for strictly pocket carrying and a larger model which will require a belt sheath. Duff will provide sheaths with each of his folders for an additional cost.

As of this writing, Duff is asking a bit under a $100 for his folding model. He clearly feels that a custom-made, folding lock-blade knife, at under $100, is a bargain in today's volatile market. Exotic materials for handles and perhaps blades made of 154CM steel will increase the price to a certain extent.

Duff has no intention of going into mass production of folder hunting knives, but he feels with proper planning and material handling, he will be able to turn out a lock-back-blade model in about a week.

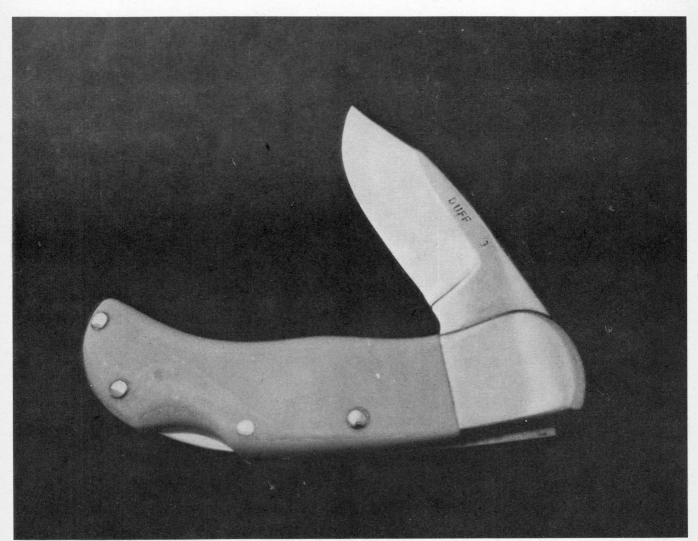

Traditionally, Bill Duff will retain his prototype models of new knives with serial number one. He calls it the Duff 801 Custom Folder. Knife may be carried in pocket for everyday use or snuggled in leather sheath for quick access.

Some of the world's most valuable contemporary knives come from the Maryland shop and forge of Bill Moran.

Chapter 8

FORGING AHEAD

This Technique For Knife Craftsmanship
Is Ages Old But Still Respected

ACCORDING TO Webster's New World Dictionary, one definition of the word *forge* is *to form or shape (metal) by heating and hammering; beat into shape.*

In today's world of knifemaking, there are perhaps two hundred more or less serious cutlers, but, of this number, less than ten use the forging procedure to the exclusion of any methods. As recently as twenty-five years ago, however, most custom knives were forged.

Why do most present-day cutlers elect not to forge? Some of the most frequently stated reasons include "The many excellent steels available from the mills make forging unnecessary"; "Frankly, I don't know how to forge"; "The possible advantages are too minute to justify the additional time and trouble"; "I don't have the equipment"; et cetera. One reason that almost never is verbalized, but which is

For centuries forging has been the traditional method of producing arms and armor. The Damascus short sword below was hand-forged by Bill Moran.

evident is that forging is hard work; to do it properly requires more training than stock removal.

Ordinarily, a cutler who forges is called a smith, while those who do not are designated as makers. The smiths defend forging with such statements as "Proper forging tends to align the grain of the steel with the curvature of the blade"; "Forging is the traditional way to make a blade"; "Forging eliminates stress within the steel"; and "Forging allows the smith to put varying degrees of hardness within the same blade — the edge can be very hard for maximum cutting efficiency, while the back can be comparatively soft for maximum strength."

Generally speaking, forging consists of taking a piece of steel and heating it in a forge — hence the name — then hammering it. The process is repeated until the metal assumes the desired shape and thickness. From this point, the technique of the smith is similar to that of the maker with this important difference: all smiths do their own heat-treating, but only a relatively small percentage of the makers do theirs, the majority preferring to farm out this operation to a commercial firm.

Most smiths heat-treat their knives one at a time and, as mentioned earlier, it is well within the capabilities of a trained smith to vary the hardness within a single blade.

Concerning this technique, Bill Moran, considered by his contemporaries as today's most-famous smith, states: "A Moran blade is hard from the center to the edge. The back is tempered to about the consistency of a spring. The point is less hard than the edge, while the tang is annealed for maximum tensile strength. Such unique tempering results in a blade that combines strength and edge-holding ability to a degree unattainable by any sort of production line methods. The blade has to be tempered by hand and cannot be tempered in a furnace."

The excellent quality of today's steels has contributed greatly to the decline in the number of practicing smiths. Virtually everyone agrees that when grinding equipment was comparatively crude, metal could be moved faster by forging than by grinding, and, too, when cutlers used just about anything that came to hand for blades — files, car springs, plowshares — the steel did need improving, and forging accomplished this. Now, most maintain that the current steels are almost perfect as they leave the mills and forging contributes little or nothing.

Speaking in terms of high-alloy tool steels, it is agreed generally by makers and smiths alike that forging is not a sage idea. Corbet Sigman, one of the best-known and most-talented modern cutlers, made a systematic study of steels and feels that while the advantages of forging tool steel are slight, they are nonetheless real and present. Conversely, it must be noted that since Sigman has changed from W2 to 154CM steel as his standard blade material, he no longer forges.

There are several well-known smiths who feel that the extra work involved is worth the trouble. These include W.D. "Bo" Randall, R.H. Ruana, Bill Bagwell, Don Hastings and Moran. In addition to these men, a limited number of

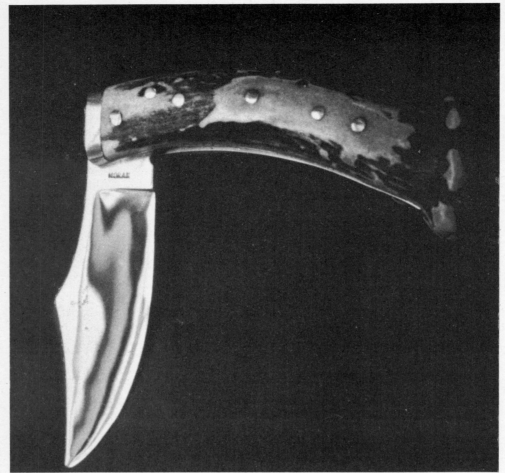

Another knife by knifesmith Bill Moran; a folder with crown stag handle slabs.

other cutlers, including Dan Dennehy and Jimmy Lile, offer a few models with forged blades, although the bulk of their work is made via the stock-removed method.

At the 1973 Knifemakers Guild meeting in Kansas City, Moran unveiled a number of forged knives featuring genuine Damascus blades. Some of those blades had as many as 1024 layers of steel and were capable of being bent to a considerable angle, then springing back to their original configuration. Since then, we have tested a number of Damascus blades, and their strength, edge-holding ability, and ease of sharpening are a delight. The procedures used to make such blades are impossible for a nonsmith.

Since Moran first displayed his masterpieces at Kansas City, at least two other smiths — Bagwell and Hastings — have developed their own Damascus blades. It is said that perhaps one or two other men are also offering blades with Damascus patterns, but there seems to be some question about the strength and edge-holding characteristics of these cutlers' work.

Just exactly what is this age-old super steel? The Encyclopedia Britannica states that Damascus is *a steel with a watered or streaked appearance....This appearance was the result of repeated twisting and forge welding together strips of steel of different qualities.*

The Encyclopedia Americana has this to say on the subject: *Damascus swords were probably made by hammering alternate layers of iron and steel into thin bars, cutting the bars into shorter lengths, bundling them together, reheating them and forging them together again into a thin bar....When the finished blade was slightly etched, the composite structure resembled the watered pattern characteristic of the Mohammedan damask fabrics. This "watered steel" has been called "the ladder by which the faithful ascended to Heaven."*

Some fantastic claims have been made for Damascus steel. For example, it is so flexible that a blade can be bent so as to allow the tip of the blade to touch the handle; a Damascus blade will taste salty to the tongue; such a blade could bisect a feather floating in the air; a strong man could chop down a tree (size not specified) with a single blow with a Damascus sword. Of such are legends made.

Frankly, we know of no Damascus blade, antique or modern, that can be bent that much! We haven't tried the feather bit, but it does not sound totally impossible. The tree trick has been accomplished — of course, the knife was pretty big, and the tree was rather small. A Damascus blade does indeed have a salty taste similar to that of blood. Suffice to say that a good Damascus blade is excellent by any standard.

Why do Moran, Bagwell and Hastings charge such high prices for their Damascus blades? Perhaps the best answer is that there is no shortcut to turning out such a blade, and a finished knife may represent as much as a hundred hours of hard, dedicated labor; in some cases, even more. In addition, it is not possible for the smith to know whether the blade is perfect until it is completely forged, ground and hardened. If it is not satisfactory, all the work on that particular blade has been for naught.

Here is the procedure used by Moran to turn out a Damascus blade:

He begins with a bar of iron and a bar of steel. The proportions must be exact, and the steel must be of the correct type with just the proper amount of carbon. Just exactly what this steel is, Moran doesn't say.

These two pieces of metal then are welded together in the fire of the forge in the age-old manner. The heat must be exactly right for both the iron and the steel. If the metal is too hot, the steel will be ruined; if it is not hot enough, it will not fuse properly. As for how much heat is required, Moran, Bagwell and Hastings do not divulge this bit of information. The bar then is folded and welded again. This is a gross oversimplification, but the operations not covered remain privileged information.

At this stage, the smith has four layers, the bar is approximately three inches square. Now the bar must be hammered out to a length of approximately six inches, and again folded and welded. This process is repeated until the desired number of layers is reached. Should you try your hand at this, you'll discover that the layers do not want to weld together in a satisfactory manner. The secret remains.

"I have tried everything from sixteen to 2048 layers," Moran stated. "The best blades and the most beautiful patterns can be achieved with 512 layers. If you go too high, the layers tend to become carbonized all the way through, and you are back to a solid bar of carbon steel. To achieve the many different patterns, many and varied techniques must be employed at certain stages of the forging. The more closely the blade is forged to the finished size, the better the blade will be."

The smiths can control the basic patterns of each blade, but they are quick to add that each blade is unlike any other. "The patterns are as different and individual as the human fingerprint," Moran told us. "Each has a character of its own. I sometimes feel that a part of one's personality goes into each Damascus blade."

The final step in finishing a Damascus blade is to treat it with a certain strong acid that brings out the figure of the grain.

Again, it should be emphasized that simply because a blade has a pattern, it should not be compared with those offered by Moran, Bagwell and Hastings. A good Damascus blade should be comparable in every respect — edge holding, flexibility, tensile strength — to the finest blade made from the most-modern cutlery steel. Beware of those

Daryl Meier hand-forged these tomahawks. Although they certainly are not folding knives, they do demonstrate the art of the smith at the forge. Meier offers these works of art in various configurations.

who offer so-called Damascus blades that will not hold an edge, or are not recommended for use. Originally, a Damascus blade was an object upon which a warrior staked his life.

Perhaps, at this stage, you are awaiting the moth-eaten debate of which procedure — forging or grinding — will result in a tougher, stronger blade that will hold its edge for the longer period of time. We cannot resolve this debate. We can only say that if a knife is made by a first-class cutler and heat-treated in a proper manner in a forge or an electric furnace, the resulting blade will be good. Which is to say that a first-rate forged blade is as good as any currently available.

The list of current smiths who offer folding knives is small, because there are relatively few smiths, and less than half of them offer folders. The most-famous forged folding knives of today are those offered by Moran. Lile, we understand, offers a few folding models with hand-forged blades on special order, and Bagwell makes a few such knives, some with Damascus blades. His most-popular blade

material currently, however, is one which he terms "double extra forged."

This procedure, to quote Bagwell, "enhances the qualities of my standard forged steel through a special hammer technique combined with a very high blade temperature, then a different hammer technique at a very low heat. This procedure is used over and above all normal forging techniques and practices." Although Bagwell does not claim that this double extra-forged steel is as good as his Damascus blades, he contends that it does approach such blades. Obviously, they are much lower in price than the Damascus models.

Recently, the American Bladesmiths Society was formed, with Moran named chairman, and the following named to the board of directors: Bagwell, Hastings, Lile and B.R. Hughes. Moran and Lile both have served as president of the Knifemakers Guild, and Moran is quick to point out that the society is not designed to be in competition with the guild.

"Most of us are members of both groups," he emphasizes, "and the expressed purpose of the society is to

Damascus steel blades are rare enough in themselves, but a Damascus folder must rank among the rarest. Bill Bagwell from Louisiana created this outstanding stag-handled folder. Bolsters are also made of Damascus.

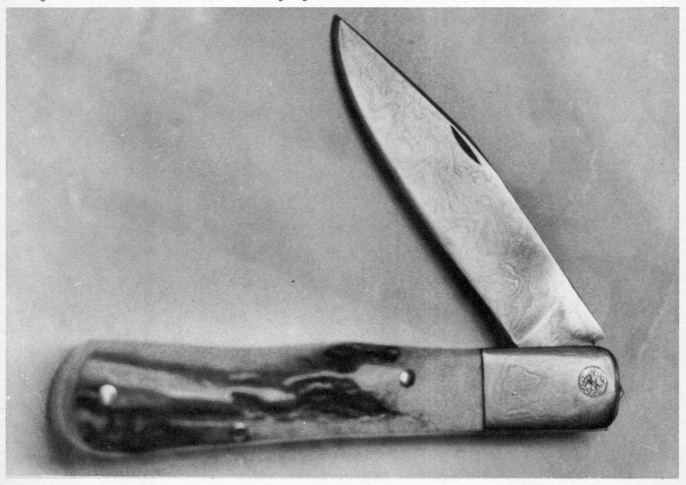

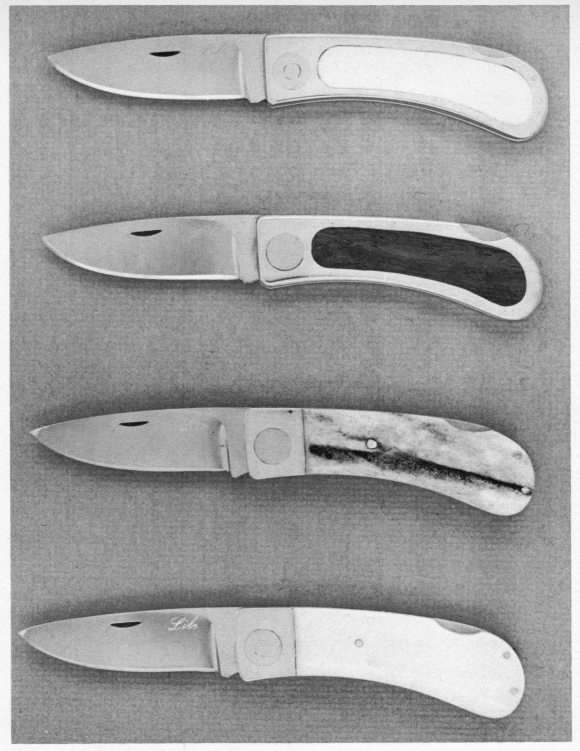

Jimmy Lile has been producing his folders for some time from standard steel. Lile has announced plans to offer a limited number of forged blade folders available on special order. Delivery time is unknown.

encourage and promote interest in the art of the forged blade."

Moran feels there is currently much more interest in the art of the smith than was the case perhaps five years ago.

"Almost daily I receive letters or phone calls from individuals who want to know more about forging," he reports. "This was not the case a few years back."

Things apparently are looking up for the smith and for the customer who desires a knife made via the forging process; this is all to the good. Even if you should honestly feel that the resulting knives are no better, if as good as those made via stock removal, honor still is due to that handful of men who continue to use the methods that smiths have used for thousands of years to produce blades.

Chapter 9

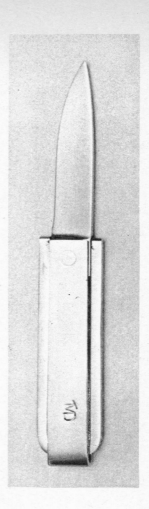

NONTYPICAL FOLDERS

Some Originality

Of Design Has

Resulted In

Unusual But Still

Practical Cutlery

Everyone KNOWS what constitutes a folding knife, right? It's a knife with a blade or blades that open and close in a manner that is familiar to every boy scout. Some models require you to push a lever to close the blade, but they are all pretty much the same, right?

Well, usually, but not always.

There are a number of folding knives on today's market that do not fit this normal mould, and we have elected to term them nontypical folders. Some are novel, some are downright ingenious, and more to the point, most are extremely functional.

That last point is important. It is not enough for a knife simply to be different. Virtually anyone can come up with a unique idea that is different, but in order to take that idea to the bank, it must be functional.

Perhaps the first nontypical folding knife we ever saw was a Philippine design called the balisong, which was also

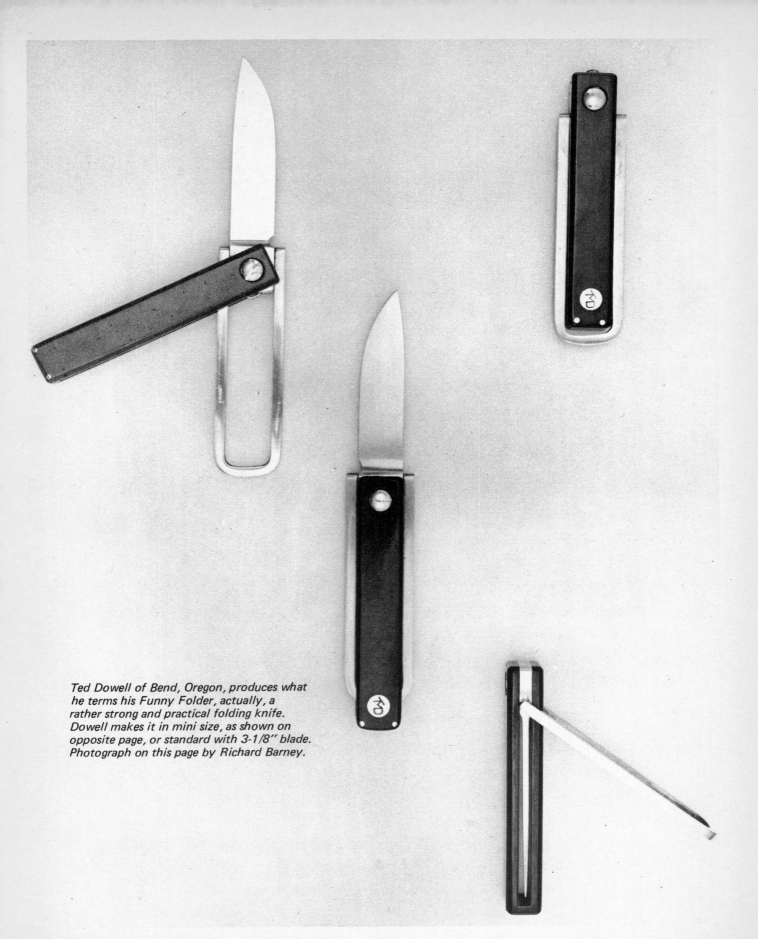

Ted Dowell of Bend, Oregon, produces what he terms his Funny Folder, actually, a rather strong and practical folding knife. Dowell makes it in mini size, as shown on opposite page, or standard with 3-1/8'' blade. Photograph on this page by Richard Barney.

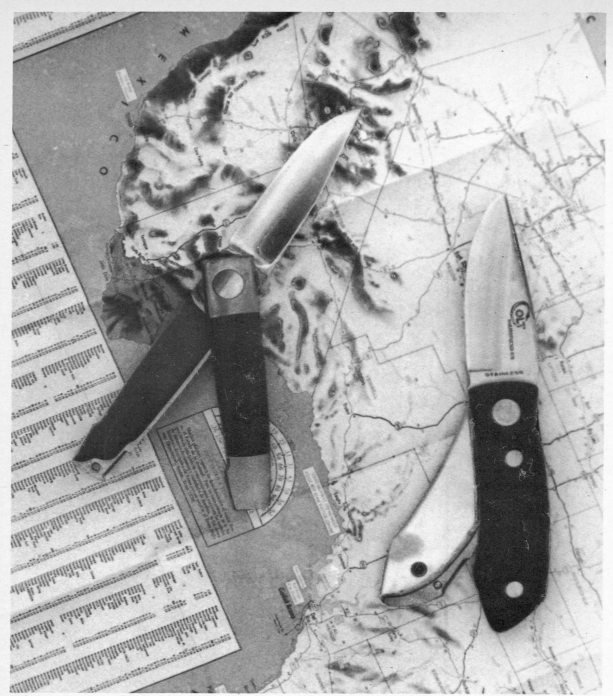

Folder at right is the Barry Wood design that was marketed by Colt a few years ago. The Wood knife at left features a blade made by R.W. Loveless. The Loveless blade has become a genuine collectors' item.

termed a click-click knife by the GIs. The handle is divided into two parts that swing around the blade on a central pin. Closed, the two sections completely surround the blade; open, they form a much sturdier handle than you might imagine. Quite a few of these knives were brought back as souvenirs by our victorious troops, but the workmanship and overall quality of these trophies is second-rate by modern standards.

A number of years ago, the Garcia Corporation imported from Finland a well-made version of the balisong made by Hackman. In that preinflation era, the importers were able to sell it for the remarkably low price of $7.50. According to reports, however, the knife did not sell well. When asked by the feds to stop importing it, Garcia complied without putting up much of an argument. Apparently the federal boys considered it a type of switchblade, and, in truth, it

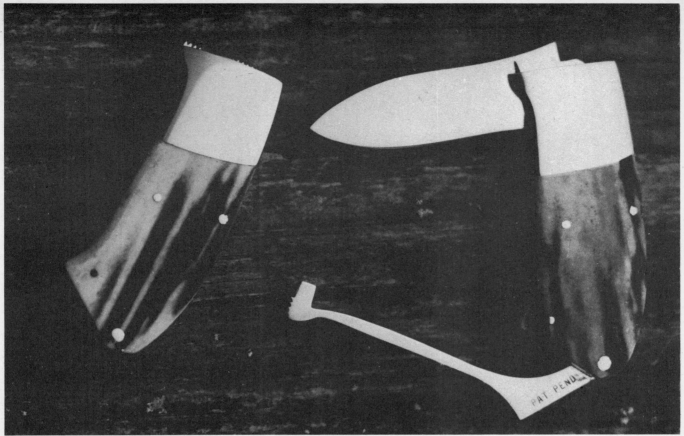

Leon Pittman calls this folding knife the Worm. It operates flawlessly with no spring but locks open or closed. Note the serrations above the bolster of the closed knife. Definitely nontypical.

could be opened with only minor effort and delay with one hand. Cheap imitations of the Hackman still can be found, most of them made in Hong Kong, priced at less than $5. The original Hackman knives, when one can be found, are bringing four and five times their original price as a novelty of collector interest. But before you buy one, check on local legal ramifications.

Then there is Ted Dowell's so-called Funny Folder. We saw this knife for the first time back around 1969 or so, and it is, to say the very least, unusual and useful.

Here's what Dowell has to say about this model: "This design is not original with me — the adaptation of this design to a hunter-sized folding knife may be, though even this idea was given to me by a good friend and I cannot claim it.

"It is funny only in that it's unusual. Actually, it is a very strong folding knife. We've used it to push through the briskets on small bucks many times with no problems."

Dowell makes this model with a 3-1/8-inch blade that is three-sixteenths-inch in thickness with either D2 or 440C as a blade material. The total weight, with micarta slabs, is only four ounces. The last time we checked, the price was $90, but one should be prepared to wait about three years for delivery.

Describing this knife is tough. Suffice to say that the blade fits into an elongated U-shaped piece of steel, the micarta slabs revolve around, the blade pivots out of the U,

The Barry Wood Mark 2 special folding knife. The handle halves rotate around until they catch in either the open or closed position. This handsome knife operates as well as it looks.

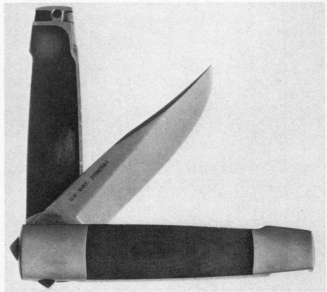

Arkansas' Jimmy Lile has designed his locking system as a push button. Knife is popular at about $200.

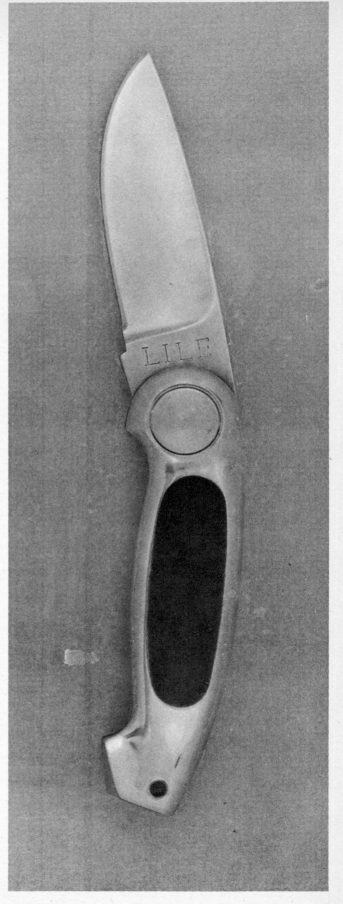

and the slabs, together with the piece of steel, becomes the handle.

It sounds complicated, but in reality it is ultra-simple. Pictures perhaps show it better than words can express.

Another novel folder is offered by Leon Pittman, who markets his knives under the name *Worm*. Don't ask us why. Leon calls this model his Hidden Blade Folder, and that's a graphic term.

Imagine a fixed-bladed hunting knife of the full-tang variety. The guard is simply a slight extension of the front of the bolster; this extension has a serrated section. Push down and out on this section, and the front half of what normally would be the tang swings down, revealing a slot for the blade. There is no spring on the blade, and it simply moves down into its receptacle without resistance. Now swing the front of the tang back into its original position and you have what is apparently a well-made handle sans blade.

Pittman offers this model in two versions: one a 2-3/8-inch blade made from one-eighth-inch stock at $175, and a slightly larger model made from three-sixteenths-inch stock sells for $225 at this writing. His standard blade material is D2 and standard handle materials include rosewood, walnut micarta and linen micarta. Genuine stag and white micarta are available at slightly higher prices.

The waiting period for one of these custom-built *Worm* knives is less than a year as these lines are written, and this one must qualify as one of the most unusual folders on today's market.

In our book, perhaps the most functional of today's nontypical folders may well be those offered by Barry Wood. This design is familiar to most knife buffs, as it was offered first through Indian Ridge Traders a number of years ago, then was marketed by Colt. For a brief period it was possible to purchase Wood knives with blades made by R.W. Loveless. If you have one of these, you have a bona fide collector's item!

For the past few years, however, Barry Wood has sold his knives under his own name. The two halves of the handle and the blade are pinned together at one end; the handles simply revolve around the blade, which itself stops revolving halfway around, leaving one-half of the handle in the traditional open position. The other half of the handle completes its journey, and there you have it! We once asked A.G. Russell, the knife authority, what he thought of Wood's invention and he replied, "It has enormous merit. It is strong and can be easily operated even with very cold fingers."

Wood currently offers several different models, ranging in price from $85 to $150. You can, of course, spend more if you desire stag slabs, a high polish on the blade, et al.

Wood's standard blade material is 154CM, with the handle plates made of 17-4PH stainless steel.

Our special favorite in the Wood line is the Mark 2 Special, which features a 3¼-inch blade made of one-eighth-inch steel, and a price tag of $125. At this price, you can select from a variety of micartas, including black, cordovan, natural or green.

But be prepared to wait at least thirteen months for a

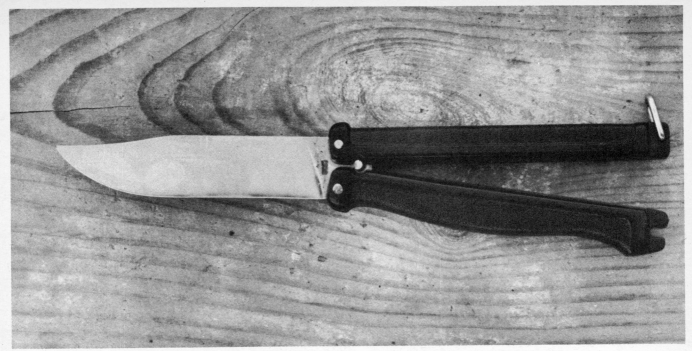

This knife is a copy of the Philippine balisong or click-click knife as it became known. Slabs fold down to form the handle. When closed, handles surround blade. Garcia imported a similar model a few years ago.

Wood knife — longer if you desire extra features. The finished product, however, is worth the time lag, we feel.

Then, there is a new breed of lock-blade folders that some may consider traditional. However, since the lock is a button device incorporated with the hinge pin, we feel otherwise.

Gerber Legendary Blades has its Paul Folder, with prices beginning at around $55. When we talked with Gerber's Al Mar at the 1977 Expo in Dallas, he indicated that his firm's only problem with this model is keeping up with the demand. It's a real looker, and up to normal Gerber standards of high quality.

A larger handmade version of the button lock is available from Jimmy Lile, and it is not a copy of the Gerber. These were developed separately, which, we suppose, goes to prove all the things said about great minds following similar paths.

The Lile lock button is a well-made knife suitable for field dressing big game. One can be yours for $200 with a waiting period of six to eight months. Lile ordinarily uses D2 for his blades, but other steels are available if you prefer. The handle inserts are available in rosewood, cocobolo, various micartas, ebony, stag and even ivory at varying prices.

In foreign climes other types of nontypical folders are encountered occasionally, such as the Scandinavian barrel knife, but those discussed in this chapter pretty well cover what is normally available in this country.

Some are more expensive than others; some are better made than others; some are more functional. They have one thing in common, however. All are interesting, and a fascinating collection could be assembled featuring these nontypical folding knives.

Gerber's Paul folding knife has a push-button lock similar to Lile's. Each was developed independently. This new model is on the market for about $60.

Chapter 10

SELECTING THAT EVERYDAY POCKETKNIFE

There Are Good Knives Aplenty, But Some Are Even Better!

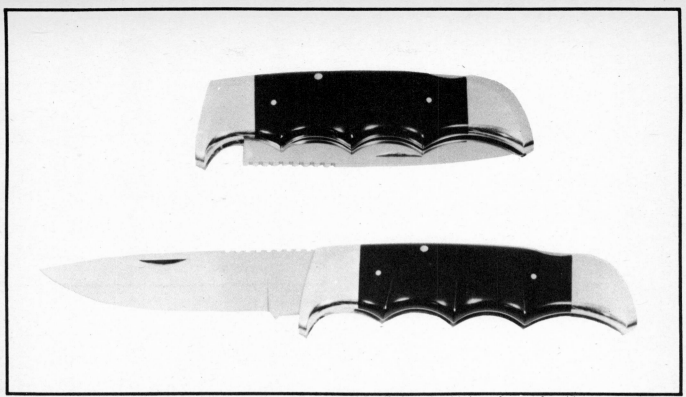

At left is an array of folding knives of various sizes. The one at right of photo is a bit large for comfortable carrying, while the one at the bottom is too small to be of great practical use. The other two are considered about right by the authors. (Above) This Kershaw folding filed knife is fine for the field, but not for the pocket. It comes with a scabbard so that it may be carried, folded, on the belt. Such knives are not designed for everyday use.

MOST BONA FIDE knife buffs, whenever they go hunting, slip a folding knife into their pocket in addition to carrying a sheath knife on their belt. The game might be duck, quail, deer, bear, moose, dove, or what-have-you, but a second knife invariably goes into the pocket. This pocketknife might be a Puma Backpacker, a Buck Esquire or Cadet, a Schrade 3-9/16-inch stock knife, a Gerber Classic, or any one of several handmade knives.

Admittedly, we are dedicated knife buffs, but it is our considered opinion that no man should ever put on a pair of trousers without slipping a folding knife in one of his front pants pockets.

The next chapter is devoted to selection of a folding knife for hunting purposes, so here we are primarily concerned with choosing a folder for everyday wear. It should not matter a whit if you're going for a drive in the hills in your family auto, heading for a favorite fishing spot in a pickup, taking your best girl to the movies, sitting in church on Sunday, or headed afoot for a quart of milk at the corner convenience shop. And if you develop this habit of having a folding knife in your pocket, it should feel right at home there.

Mind you, we are not advocating such a practice from the standpoint of either protection or survival. A handy folder with a 2½-inch blade is not the greatest thing in the world for protection, and it is virtually worthless for offensive purposes, although it does beat nothing at all. Moreover, a relatively good case could be made for such a knife's usefulness in a survival situation; a survival knife is, after all, what you have handy when disaster strikes. If excreta hit the fan while you're driving around town, your survival knife is going to be what you have with you, and your

beautifully designed and crafted combat and survival models that are back home in their rugged sheaths are about as worthless as a Confederate $5 bill!

Actually, we are discussing a knife that will be used to open envelopes at the office, cut twine when wrapping a package, snip a thread from your double knits, scrape the mud from your boots, clean a pipe bowl, pare your fingernails, whittle, sharpen a pencil, or perhaps even dress some small game.

How does one go about selecting such a faithful companion where there are literally hundreds of makes and models from which to choose?

Perhaps the first thing to examine is the overall size and shape. If a closed folder is four inches or more in length, you can write it off as an everyday associate. It may be just the ticket for dressing out deer, and it may ride easily enough in your jeans, work pants or hunting trousers, but it won't feel right in your business suits or dress slacks. If you'll permit personal opinion, our vote goes to a knife that is no more than approximately 3½ inches in length, and if it is more than one-half-inch thick, it will not get our vote!

If the size appears suitable, take a close look at the knife with the blades closed. All corners should be rounded; no point of any blade should ride up above the handle; there should be no obvious gaps in the back of the knife — everything should be well-fitted. The nail nicks in the blades should be large enough and readily accessible; and no blade corner should protrude more than one-eighth of an inch or so. This latter point is one that disqualifies many otherwise perfectly suited knives. If a corner protrudes to any extent, it is guaranteed to wear out the lining of a pocket *muy pronto!*

Concerning those nail nicks — believe it not, we saw one

folder the design of which made it impossible to open one of the smaller blades unless the largest blade was opened first. The nail nick had been put in the wrong place on the small blade. Shun such designs like you would the plague!

Let's assume that you have picked out something that fills the bill up to this point, no pun intended. Open all of the blades, then close them one at a time. When a blade is opened, it should hesitate at the halfway position. Each blade also should close in the same manner. The blades, all of them, should open and close with a click. The only term we have ever heard used to describe this hesitating, then opening or closing with a click, is "walking and talking." Any good knife should do just that.

Granted, getting a knife to perform in such a manner does require considerable skill when the component parts are fitted. This is generally accomplished with a deft hand and the proper file. Even on mass-produced knives this is done through hand operations, so when we speak of folding knives, any such knife of good quality is in fact a partially handmade model. It is a tribute to the knife factories that versions with three and four blades can be made to "walk and talk" and still be sold for a profit with a list price of under $20.

If the knife you are considering will not pass this test, reject it. If none of the knives in the shop can pass it, you're in the wrong store. Any good-quality factory folder should pass this phase of the examination.

The knifemaker who turns out handmade custom folders can produce a knife that will not hesitate or click, if the man laying down the long green so desires, and there are those who want their folders to open and close in a soft manner. No really good explanation of why a person would desire this has ever been advanced within our hearing — we like 'em to walk and talk!

The matters of materials and blade shapes already have been discussed at some length. Suffice to say that we cannot recommend an everyday knife that has more than three blades, and there is much to be said for some two-bladed models. If it's the right make and model it will be light, compact and up to most chores.

On a two-bladed knife, one blade should be the so-called long clip, and we vote for the spey design for the second blade. If a third blade is desired, it probably should be a sheepfoot, which also makes a dandy patch knife if you're a black powder shooter. Such gadgets as cap openers, screwdrivers — regular and Phillips — awls, et al., have their place in the scheme of things, but not on your everyday knife.

Some favor single-blade folders, and with a three-inch blade there is much to be said for such a model. These frequently are called jackknives, and probably only the multitude of extremely poor-quality knives made in this guise keep this style from being more popular.

There was a time in the dimming past when one could specify a desired handle material, even on factory knives, from a selection including bone, stag, pearl, ivory, rosewood and gutta percha. Now, you pretty well take what you are offered. Synthetic materials are in and handles such as those offered by Schrade for their Old Timer and Uncle Henry lines have proved themselves both attractive and durable. The same can be said for Buck's handles. On a custom model, stag is never a mistake, but you'll probably have to settle for micarta. Real mother-of-pearl and ivory are probably the poorest possible selections. Both are brittle and costly.

The Schrade Model 837Y is a fine everyday model, although some buffs might tend to object to the lack of bolsters.

There's much to be said for the faithful, old Barlow design, provided the size is right, workmanship is good.

Everyday choice of coauthor Bill Hughes is this Schrade Model 897UH. With knife closed, no corners protrude.

For the man who wants a single knife to open up deer in the field as well as envelopes in the office, this petite folding blade model Camillus is a wise choice. It is relatively inexpensive, but is well constructed.

On custom folders that are to be carried and used — you'd be surprised at how few fit into this category — micarta is the best handle material. The handmade lads offer it in a variety of patterns and colors. Today's favorite, according to these makers, is ivory micarta, which the average person cannot distinguish from genuine ivory at a distance of six inches!

As suggested earlier, we feel that nickel-silver bolsters are somewhat more desirable than brass, although brass liners are great for pocketknives.

On that everyday knife, we strongly urge you to consider stainless steel as a blade material. Most people clean a hunting knife after each use, but a knife used daily will not, in all probability, receive a daily cleaning.

Gerber is now using 440C on most of their folders and this steel is about as good as any and better than most. Since a small folder is not expected to handle heavy chores — or should not, at any rate — such a blade should be hard; say Rockwell C 62-64. Hardness and brittleness are not one and the same, but are definitely related.

Most of today's handmade folders are designed as hunting models, so there are not many custom knives made today that can qualify for everyday wear. Jess Horn, Harvey McBurnette and G.W. Stone, to name three, do offer compact custom models that are things of beauty.

On the other hand, for less than $20, it is possible to purchase a well-made pocketknife with two or three blades

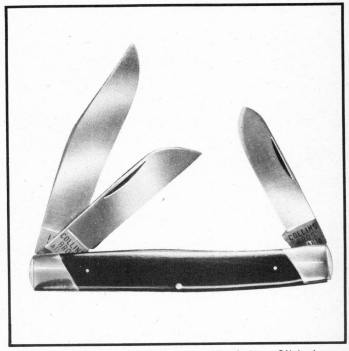

A knife with an overall closed length of about 3½ inches is ideal for everyday carrying. Large enough to earn its keep, it isn't large enough to wear out pocket linings.

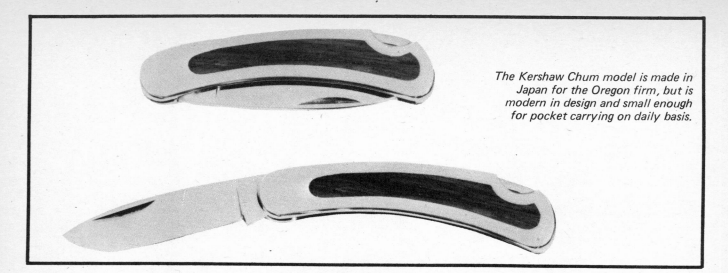

The Kershaw Chum model is made in Japan for the Oregon firm, but is modern in design and small enough for pocket carrying on daily basis.

bearing such names as Buck, Camillus, Browning, Western, Case, Ka-Bar or Schrade. Said knives are well-made from good materials and will "walk and talk" with great aplomb! Such a knife is actually a lifetime investment, provided you take reasonable care of it and don't lose it. Consequently a little time spent in the selection of this type of knife does not seem out of line.

Keep in mind that a carrying knife is for using. We recall one incident wherein a gentleman-sportsman and his wife went to a barbecue where the eating utensils provided were plastic! Have you ever tried cutting a healthy chunk of barbecued beef with a flimsy plastic knife?

The husband, much to his wife's dismay, pulled out a

Schrade Uncle Henry 897 and proceeded to eat his meal with gusto. Finally, faced with starvation, his better half requested the loan of the little folder. Soon, almost everyone at that table was using the Schrade. Chalk up another use for the everyday knife.

We've been packing everyday pocketknives for years. Of course, it's not always the same knife, and literally dozens of various makes and models have held the title of "Old Favorite" for varying periods of time.

However, you can bet your favorite pair of hunting boots that the next time you run into one of us, we'll each have a folding knife in our respective pants pocket. We feel undressed without them.

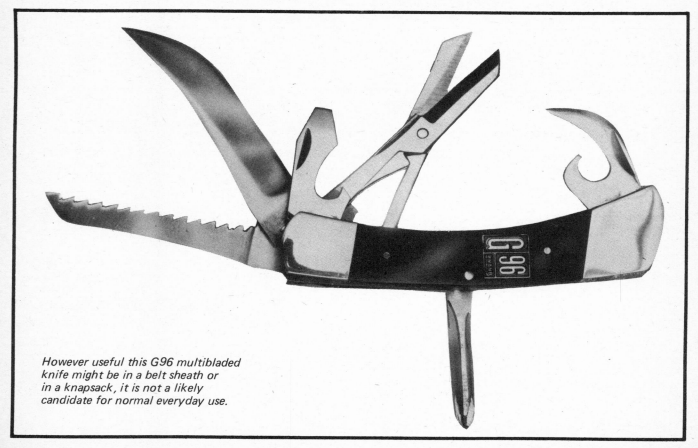

However useful this G96 multibladed knife might be in a belt sheath or in a knapsack, it is not a likely candidate for normal everyday use.

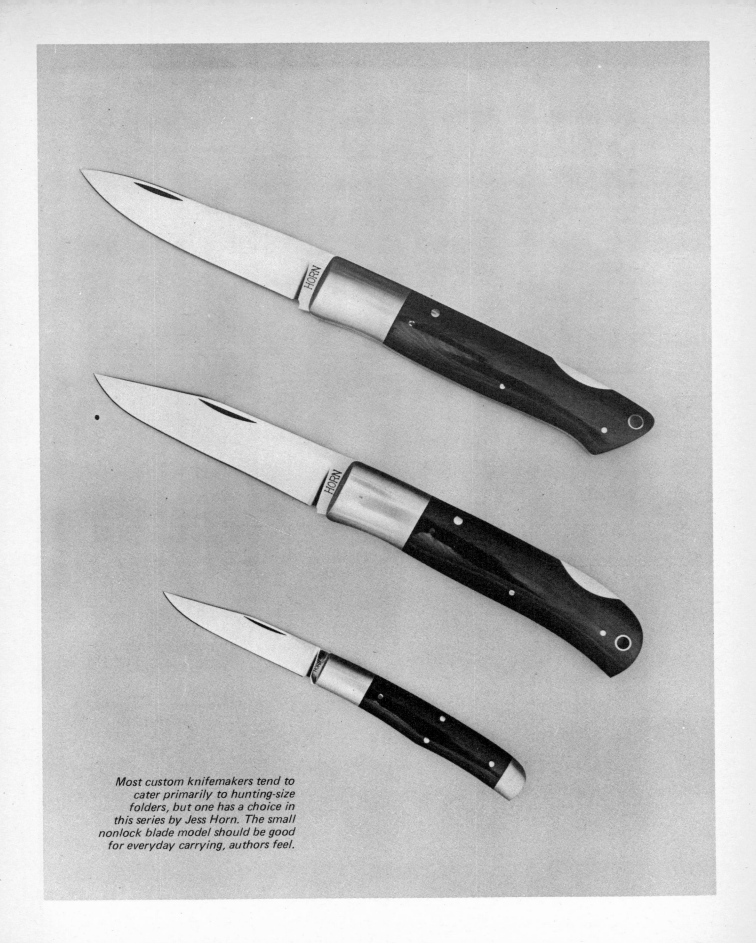

Most custom knifemakers tend to cater primarily to hunting-size folders, but one has a choice in this series by Jess Horn. The small nonlock blade model should be good for everyday carrying, authors feel.

SELECTING THE FOLDING HUNTER

Chapter 11

The Right Knife In The Field Can Save Time, Discomfort And Temper In Dressing Out Game

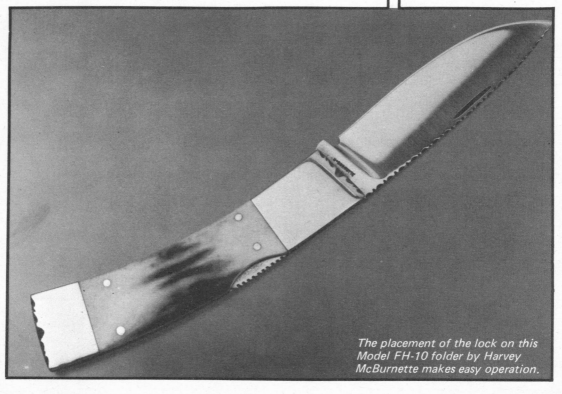

The placement of the lock on this Model FH-10 folder by Harvey McBurnette makes easy operation.

B.R. Hughes once used a small Buck Cadet pocketknife to dress out a forkhorn buck he had taken.

SEVERAL YEARS AGO, B.R. Hughes, one of the coauthors of this book, found himself on a whitetail hunt, miles from home, and his only knife was a Buck Cadet.

This was a definite oversight. With a couple of dozen larger models waiting for the opportunity to go hunting, Hughes had wandered out in a mental fog with only his petite pocketknife on his person. As most knife buffs know, the Cadet's longest blade is only about 2½ inches long, and it is not the type of knife that comes immediately to mind when big-game hunting is mentioned.

To make a long story short, at about eight o'clock that morning, Hughes dropped a nice forkhorn with his .264 and the little Buck Cadet did the job — not as quickly and perhaps not quite so neatly as a larger knife would have done, but it did suffice. Next time, however, Hughes made certain he had a better tool for the job at hand.

A number of years ago, when it was considered fashionable to pack a sheath knife with a five or six-inch blade, not so many folding hunters were available. The first model that won general acclaim for hunting was the large Buck lock-blade folder, and this is still the big seller in many areas.

A folding hunter makes a lot of sense these days. Most custom makers report that their best-selling sheath knives have blades ranging from three to four inches in length. In

One of the first folding hunter models to gain acceptance with the outdoor fraternity was the Buck.

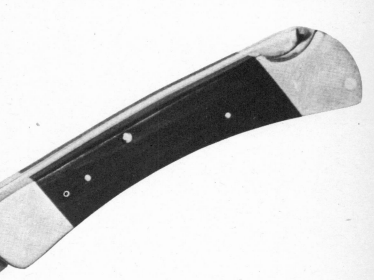

truth, anything that such a knife can do, a folding knife can do equally well. There is an added advantage for the folding model in that, when such a knife is in the closed position, it is approximately half as long as a sheath knife. Thus, you don't find a folder carried in a belt sheath poking the car or truck seat, the bench in your duck blind, or whatever you're sitting on in a deer stand. Neither does it attract as much attention when you stop at the diner for a cup of coffee returning from the hunt.

Let's assume that you have decided you desire a good hunting folder. What do you look for when you walk into the knife shop?

First, you should decide whether you want a lock on your blade. There is much to be said for a lock and little that can be stated against one. We haven't had a lot of nonlocked blades slam closed on our fingers in actual using situations, but it has occurred, and, we assure you, this is not a habit-forming occurrence! A good lock keeps that blade open until you are ready for it to be closed. That is how it should be.

An objection to the blade lock is that it is difficult, though not impossible, to close the knife using only one hand. Theoretically, this may be a drawback, but it is more theoretical than real.

If a knife is to be used primarily for hunting, we recommend a lock on the blade, but the lock should be easy to operate. We tried a model once that was on the market only for a year or so that was virtually impossible for anyone with less grip than King Kong possesses to operate the lock latch. No children, few women and only some men could make it work! Add to this wet and/or bloody hands and cold temperatures, and you have just about the most impractical lock-blade folder that has yet to be created. Needless to say, it's not around these days.

Some locks are easier to operate than others. Among the ones that we really like are those offered by Ron Lake, Harvey McBurnette, Jimmy Lile, Gerber, most Bucks, Camillus, Case and a couple of others.

The blade or blades should be easy to open, but should not fall open without some effort; the blade should stay put until you are ready for it to open, and, at this point, minimum of effort should be required.

One of the best opening knives we have used are those of Barry Wood's design. They are not traditional folders but they are certainly folding knives. These were covered at greater length in another chapter.

A blade lock on a folding hunting knife is not mandatory, as illustrated by this functional model which is the work of cutler Ron Little.

Puma's folders, for the most part, open with little effort, as do those made by Lake, Lile, McBurnette, Bill Moran, Gerber, Buck, et al. If, however, a hunting folder has a blade that seems tough to open, once again think of those cold, wet, often bloody fingers. If you have problems in the sporting goods shop, those problems will be magnified a hundred fold in the field.

One blade or two? This is a moot point, because there is as much to be said for the trimness and comfortable grip of the single-bladed knife as for the versatility of the two-bladed models. It is true that when one blade gets dull on a multibladed knife the other — or others — will still be sharp, but this may not offset the additional cost and bulk. Each hunter must make up his own mind on this issue. We favor single-bladed knives, but it's still a relatively free country.

Knifemaker-guide-hunter Jim Barbee has introduced a line of folders. Barbee tests his custom knives in the field and knows what a good folder should be.

The hunting blade should be a minimum of three inches in length, if it is to be superior to the so-called pocketknife. A blade this long can handle just about any outdoor chore, but if you should prefer one slightly longer there are plenty available.

There must be at least two dozen factory models that would more than adequately meet the needs of the sportsman in quest of a folding hunter; in addition, there are at least sixty makers of handmade cutlery who will furnish such knives with the customer's choice of handle material, blade hardness, etc. Price-wise, these knives range from less than $15 to — well, the sky's the limit.

It would be impossible to list all the good factory folding hunters, but here are a few that are impressive: Buck's Ranger, standard folding hunter, and Esquire; Case's Shark Tooth; Camillus' No. 88 lock blade; Camillus' No. 26 sans lock; Gerber's entire line of lock-bladed folders; Puma Game Warden; Western's No. 932, a monster that comes with a saw blade as well as a flat-ground blade; Schrade's No. 127 Uncle Henry sans blade lock; Western's brand-new lock-blade hunter dubbed the Model 532; S&W's lock-blade hunter; Bowen's Remington Bullet copy, ad infinitum.

There are so many excellent handmade folders that we can only name a few favorites: Jess Horn offers several excellent models; W.T. Fuller makes a complete line of

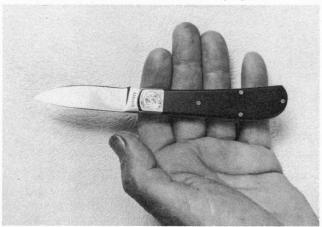

Georgia custom builder Jack Barrett produces a folder that measures four inches overall. He says the length is the practical maximum for pocket carrying.

easy-opening lock-bladed hunters; Jim Barbee has just introduced a line of lock blades that promise to be real winners (Barbee is a hunter who knows what hunters are looking for); McBurnett's hunters with the lock located high on the back of the handle are a delight to use; Jimmy Lile's models have been long-time pals; Ted Dowell's work is always excellent; Buster Warenski is just beginning to get his fine models out in limited numbers; Ron Lake is in a class all to himself; Bill Davis' lock-blade models are lightweight marvels; no one's work holds an edge longer than does the old master, Bill Moran; Russ Andrews promises to be one of tomorrow's big names.

Concerning the handmades, virtually any maker listed in our directory could easily make up a lock-bladed folder that will meet the demands of the most discriminating sportsman. Just remember, the price will probably be a minimum of $60, and you will probably have to wait at least six months for delivery, maybe longer.

Should you decide on a custom model, you will need to specify handle material and, in most cases, a blade steel. The best handle material for the hunting folder, no questions asked, is micarta. Some object to the fact that it is an artificial material, but the average person cannot distinguish between a handle made of genuine ivory and one made of ivory micarta, which is one way of saying that a properly made micarta handle is attractive and really is quite durable.

One drawback to the folding hunter is that such a knife is more difficult to clean than a standard sheath model. Thus, a good case can be made for blades made from

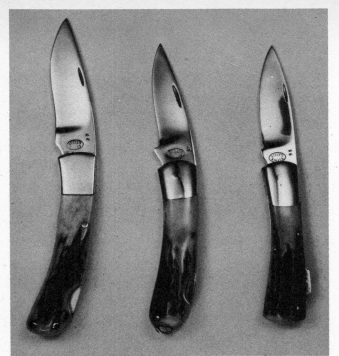

Steve Davenport has built an enviable reputation for making a number of rugged, handsome folders that are well designed for the sportsman-customer in the field.

(Below) Jess Horn has been known as one of the best folding knifemakers for years. The reason is obvious.

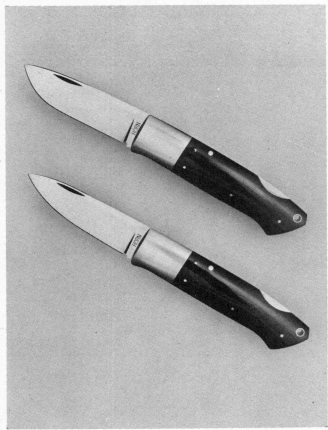

Two sizes of the Remington Bullet model folding knife by Bowen are offered. Either will do a job on game.

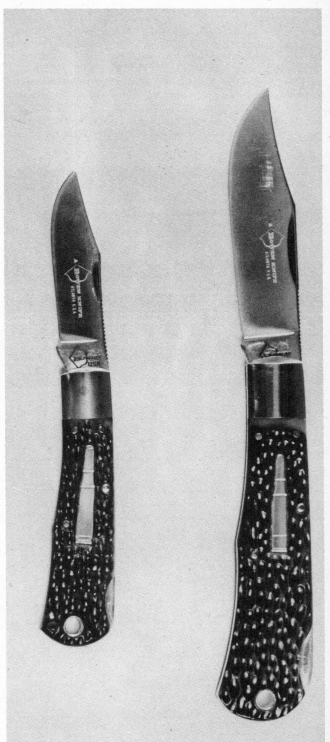

stain-resistant steels such as 154CM, 440C and D2. A properly heat-treated blade made from any of these steels will be good.

The folding hunter also will be difficult to sharpen once it gets dull. One of the best blade steels around today is 01, which is one of the older materials. The late Red Watson, who would have become one of the all-time greats had he lived out his allotted years, once told another knifemaker that he made knives out of 154CM for customers, but used 01 steel for knives that he made for his own use. That should tell you something.

Don't make the mistake of having your blade treated too hard. Around 56 to 58 on the Rockwell C scale should handle most sporting functions, and it will make for a tough, durable blade that will hold an edge better than most, yet be comparatively easy to sharpen once dull.

Although it will be somewhat difficult, as mentioned earlier, clean the knife after it has been used. Of course, a folding knife designed for big-game hunting will not see daily usage, so one or two thorough cleanings per season are not too much to ask for a faithful companion.

No question about it, the folding hunter is much more popular today than was the case only a few years ago. The trend toward shorter blades has had much to do with this state of affairs. Fashion also has had its impact, currently the folding hunter is the "in" item in the cutlery world. Moreover, unless it is a really large folder, such as Western's 932, it can be packed in your jeans pocket on weekends, although a folding hunter will hardly do for day-in, day-out carrying — too rough on pockets!

The big thing in favor of such knives, however, is that they work, and that's the bottom line.

Although relatively new in the folding knife market, the series of lock blade hunters by the Nolen Brothers has proven popular with buyers. Most custom knifemakers are quoting rather long delivery times for orders.

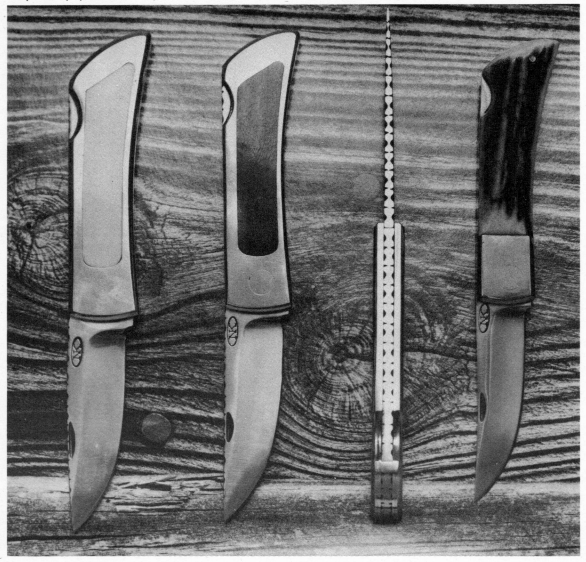

One of the real monsters in the field is the Western No. 932. It must be carried in a belt sheath but can handle the roughest job.

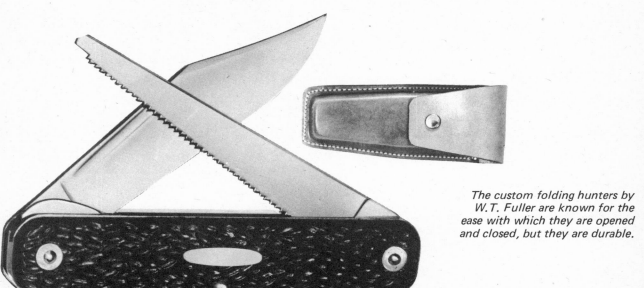

The custom folding hunters by W.T. Fuller are known for the ease with which they are opened and closed, but they are durable.

Chapter 12

Henry Baer, president of Schrade Cutlery, is the original Uncle Henry, who takes an active part in the day-to-day operations. He uses one of his firm's Honesteels to put an edge on one of the knives from the upstate New York plant.

MADE BY SCHRADE

A Lifetime Guarantee Should Be Evidence Enough Of This Firm's Faith In Its Product!

WHAT SHEFFIELD is to England, upstate New York is to cutlery in this country and one of the leaders for more than a century has been what now is Schrade Cutlery.

Oddly enough, it was the Sheffield experts in steelmaking and knifemaking who migrated to the area and founded the industry in this country. From the early Nineteenth Century until after World War II it was that area of the Catskills from which came most of the folding and hunting knives of the extended era.

Before the introduction of electricity into the area during the Twenties, the mountain waters of the surrounding Catskills powered the machinery and the grinding wheels. As many as 3500 knifemakers were gathered in the factories of Orange and Ulster Counties in those days.

Today, Ellenville, New York, is the seat of the industry. It was there that a group of Sheffield-trained cutlers began plying their craft in 1871, with the founding of the Ellenville Cooperating Cutlery Company. A couple of years later, one Major Dwight Devine purchased the firm and changed the name to the Ulster Knife Company.

Three brothers, Joseph, Louis and George Schrade,

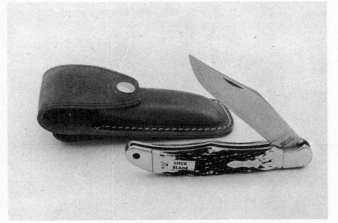

Uncle Henry's unique lock-blade design is described by the firm as a folding Bowie, measuring 5½ inches closed, with a sheath; each of the knives has a serial number.

The Model 610T, one of the originals in the Old Timer line, measures four inches closed and is described as a slim stock style with Turkish clip, sheepfoot, spay blades.

began producing knives in Walden, New York, thirty miles from Ellenville, in 1904. The brothers introduced dies and accurate reproduction tools at that time to get into the mass production phase of knifemaking.

It was after World War II — in the late Forties — that the legendary Uncle Henry Baer and his brother, Albert, purchased Schrade Cutlery and made it a division of their Imperial Knife Associate Companies. At that time, the firm became known as Schrade-Walden and it was only in the last several years that the name again has become Schrade Cutlery. There are those who feel this may have been a bit belated, since it was more than two decades ago — in the

early Fifties — that the entire operation was moved from Walden to Ellenville, where the modern Schrade plant nestles in the foothills of the Catskills. Executive offices are maintained at a Broadway address in New York City.

As a part of the Imperial Knife Associated Companies, Schrade finds itself in an odd position. True, there are demands for all sorts of knives, but with the associated firms ready to make some sizes, shapes and types, this allows the Schrade craftsmen to concentrate on a smaller, concentrated line of knives specifically for outdoorsmen.

There are a lot of modern engineering and manufacturing techniques used in the Ellenville factory these days, but, according to Tom Taraci of the home team, "There are over a hundred hand operations in every

Schrade's Middleman jackknife is a medium stockman's knife with hand-glazed clip and pen blades. It measures 3—5/16 inches closed, and has handles of saw-cut Staglon.

The latest folder to come out of the Old Timer line in 1978 will be the Model 510T, a husky lock-blade style.

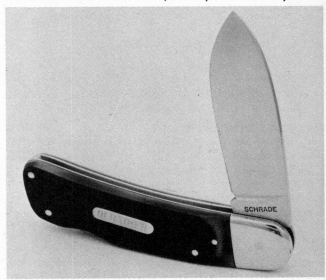

pocketknife. Each blade is hand-honed razor sharp. Second and third generation cutlers make certain each one clicks open smoothly and snaps shut (walks and talks in the vernacular of the trade). This care results in a product that Granddad would be proud to own."

Taraci feels that Schrade blades are superior and explains why. "If you've ever run your fingers across an envelope you know how easily you can be cut. What is this property, found in a flimsy piece of paper, that allows it to cut so sharply? It's thinness. And it's this thinning of the blade, known as whittening, which gives Schrade knives their superior cutting ability."

Two separate hand-grinding operations are performed on every blade. First, special care is taken to grind each blade individually. Then in a second hand operation, each blade is whittened or thinned to prepare it for its original razor sharp

"These handsome folding and rigid blade knives are superb examples of the old-time cutler's art. The finest blade steels, solid brass linings, solid nickel-silver bolsters and unique saw-cut Staglon handles assure beauty and performance," Baer says. Each knife carries the Old Timer shield and comes in its own gift box.

Latest out of the Schrade plant are the Uncle Henry knives. Each of these knives is serialized and guaranteed against loss for a full year! Hand-crafted to custom quality standards, according to Henry Baer, these knives also have solid brass linings, nickel-silver bolsters and handles of

Several knives may be cut from the same sheet of steel, as has been done in this instance with a Sharp Finger blanking die. Blades for the folders are done in the same manner. (Below) Don Lewis, head of quality control, checks a Rockwell reading.

edge. It's this thinning of the blade that not only makes Schrade knives super sharp, but easier to resharpen, according to the factory expert.

At present, the New York firm offers three different lines of knives.

The original Schrade line that made the firm known for high-quality, rugged construction and practical design continues unabated. According to Tom Taraci, "Each blade goes through two edging cycles. After the first hand-edging, they are precision ground and tapered horizontally and vertically to re-edge." There's a style for every outdoor need, with some patterns dating back to the beginning of the company.

More recent is the Old Timer line, which Henry Baer describes as "authentic handmade American classics."

antler-like Staglon. The blades are of Schrade Plus Steel. Each blade has a polished edge that is long lasting and easy to resharpen, according to factory technicians.

"The special analysis high-carbon steel used in Schrade knives was chosen after many years of testing for its proven strength and edge-holding qualities," according to Taraci. "Electronically controlled heat-treating equipment and continuous Rockwell testing assure uniform strength and

Left: Six pocketknife blades are being lifted out of a bath of molten lead. This is a part of a hardening process that Schrade officials say the custom cutler cannot duplicate.

Another step in the complicated process for hardening and tempering is to oil-quench blades for standardizing.

hardness." Incidentally, all Schrade knives measure 57 to 59 on the Rockwell C scale.

The Schrade Plus Steel mentioned earlier is a special analysis, super-hard carbon steel, according to Taraci. The blades are rust resistant and inhibit staining and corrosion. These properties make them easy to care for and especially functional in wet conditions, Taraci claims.

As for the mysterious handle material called Staglon,

their minds, making sure that each knife we produce will walk and talk."

With the pick bar, the cutler rapidly opens all blades of the knife, lays them on a small anvil and begins tapping them with his hammer. Thus the cutler's hammer becomes an extension of his hand and the pressure of his grip wears down the solid wood handle in just six months or so!

While the cutler and his hammer are important, they can

The cutler's hammer, wielded in the hands of an expert, is one of the most important tools of the knifemaker's trade. Note that the handle held in artisan's hand has been badly worn. Such wear can take place in six months.

this is a virtually indestructible formula developed during the space program, when NASA scientists needed a durable material that could withstand tremendous heat, yet would be light in weight. The folks at Schrade must have a lot of faith in it, since they say it is chip-proof, flame retardant and they guarantee it against breakage for the life of the knife.

"Of the various skilled craftsmen who are involved in making a quality knife, none requires greater skill and dexterity than the cutler," Henry Baer insists. "These artisans with thirty or forty years' experience are able to work at a rapid pace with the rhythm of the ancient craft in

hardly be considered the ultimate in Schrade knife building. There are a lot of other factors that go into making the folding knife before it gets into your pocket.

A great number of the craftsmen working at the Schrade plant are third generation workers, who take a great deal of pride in their workmanship.

Of the five cutlery factories that once made Ellenville and nearby Walden this nation's cutlery center, the huge Schrade facility in the former community is the one that survives today, its continuing flow of cutlery handled by some three hundred employees. To handle the growing production requirements, the plant was greatly expanded in

1973-74, but Henry Baer insists that the methods on which the firm's reputation is based be continued — skilled craftsmen continuing to maintain the basic role in producing the entire line of knives.

Many well-known plants in Europe — primarily England and Germany — have gone in heavily for automation in recent years. Henry Baer and his staff of advisors have steered away from this approach purposely. Instead, they have maintained the staff of craftsmen who perform the same hand-finishing techniques that were used nearly a century ago by their ancestors in the same environs.

Perhaps the greatest surrender to today's automated techniques is in Schrade's heat-treating facility, where expensive and complex electronic controls and test equipment have been installed for the sake of regulating a standard. It is also possible to check and double check that

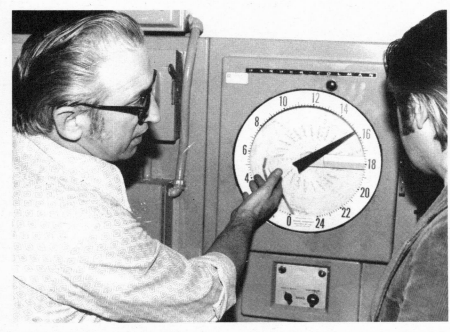

Don Lewis checks the controls for the tempering heat pit at the New York plant. A great deal of new electronic equipment now is in use.

Blades are lowered into the heat pit at Schrade for tempering. The unit is an electric temperature furnace.

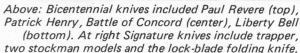
Above: Bicentennial knives included Paul Revere (top),
Patrick Henry, Battle of Concord (center), Liberty Bell
(bottom). At right Signature knives include trapper,
two stockman models and the lock-blade folding knife.

proper temperatures are reached before the steel is quenched and tempered for proper hardness in the finished product.

Quality control is the watchword at Schrade, especially in the heat-treating operations. The blades not only are Rockwell tested for degree of hardness, but a specified number are broken from each load during the hardening process. Thus technicians are able to determine that the proper molecular proportions are maintained. This also has a great deal to do, we are told, with how a blade will accept and retain its cutting edge.

The Schrade management team has worked closely with one of the larger testing laboratories to develop the sophisticated equipment now in use at the Ellenville plant.

This equipment is used in testing comparable cutting potentials of the various blade designs and edging techniques. As a result, designs have been developed that Schrade technicians feel are superior to those utilized by their competitors in the cutlery field.

During the Bicentennial, Schrade got into the commemorative business with a vengeance. First was a set of folding knives dedicated to observing the anniversaries of the founding of each of the three major armed services: the Marine Corps, the Navy and the Army. Other Bicentennial styles, all in folding stock knife configurations, noted such American institutions as the Liberty Bell, the Battle of Concord and historical figures like Patrick Henry and Paul Revere.

The latest innovation at Schrade is
the series of scrimshawed knives
that already are collector items.

Left: Grand Dad's Barlow, another in the Old Timer line, follows the design of the original, with a heavy-duty clip blade, pen blade and extra-long embossed bolsters.

As early as 1974, to celebrate their seventieth year of cutlery manufacturing, Schrade introduced what became known as Grand Dad's Old Timer in collector series. In 1975, due to demand, Schrade introduced the Grand Dad II. Each hand-finished knife in this limited edition had an engraved serial number on its unique solid-brass bolsters. The back of each knife was diamond engraved, the blade etched and a commemorative shield added.

With the sudden interest in the ancient art of scrimshaw, Schrade has introduced a series of such designs on unbreakable ivoryite handles, each depicting a patriotic scene. These designs are meeting with immense success among collectors and simply those buyers who want to carry a knife, but want it to be a conversation piece at the same time.

Perhaps the greatest testimonial to the firm's faith in its product is the standing guarantee against defects in workmanship and materials. Each knife is guaranteed for the life of the original buyer. If the knife proves defective, it will be replaced.

Uncle Henry's Pro Trapper Model has a long skinning blade and utility sheepfoot blade, Staglon handles.

The King Ranch model is a stockman's knife with clip, sheepfoot, spay blades, brass linings, solid nickel-silver bolsters. The knife measures four inches closed.

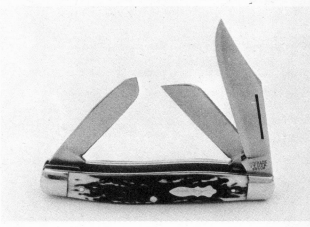

Another sheath-type folder is the No. 250T from the Old Timer line, with clip and skinning blades. This style measures 5¼ inches closed, has Staglon handles.

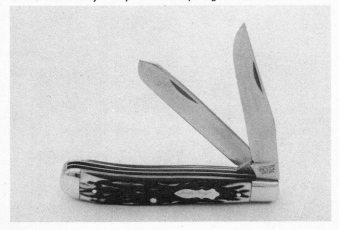

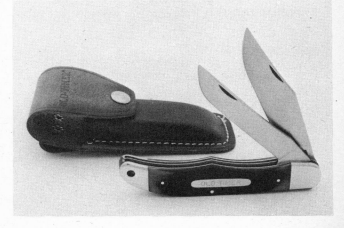

Chapter 13

*It's A Long Way From Upstate New York
To Boulder And There Were A Lot Of
Blades Along The Way!*

THE WESTERN WAY

*Below are the component parts of a Western
Cutlery Company hunter and folding knife.*

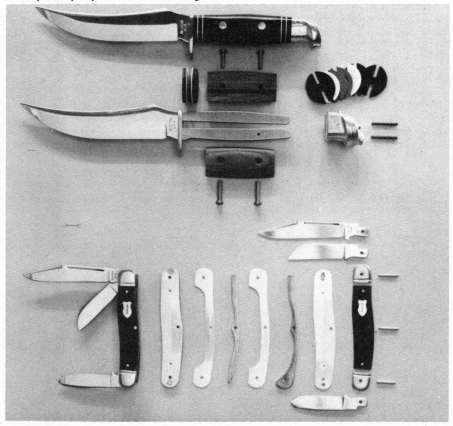

IN THE FOOTHILLS of the Colorado Rockies is a low one-story building, the home of an industry that, for all practical purposes, had its beginnings in Sheffield, England, nearly a century and a half ago.

Western Cutlery, one of the leaders in production of all types of sporting cutlery, operates out of a modern factory complex under the guidance of an executive staff that includes Harvey Platts and Harlow Platts, carrying on the traditions of the founder of the firm, Charles W. Platts.

Charles Platts was born in Sheffield in 1838, starting at an early age to learn the cutler trade and ultimately mastering all of the intricate knowledge of the trade.

The Platts' father had been an expert knifemaker before him, also having served a lengthy apprenticeship in the Sheffield cutlery plants. And there had been ancestors in the trade even before that. Records of the historic Sheffield artisans date back for hundreds of years and list the members of the old guild system where apprenticeships and standards of the Sheffield cutlers were strictly regulated. Perhaps not surprising is the fact that the Platts' name is

Hardening is first step in heat-treating metal. Next step for these blades will be quenching in oil.

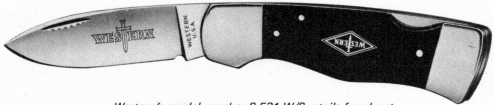

Western's model number S-531 W/S retails for about $30 and features 3-inch lock blade, deep black handle.

Above, still-hot blades are drawn out of special oil bath as part of treating process. At left, drilling pocketknife scales and covers requires highly skilled hands.

Blade grinders are set up in left and right hand pairs. Operator switches blades from one grinder to the other. Automation speeds production.

repeated numerous times in these records, dating back as far as the 1600s.

Charles Platts worked at his trade in Sheffield until he was qualified for a a superintendent's post. However, he passed this up, deciding to migrate instead to America. He arrived in Northfield, Connecticut, in 1866, being employed almost immediately as a superintendent at the historic Northfield Knife Company.

In time, Platt and his wife, Sarah, raised five sons, all of whom went to work at early ages in the Northfield knife plant, learning the cutler's trade under their father's firm supervision. The elder Platt continued with the Northfield company until 1894, when he suddenly moved to Little Valley, New York.

Actually, H.N. Platts, the second eldest of the five sons, had been the first to settle in Little Valley and had become a foreman in the grinding and finishing department of a local knife factory. His father became superintendent of the same plant upon arrival.

Father and son decided to start their own knife factory in 1896 and found a building in the nearby village of Gowanda, where they began the initial manufacture of pocketknives with their own Platts markings. Ultimately

L44

L49

Two old Western States sheath knives showing the evolution of the curved end knob.

Pocketknife stamp 1911-1950.

Pocketknife blade etch 1920-1930.

WESTERN
BOULDER. COLO
PAT. NO. 1.967.479

Sheath knife stamp 1931-1950.

Pocketknife blade etch 1928-1940.

After hardening, knife blades are tempered at medium-high temperature in special electric furnace.

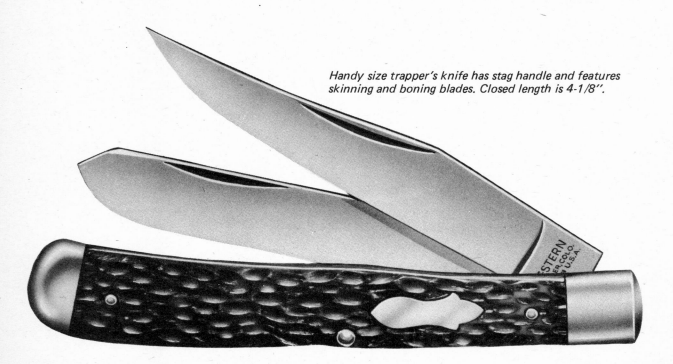

Handy size trapper's knife has stag handle and features skinning and boning blades. Closed length is 4-1/8''.

the other four sons joined the operation and Platts knives found immediate acceptance. This almost instant success found the father and his five sons soon outgrowing the capabilities of their small village factory and a year after the firm's founding, they moved to larger quarters in Eldred, Pennsylvania.

Today, serious collectors of folding knives do not consider their collections complete if they do not have included a C. Platts & Sons model with the Gowanda, New York, markings. Inasmuch as the firm operated in this location for only a year, such knives are considered quite rare.

In the new Pennsylvania location, the business continued to flourish, with the family craftsmen concentrating on quality pocketknives that were sold throughout the country. With the death of Charles Platts in 1900, the company's trademarked name was shortened to *C. Platts' Sons.*

It would appear that, following their father's death, the lack of his guidance was felt. By 1905, H.N. Platts had arranged to buy the company stock held by his four brothers, thus becoming the sole owner. That same year, the new owner moved the entire operation to Bradford, Pennsylvania, where he combined it with a knife business then operated by his wife's family. In this combined operation, H.N. Platts remained a principal stockholder and continued in charge of all manufacturing until 1911, when he sold his interest in the firm and moved to Colorado.

Meantime, in 1907, three of H.N. Platts' brothers — Frank, Charles, Jr., and Joe — established a firm known as

Pocketknife No. 06245½ with buffalo trademark etching. Illustration not actual size.

Pocketknife No. 6345½P with "sharp" trademark etching. Illustration not actual size.

Double tang handle construction patented by Western States.

Machine cuts leather sheath parts from hide in quick operation. Western has made own sheaths since 1954.

Western supports retailers with several shapes and sizes of attractive knife and ax displays.

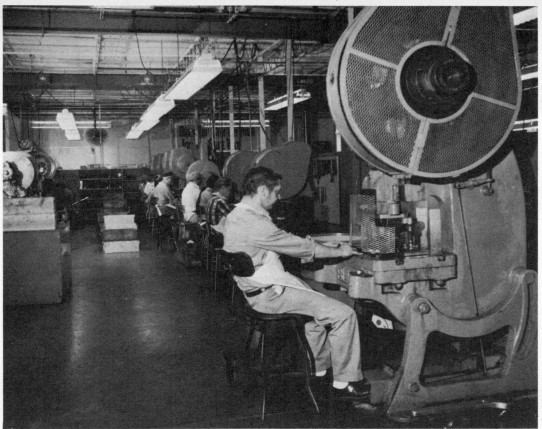

Light stamping and piercing of small parts is done on double row of presses.

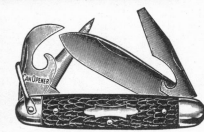

No. 6490 campers' pocketknife as supplied to U.S. government in WWII.

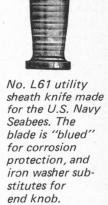

No. L61 utility sheath knife made for the U.S. Navy Seabees. The blade is "blued" for corrosion protection, and iron washer substitutes for end knob.

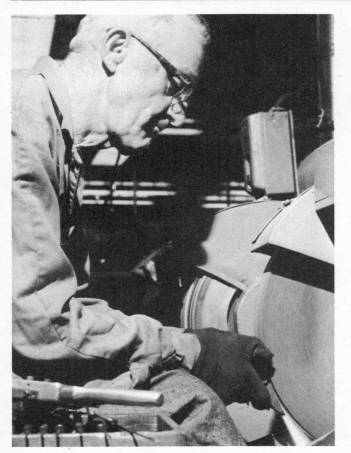

Pocketknife parts are dressed by hand on grindstone.

Platts Bros. Cutlery Company, in Andover, New York. They continued in business at this site until 1911, when they sold their interest in this factory.

H.N. Platts set up shop in the mountain town of Boulder, Colorado, forming what he called the Western States Cutlery and Manufacturing Company. He was 45 years old when he established the firm, coming up with a trademark that incorporated the words, *Western States Sharp Cutlery,* with an artist's impression of a buffalo skull.

Population of Boulder in those early days was less than 9000 people, and the new firm, established in a new two-story brick building, was one of the community's earliest manufacturing plants.

In the beginning, Platts had been farseeing enough to bring with him to Colorado a basic crew of the experienced cutlers that had worked for him in his Pennsylvania factories. It was these men who formed the basis for his work force, training the local pioneers who became interested enough in the new factory to want to learn the cutlery trade.

Big 8" blade on this vanadium steel knife may be used to clear trails, skin game or chop light kindling.

Western Cutlery's saber ground blade is 5". Knife is 9¼" overall.

Three-bladed folder has short pen blade, sheepfoot blade and California clip blade.

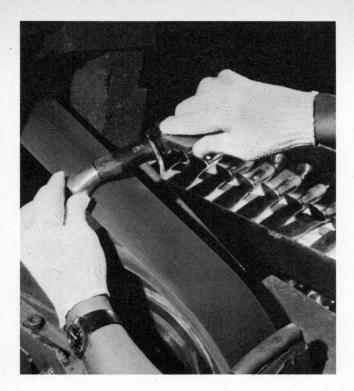

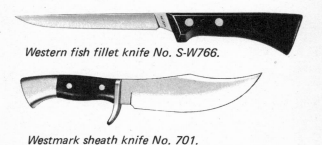

Finishing sheath knives to their final shape is done by hand on belt sander. The process is called hafting, a holdover from English cutlers.

Western fish fillet knife No. S-W766.

Westmark sheath knife No. 701.

Adjusting folding blades to "walk and talk" is yet another skill to be done by hand, not machine.

For nearly two decades — until about 1930 — the Western States' product line was made up almost exclusively of folding or pocketknives. It was in the height of the so-called Depression years that the firm embarked upon the line of sheath knives. These fixed-blade knives had a patented double-tang design, which Western States' technicians had developed.

In a total departure from their earlier efforts in the folding knife field, the fixed-blade knives had a symmetrical aluminum end knob that was similar in design to other knives of the era. However, in the mid-Thirties, Western designers came up with a new end-knob shape that has been copied over the years by many other commercial knifemakers both in this country and overseas.

Most of us develop attachments for certain knives. Both of the authors agree that should they venture out of the house without a particular knife tucked away in their pocket, they tend to feel only partially dressed until the lack is remedied. Many others tend to feel similar feelings of depression in like circumstances, we have learned.

During World War II, Western States Cutlery became involved in the war effort, turning out thousands of knives for servicemen. A good many of those knives still are in the possession of men now in middle age, who carried them through campaigns in Europe and the South Pacific. We know of several instances where those same knives are being carried by a third generation, which has to speak well for the hurried wartime production methods in spite of material substitutions that became necessary.

Immediately after the attack on Pearl Harbor, Western States Cutlery volunteered its facilities to the war effort and was assigned to produce knives for the Armed Forces.

The most popular model and the one still seen is their No. 6490, which had been introduced originally as a camper's knife, but was adopted as the all-purpose tool that every fighting man in the field should have.

The firm also made a utility sheath knife for the Navy Seabees as well as survival knives for airmen. Perhaps the most unusual knife to come out of the Western States factory was one that didn't really look like a knife at all. In

After stitching, leather sheaths are riveted at stress points for strength. Leather is specially tanned.

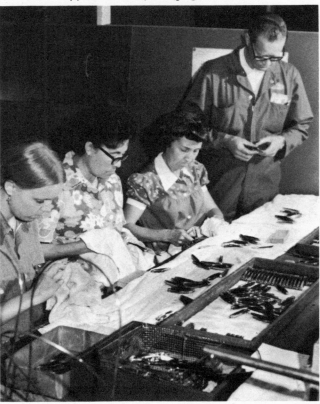

Final inspection and cleaning by skilled hands is last stop for these folders. A protective coat of clear wax is applied before packaging knives.

fact, it didn't look like much of anything by which a comparison can be made. The handle was of wood and there was a curved nonpointed blade. The blade, itself, was punched with holes that were meant to reduce the weight and make it a floating knife. It was designed primarily for airmen's survival kits, so that pilots could cut themselves out of their parachute harness if shot down.

During this period, incidentally, the firm realized that production could come to a standstill if their power supply was cut off, so in 1940, a large diesel-operated generator was installed and this furnished power for the entire plant until as late as 1951.

As suggested, the war years brought some temporary substitutions of materials. For example, the camper's pocketknife issued to troops did not have the nickel-silver bolsters that had been standard on civilian production models. Instead, the bolsters were of iron. Likewise the handle scales, in many instances, were of brass-plated iron, instead of bone. Sheath knives issued for military use had iron washers or even moulded plastic in place of the familiar aluminum end knobs, with iron or plastic being substituted for brass in the guards.

During the war years, Boulder had grown and officials of the firm found themselves suddenly hemmed in, unable to expand. As a result of wartime exposure, sales had increased in the civilian market by the early Fifties and distribution had been expanded to cover the entire nation. In 1954, a leather department was incorporated, workers making the sheaths and scabbards that previously had been contracted elsewhere. Finally, in 1957, the entire operation

was moved from the crowded downtown site to a new structure in the Boulder Industrial Park. Meantime, the name of the firm had been shortened to *Western Cutlery Co.* in 1956.

The Sixties saw the introduction of many new products and continued additions to the Boulder facilities. The size of the Western Cutlery Building was doubled with additions in 1964-65. By 1967, a full line of stainless-steel pocketknives and sheath knives had been introduced.

The trademark of the firm has gone through numerous changes along the way, since the move west and the initial use of the buffalo skull drawing. The numerous variations on the name alone have become subjects of interest among collectors, although the original insignia was used until the early 1940s, when the word *Western,* suddenly began to appear in rope-style script. More recently, registered trademarks have incorporated the name of the company with a knife running through the middle of the word.

In 1970, the Westmark Custom Quality line of sheath knives was introduced and the *Westmark* designation also has been trademarked by the firm.

In today's modern Boulder factory, knifemaking begins in a large, well-lighted press room. In this room, mechanical presses ranging from twenty-two to four hundred tons

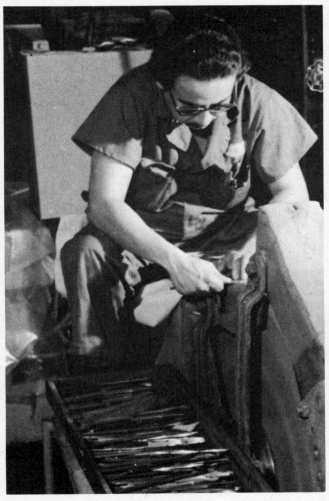

The old skill of free-hand grinding on large diameter stone wheels is still done much as it was in 1890s.

Fixed-blade knives and some folding knives by the Colorado cutlers are supplied with leather sheaths.

capacity cut out the hundreds of different component parts. Some of the presses are hand fed, while others are fed automatically from coils of raw materials and operate at high speed.

Each year, these presses process countless tons of steel, brass and nickel silver, as well as large amounts of aluminum strip, vulcanized fiber, and many types of wire.

The hundreds of different parts in the Boulder firm's product line require many different types of tooling for each part. Thus a fully equipped tool and die shop is maintained on the premises with experienced tool and die makers maintaining the equipment and developing new tools or dies as needed.

In spite of automation, the personal touch is not ignored, as more than 150 hand operations are required in the building of what appears to be a simple stock knife.

Several types of special analysis alloy steels — including both stainless and chrome-vanadium steel — are used for blades. These steels are made to Western's own specifications in the Eastern steel mills and shipped into Boulder. The inspection facilities look like the set for a *Star Trek* television segment, with a great variety of electronic and computerized equipment used to assure that quality remains a constant.

In heat-treating, the temperatures required for each type of steel are monitored to keep them within the close heat limits required. At each step in heat-treating, skilled craftsmen conduct tests for hardness, bending and breaking. All of the blades and springs that go into a folding knife are treated at the in-plant facility.

Hardening is the first step in heat-treatment. The blades are heated to the high temperature at which changes take place in the microstructure. The heated blades are quenched immediately in a special oil, which leaves them hard, but brittle. In addition, the blades made from some steel alloys then receive a deep-freeze treatment to complete their transformation.

Tempering is the next operation. This toughening — done properly — causes a blade to resist breaking or

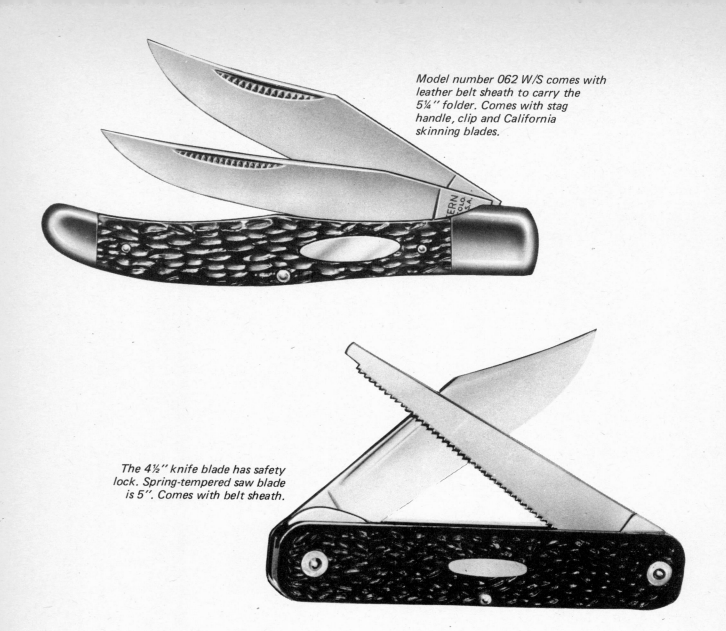

Model number 062 W/S comes with leather belt sheath to carry the 5¼″ folder. Comes with stag handle, clip and California skinning blades.

The 4½″ knife blade has safety lock. Spring-tempered saw blade is 5″. Comes with belt sheath.

chipping. This process often is called drawing, since it draws out the brittle quality.

During this phase, the blades are heated again, but only to what is termed a medium-high temperature, then are slowly returned to room temperature. Done properly, this process of tempering should give a blade a tough quality without greatly reducing the quality of hardness. This combination also results in the ability of a blade to take and maintain a sharp edge.

In the grinding and polishing operations, the rough blade blanks are shaped and contoured, then each blade — whether for a folding knife or a sheath knife — undergoes a grinding operation on each surface.

Since grinding is basic to knife manufacture, rows of automatic, cam-controlled precision-grinding machines are found in the Western factory. They speed the routine cutting-away of metal required to get the blades ready for handwork.

These grinding machines have been set up in pairs, so that, when one side of a blade has been ground properly,

the operator switches the blade to the other machine and the opposite side of the blade blank receives a matching grind. The grinding is conducted under a circulating stream of liquid that keeps the blade cool and, at the same time, washes away the metal grindings.

Although machines are utilized to make the first heavy grinds on a blade, skilled hand grinders have an important role in producing Western knives. Each grinder uses one hand to press the blade against the wet grindstone, which rotates away from him. At the same time, the other hand is used to set the angle and draw the blade across the stone. Hand grinding requires steady, trained hands, of course, and it takes years to develop the right feel in working each blade. After the grinding process, the blades are put through several different polishing operations to complete the finish on the surface.

In the section devoted to assembly of pocketknives, after the blades and springs have been hardened, tempered, ground and polished, and the numerous components similarly finished to size and shape, assembly is done by a

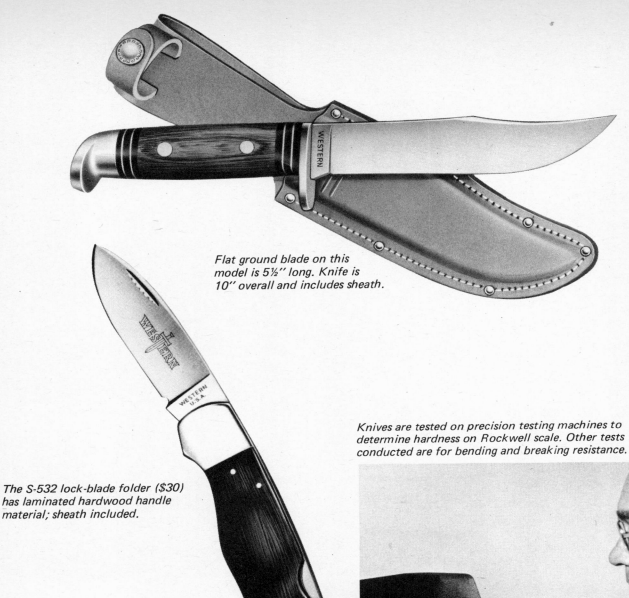

Flat ground blade on this model is 5½" long. Knife is 10" overall and includes sheath.

The S-532 lock-blade folder ($30) has laminated hardwood handle material; sheath included.

Knives are tested on precision testing machines to determine hardness on Rockwell scale. Other tests conducted are for bending and breaking resistance.

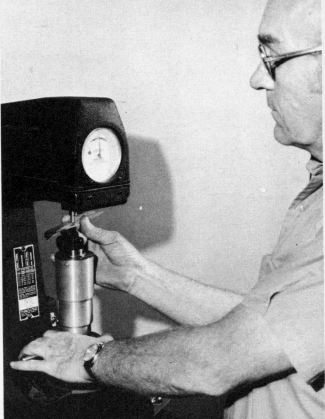

combination of many skills, the work accomplished by hand at individual benches.

Each blade must be adjusted to open and close properly. This is accomplished by individual craftsmen working with their cutler's hammers, the final shaping and polishing is done on special belts and wheels, each surface receiving a separate operation.

Hand honing each blade is one of the last of the more than 150 hand operations required in each pocketknife. Finally, each knife is cleaned, inspected and given a final protective coating of clear wax to protect it during shipment and storage.

Today, the traditions and crafts of the past, begun in what was little more than a pioneer village, are being carried on with that same knowledge, skill and efficiency in modern surroundings.

Chapter 14

KA-BAR,
THE LIVING LEGEND

Series of folding knives from Ka-Bar range in size from the 5¼'' single lock-blade hunter with thumb release at top, to 2-3/8'' clip blade (bottom).

An aerial view of the Olean factory as it looked in the early 1940s. Note the automobile models.

Since 1912, through a series of product names, the Ka-Bar Cutlery Company has produced knives in Olean, New York.

Supposedly Derived From A Fur Trapper's Tale, The Ka-Bar Trademark Is Recorded In The United States' Military History

KA-BAR, a historical name in American cutlery, was founded in 1898 by Wallace Brown in a warehouse-type building fronted by a wooden sidewalk and dirt street in Tidioute, Pennsylvania. The name of the founding company was the Union Razor Company, which reflected its emphasis on the production of straight razors, although it included folding knives, fixed-blade knives and household cutlery in its extensive line.

From the beginning, Wallace Brown was dedicated to producing quality products, and collectors and knife enthusiasts fortunate enough to have acquired one or more of the early Union Razor Company folding knives tang-stamped Tidioute, and those later produced in Olean, New York, value these highly in their collections and have only praise for the workmanship and materials evidenced in these historically significant knives. This is a rather outstanding testimonial to the ability and dedication of

Wallace Brown to organize and train a staff of cutlers capable of achieving these quality goals from the initial start-up of the company.

The Union Razor Company's tenure in the Pennsylvania community was rather short-lived as it lasted only those fourteen years between 1898 and 1912. About 1900, the city of Olean, New York, in a drive to entice industry into the city, offered the company attractive incentives that Brown accepted.

During the next two years, the company went through the process of moving to its present location at 434 N. Ninth Street, Olean, New York. This move, completed by 1912, started a period significant to collectors, because the knives now were stamped Olean, New York.

Although the company started with its main marketing aspirations centered around razors, the folding and fixed-blade knife segment of the business rapidly gained in

Replica of original Union Cutlery Company letterhead, Olean, New York. The Union name in North American continent became trademark stamped on early knives.

importance until the board of directors had to recognize the fact that the corporate name, Union Razor Company, no longer was descriptive of the business.

They voted on January 25, 1909, to change the name to the Union Cutlery Company. To the modern knife collector this started another phase in the development of the company as the tang stamp markings became Union Cutlery Company, Olean, New York, or variations such as Union Cut Co, UCC or just Union.

There was, of course, a transition period of mixed marks as the company completed work in process in the change-over to the Union Cutlery Company name. During this period, they also adopted additional trademarks, such as Olcut, Keenwell and Ka-Bar.

It was also in the early 1920s that the highly collectible Dog's Head shield was introduced. This shield appeared on Union Cutlery Company products prior to the adoption of the Ka-Bar trademark. Knives which bear this Dog's Head shield do not show the Ka-Bar mark on any of the blades or on the shield. At a later date after the adoption and use of the trademark, Ka-Bar, this mark was added to the shield and to the master blade of the knives, although the Union Cutlery Company name also was carried on the secondary blade. Marking changes such as these add considerable interest and excitement to the hobby of collecting knives.

It is unfortunate that the corporate files of Ka-Bar do not include a catalog or any illustrations of its product line as the Union Razor Company in Tidioute, but recently the

Before adoption of Ka-Bar trademark, the Dog's Head appeared on Union knives.

KA-BAR

Original Ka-Bar trademark used print style (above).

Current script-style trademark (above) was adopted about 1951.

A somewhat feisty looking bear accompanied the Ka-Bar mark, adopted during the mid-1920s.

Crudely written letter from a fur trapper whose gun jammed, leaving wounded bear to be dispatched with knife, led from "kill-a-bar" to Ka-Bar.

Page from 1925 Union Cutlery Company, Ka-Bar Dependable Pocket Knives catalog shows large selection of shapes and sizes.

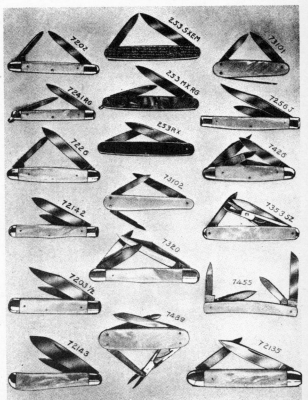

company did discover a catalog of the Union Razor Company, Olean, dating back to the early 1900s. By the time this volume is in print, this catalog should be reproduced and reprints released to Ka-Bar's Collectors' Club members and later to all collectors and knife enthusiasts. In conjunction with the circa 1925 catalog reprinted and issued in 1975 this catalog reprint will fill in a big gap in the reference material covering Union and Ka-Bar knives.

During the 1920s and onward, the Ka-Bar trademark became widely known and respected. There have been many versions of how this name was adopted, but all evidence points to a letter received from a fur trapper which turned out to be one of the most significant testimonials ever received by the company. This fur trapper wrote a note in his rough English thanking the company, because his knife had saved his life when he had to depend on it to kill a wounded bear attacking him after his gun had jammed.

In his writing he described using his knife to "Kill a-bar." The way it was scrawled on the paper it looked like Ka-Bar which was adopted as a company trademark.

Soon after the start of World War II, the Union Cutlery Company submitted a Ka-Bar branded knife to the U.S. Marine Corps which was accepted by the Corps as the standard for their fighting/utility knife. During the War, due to the dependable serviceability of this knife and the high regard with which it was held by the Marines, it also was adopted by other branches of the armed services.

Ka-Bar folding knife blades are made of high-carbon cutlery steel or 440 stainless steel hardened and tempered to retain an edge while remaining easy to sharpen. Handles are made of Kastag, natural woods or wood laminates, or other durable materials for the hard user. Pocketknives also feature nickel silver bolsters, solid brass linings and tempered steel springs for crisp blade action. Each is hand assembled and honed.

1001 3-7/8" Medium Trapper—clip and spay blades; carbon steel.

1026 3" Jack Knife—clip and pen blades.

1047 3¼" Medium Pen Knife—clip and pen blades.

1005 3¼" Bare end Jack Knife, clip and pen blades.

1030 4-1/8" Oldtimer's Trapper—clip and spay blades.

1052 2¾" Small Pen Knife—clip and pen blades.

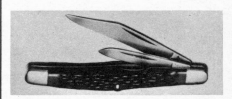

1056 2¾" Small Jack Knife—clip and pen blades.

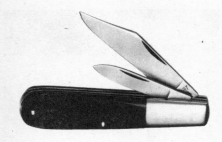

1013 3-3/8" Barlow—clip and pen blades.

1033 4-1/8" Oldtimer's Trapper—clip and spay blades, polished yellow *Delrin handle.

1063 3-7/8" Muskrat Knife—clip and skinner blades.

1019 2¾" Pony Jack Knife—clip and pen blades.

1041 4" Texas Jack Knife—clip and spay blades.

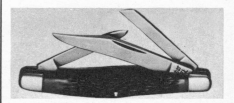

1071 2-5/8" Dress Knife—clip, pen and coping blades.

Arkansas sharpening stone comes with sheath; measures 1x3x¼".

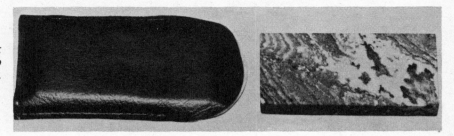

Larger stone for desk work is 2x4x½"; also sold with leather sheath.

Although it took three or four cutlery companies to supply the large demand for these knives — and many were issued under other companies' trademarks — they all became affectionately called Ka-Bars by the U.S. fighting men who depended on these knives for their everyday requirements; fixing equipment, digging foxholes, sharpening tent stakes, opening ration cans and often defending their own lives.

The World War II Ka-Bars did their job so effectively that similar versions were used in the Korean and Vietnam conflicts, but as Ka-Bar stopped producing the fighting/utility knife immediately after the end of World War II, none of these knives were produced by Ka-Bar. However, the legend of the knife continued, and as a result, these more modern versions were still called Ka-Bars by the fighting men.

During World War II, Ka-Bar also made other knives for the military. Some were folding knives such as the TL29 electrician's knife and a rigging knife used by the Navy and Coast Guard.

After the death of Wallace Brown, the presidency was taken over by Emerson Brown, his brother, and later by his son, Danford Brown, who headed the company until he died in approximately 1956.

By 1951, the Ka-Bar name had achieved such a high level of fame that Danford Brown and the directors of the company decided to change the corporate name to the Ka-Bar Cutlery Company, Incorporated, dropping the Union Cutlery name entirely. The marks on the knives changed and another transition period began, emphasized by the fact that the style of the Ka-Bar logo was also changed from the older KA-BAR to the new Kabar, script style.

This new mark was used exclusively by Ka-Bar until 1975 when a few special models, including the Ka-Bar Classics, the U.S. Bicentennial knife and the USMC Two Hundredth Anniversary Commemorative carried the old Ka-Bar marking. All of the standard production line, however, continued with the newer script-style mark.

During the presidency of Danford Brown, the company had its ups and downs. One significant down was an unsuccessful attempt to transfer the manufacturing operations from Olean, New York, to Dawsonville, Georgia. This experiment lasted only one year, then the operation was regrouped back at Olean in the original factory. Fortunately, the manufacturing facilities in the Olean plant had not been discontinued completely, so the retreat was accomplished without too much disruption in production.

Original Dog's Head folding hunter dates from early 1920s. Knife has become collectors' item today.

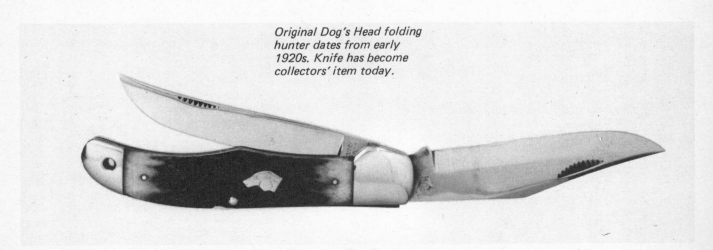

1. Fixed-blade hunting knife with unusual multicolor acetate handle. Circa 1930-40.

2. Fixed-blade hunter with pearlized handle and rare-coined grizzly shield. Circa 1920.

3. Fly-lock hunter with genuine stag horn handle. Circa 1925-35.

4. Desirable collectors' item — a folding lock-guard hunter with the famous Dog's Head shield. Circa 1920-30.

5. Early example of fixed-blade hunter with equal end guard, bare end bone handle. Circa 1900-10.

6. Dress pen knife with white celluloid or pearl handle. Circa 1920.

7. The famous U.S. Marine Corps Fighting-Utility Knife* of World War II. It served leathernecks well throughout the Pacific Theatre of Operations.
   During World War II, Ka-Bar was also proud to supply similar knives to the U.S. Navy Underwater Demolition Teams, and other branches of the military — 1941-45.

8. Bone handle outdoorsman's knife, sheepfoot and can opener blades. Circa 1930.

9. Coke bottle shape with green bone handle. Circa 1910.

10. Dog's Head folding hunter with match striker nail mark and honeycomb bone handle. Circa 1925-35.

11. Three-part mess kit. Parts slide apart for separate knife, fork and spoon, slide together into one knife with normal blade function. Circa 1920-30.

12. Striated trapper with celluloid handle. Circa 1920.

13. Sheepfoot with honeycomb bone handle. Circa 1930.

14. Swell belly folding hunter with acetate candy stripe handle. Circa 1910.

15. Rare gunstock model. Note: Repeated sharpening over 60 years of use reduced blades to a fraction of original size, but cutting edge is still excellent.

16. Hunting knife with leather handle, cast pommel. Circa 1940.

*To commemorate the 200th anniversary of the United States Marine Corps, Ka-Bar's Collectors' Division issued a limited edition of individually serialized U.S. Marine Fighting-Utility Knives in November 1976. Serial No. 0001 is displayed at the Marine Corps Museum, Quantico, Virginia.

440 stainless steel with
Rockwell rating of 54-56.

Blade locking guard.

Eight brass rivets through handle, blade and bolsters.

Hollow ground blade.

Back blade thumb serrations.

Natural birch laminate handle.

Solid brass bolsters.

The Ka-Bar Folding Hunter model 1189, retails for
$21.95. Price includes cowhide leather belt sheath.

After the death of Danford Brown, the company changed hands several times until in 1966 it was purchased by Cole National Corporation of Cleveland, Ohio.

Cole National already was involved in certain aspects of the cutlery business. An aggressive marketing operation started the Ka-Bar Company back on the road to full operations and the reestablishment of national distribution. The entire product line was reorganized with emphasis on a moderately broad range of folding knives and a complete line of fixed-blade hunting knives emphasizing the leather handled construction which had become an unofficial trademark for Ka-Bar.

In addition to reestablishing the standard product line, Cole National also created and supported the establishment of a special Ka-Bar Collectors' Division for the purpose of producing significant, commemorative knives, recreating replicas of famous antique Ka-Bar knives, while actively supporting the development and enjoyment of knife collecting in general.

The Ka-Bar Collectors' Division operates independently

*Page from today's product
catalog shows variety
of folding styles and sizes.*

1179 5½″ Outdoorsman Lock-Back Hunter—blade locks in open position, rosewood handle, leather thong.

1341 5″ Pocketknife Sheath—top grain cowhide.

1184 5¼″ Folding Hunter—saber ground clip and skinner blades.

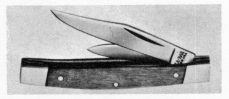

1058 3-5/16″ Medium Pocketknife—clip master blade: 2-5/16″ and pen blade—Stainless Steel.

1189 4-1/8″ Folding Lock-Back Hunting Knife—saber ground clip blade: 3¾″ Stainless Steel—includes Sheath.

1109 3-7/8″ Stockman's Knife—clip master blade: 3-13/16″ sheepfoot and pen blades—Stainless Steel.

More than 40 years of old knives, discarded for one reason or another, were recently unearthed from beneath sidewalks at the Olean plant. Many of the folders, kitchen and hunting models, are well preserved.

Gun Digest Book of FOLDING KNIVES

in the original Ka-Bar building in Olean, New York, and sponsors a special Ka-Bar Knife Collectors' Club to keep interested collectors informed of new items, to help them by making available historical information about the company, in identifying knives and in providing background information to the collector who wants to know more about his knives than just their physical qualities.

The Ka-Bar Knife Collectors' Club also provides catalogs, information bulletins and membership cards to which serialized numbers are assigned. Once a member has his personal number, this gives him the option of having this number reserved on new serialized knife editions.

Memberships in this club are free of charge and can be had simply by writing to Ka-Bar Cutlery, Incorporated, 434 N. Ninth Street, Olean, New York 14760.

As an example of the interest in history, the legend of the buried Ka-Bar knives has been around for a long time and Ka-Bar now has proven it true.

It was told that about forty years ago — and probably long before that — the Ka-Bar Cutlery Company disposed of hundreds of old knives by burying them in the backyard of the Olean factory.

These knives, described as discontinued work in progress, seconds and knives returned from customers for repairs but replaced instead, were dumped into an old well and into excavations as fill before cement was poured for construction of new buildings and walkways.

At every National Knife Collectors and Dealers Association show, Robert Reinschreiber, vice-president of marketing, and Richard Sturm, general manager of the Ka-Bar Collectors' Division, were repeatedly asked, "When is Ka-Bar going to dig up the backyard and confirm the legend?"

Drawing on the memory of some of the oldest retired employees of the company as to the locations of the buried knives, the actual dig got under way. After several attempts produced dry holes, the workers, using picks and shovels, turned over large sections of cement sidewalk and hundreds of old knives were found imbedded in the cement.

Included were folding knives, hunting knives and kitchen cutlery — styles that were discontinued many years ago and some that are still in production. As a result of this first successful probe, other areas were opened and in another spot, again, a large quantity of old knives was uncovered.

In talking with some of the old-timers around Olean, they said that one could dig and hit pay dirt all over the Ka-Bar property with some of the oldest knives buried under buildings that were constructed back in the late Twenties and early Thirties.

Although the buried knives uncovered were remarkably preserved, only a few were in what could be termed restorable condition and efforts are being made to do so. While most of these knives will never again "walk and talk" in the traditional language of the professional cutlers, they do confirm the legend.

Latest addition to the Ka-Bar line are these imported folders to be marketed under the Khyber brand name. Trailblazer model, at left, is available in three blade lengths and three handle materials, retailing from $8.50 to $15.50. Sportsmen's model, middle and lower right, may be ordered in 3, 4 or 5'' blade; all have brown linen micarta handles, selling for $11, $15 or $20. Each has locking blade.

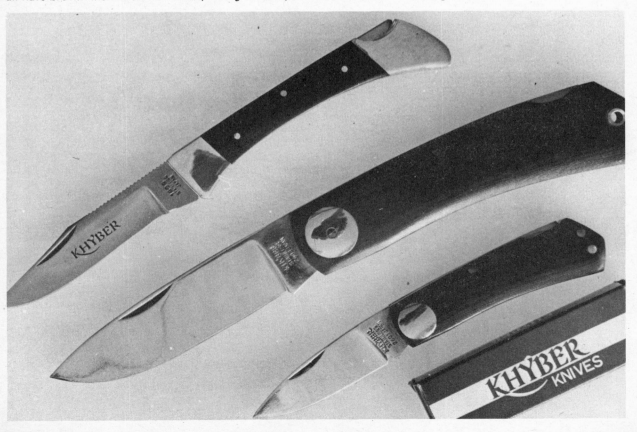

Chapter 15

*At Gerber's A Lot Of Thought
Goes Into Every New Design!*

This attractive facade greets visitors to the offices of the Gerber plant in southwestern suburbs of Portland, Oregon.

A MATTER OF LEGEND

FOLDING KNIVES are inherently more difficult to produce than are knives with fixed blades, and the folding knives with blades that lock in the open position are, in turn, more challenging from the standpoint of production.

It was this assignment that took us to visit the main plant of Gerber Legendary Blades, located at the southwestern borders of Portland, Oregon, for step-by-step observation of one of that firm's folding lock-blade knives from start to finish.

As sometimes happens, the best-intentioned plans came slightly unglued. Upon arriving at the Gerber plant, it turned out that certain operations are subcontracted, including the punch press production of the blades, as well as the brass sidepieces.

The basic raw materials are purchased by Gerber and warehoused at the main plant, being sent to the subcontractors when further production is required. The parts come back to the Gerber plant in lots of 1000 and are put up in neat bags or packs of fifty units. These fifty-packs are gathered together and fed through the factory production lines as inventory control senses a need for additional units of a given model.

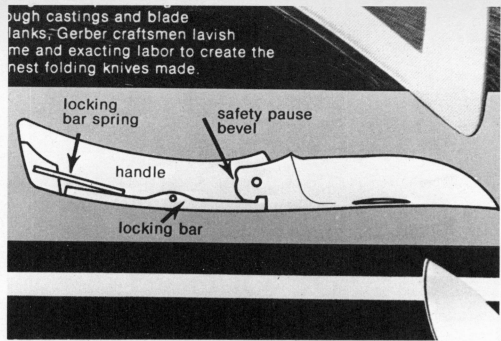

...ugh castings and blade ...lanks, Gerber craftsmen lavish ...me and exacting labor to create the ...nest folding knives made.

locking
bar spring

safety pause
bevel

handle

locking bar

This diagram, originally appearing in the Gerber catalog, helps to show the position of the working parts in relation to each other. Note the safety pause bevel and refer to photo below.

Thus, it approaches impossibility to fulfill the intended assignment, showing one given knife as it moves along the assembly line. As with many modern factories, the Gerber plant employs a sophisticated and highly efficient system of computer-programmed effort toward maintaining a balanced stock on hand of all models in the current line. It happens rarely, if ever, that any one specific model of lock-blade folding knife moves resolutely from *a* to *izzard*, in terms of total production, at any given time. Gerber has about ten different models of folding knives in their line at present and several of these are apt to be undergoing some given phase of production on any particular day. The

This Gerber Folding Sportsman shows the blade at about the point where spring pressure is taken up by the safety pause bevel (see drawing above). This aids in closing the blade safely.

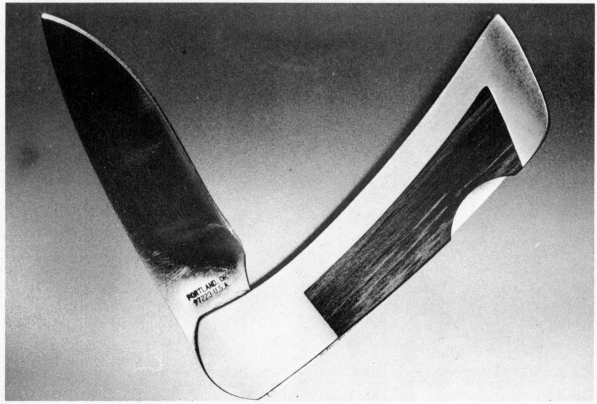

PORTLAND, OR.
97223 U.S.A.

A blade can be seen on the carrier, upper center, after having the bevel ground on left side.

A fifty-pack of blades, as received from the subcontractor, is being given the initial grinding.

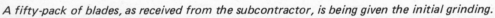

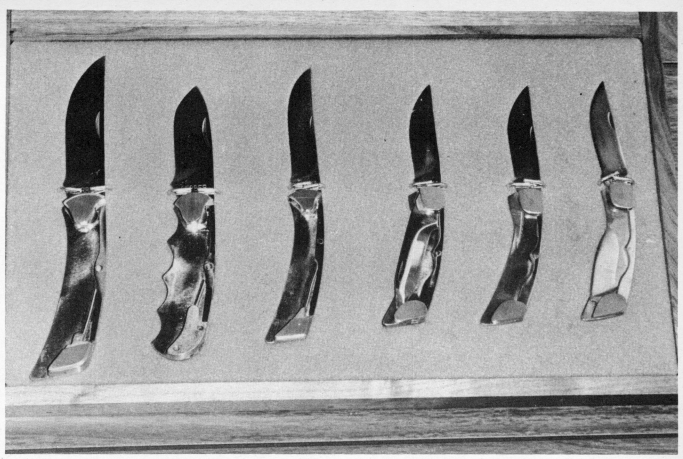

Gerber folding knives are made in a variety of sizes and basic designs, as can be seen in the partially completed display of samples on exhibit at the manufacturing plant.

Pen tip points to the ledge at the base of the blade which makes contact with the spring to protect the edge of the blade.

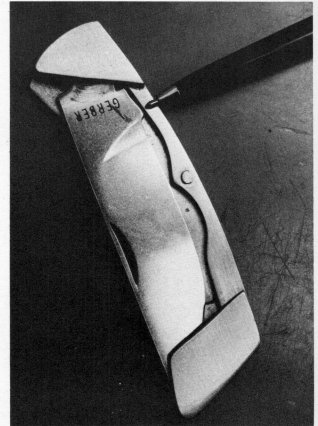

foregoing is offered as an explanation, not an excuse. The Gerber plant operates with awesome efficiency and they turn out some thoroughly admirable knives.

The steel used for the blades of Gerber folding knives is of that alloy termed 440C — 440-C surgical stainless steel, in the Gerber literature — and it is hardened to a level of Rockwell 57-59C during production. The steel does not rust, corrode nor tarnish in normal usage. The hardness level attained is an excellent compromise, offering moderate ease of resharpening, combined with excellent edge-holding abilities.

As received from the punch press subcontractor, the blade blanks are coated with a specialized, heavy grease used to prolong the useful life of the punch press dies. Even before heat-treating, 440C is a tough and obdurate alloy,

This worker has a highly demanding job, handfitting the blade on its pivot pin — as seen in closeup at top of opposite page — by means of the belt grinder running with its axis vertical. It's a cut-and-try process.

Blanks for the smaller handles are stamped on a punch press, larger handle blanks are cast of brass.

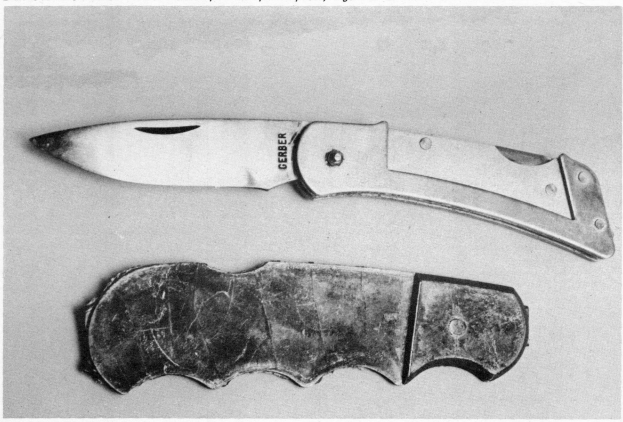

more notable for its capability at resisting blade wear than for its easy shearing qualities.

The first step consists of degreasing the blade blanks; putting them into a large, wire mesh basket and lowering them into a bath of agitated trichlorethylene solvent. This operation is performed under carefully controlled ventilation to protect workers from the solvent fumes.

A belt grinder is used to remove burrs and flashes left by the punch press, particularly from the area around the tang. The rough hole that was made for the pivot pin at the time of stamping is precision-reamed to a diameter of 5/32-inch. Reaming the hole for the pivot pin assures smooth functioning and, at the same time, prevents wear upon the pin as the knife is used, thereby greatly prolonging the useful life of the knife.

Careful inspection verifies that the blade blank is straight and flat after reaming. Straightening is performed by hand, if required. Passing this checkpoint, the blades are surface-ground to the appropriate thickness, held magnetically to the bed of the grinder as they are passed

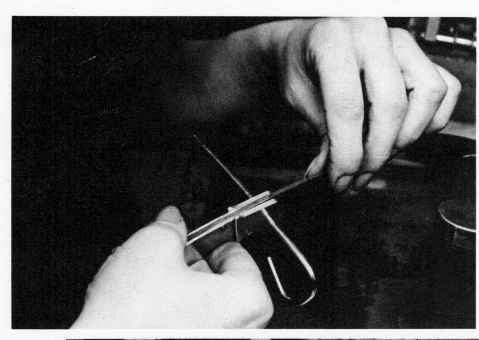

Checking the fit of the blade during adjustment, as on top of opposite page. Wire replaces pin for this phase.

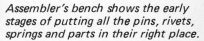

Assembler's bench shows the early stages of putting all the pins, rivets, springs and parts in their right place.

Hydraulic presses as well as hand tools are used in Gerber's assembly lines.

Once fitted, assemblies are given numbers to assure proper production. Handle scales are selected carefully to match each other.

The Asher Grinder takes off excess wood on the handle, running four-up.

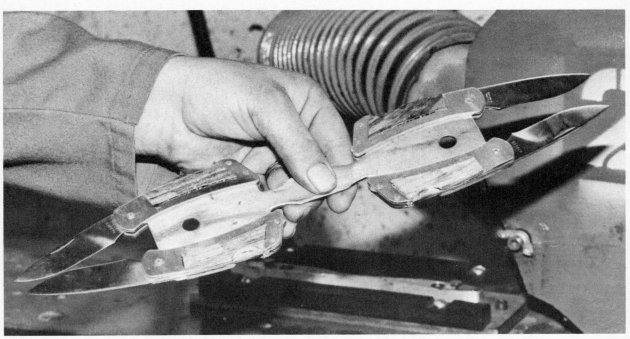

beneath a 60-grit wheel under continuous streams of coolant. Following this step, the tang area is given a finished polish with 220-grit abrasive.

To this point, the blades have not been hardened by heat-treating and the name of the maker is stamped in the exposed area near the tang, together with any other designation required. A further inspection is made for straightness and correction is applied as required.

Blades are aligned precisely in gangs of fifty and locked into the bed of a milling machine for milling of the notch that will engage the projection of the locking bar. Despite the fact that every effort is made, here and at other points during production, to assure total uniformity of dimensions, meticulous individual hand-fitting will be necessary at a later time to assure the rock-steady solidity of locking engagement. The precision expended at this and other steps does not obviate the need for hand-fitting; the intent is solely to minimize that vital phase of production.

With the lock notch milled, blade blanks are fastened individually into a jig and the crescent-shaped groove is milled near the back edge of the blade so that a fingernail can get a grip to open the blade. The useful term for this groove is the nail mark. A further buffing removes burrs that may have been left by the milling operations.

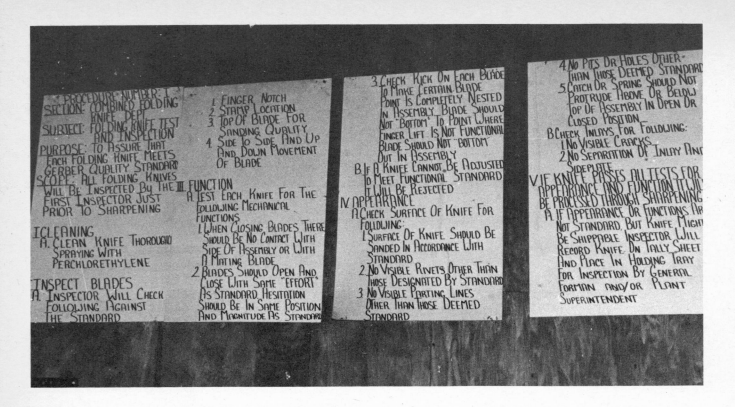

PROCEDURE NUMBER 1

SECTION: COMBINED FOLDING KNIFE DEPT.

SUBJECT: FOLDING KNIFE TEST AND INSPECTION

PURPOSE: TO ASSURE THAT EACH FOLDING KNIFE MEETS GERBER QUALITY STANDARD

SCOPE: ALL FOLDING KNIVES WILL BE INSPECTED BY THE FIRST INSPECTOR JUST PRIOR TO SHARPENING

I. CLEANING
A. CLEAN KNIFE THOROUGHLY SPRAYING WITH PERCHLORETHYLENE

II. INSPECT BLADES
A. INSPECTOR WILL CHECK FOLLOWING AGAINST THE STANDARD

1. FINGER NOTCH
2. STAMP LOCATION
3. TOP OF BLADE FOR SANDING QUALITY
4. SIDE TO SIDE AND UP AND DOWN MOVEMENT OF BLADE

III. FUNCTION
A. TEST EACH KNIFE FOR THE FOLLOWING MECHANICAL FUNCTIONS

1. WHEN CLOSING BLADES THERE SHOULD BE NO CONTACT WITH SIDE OF ASSEMBLY OR WITH A MATING BLADE
2. BLADES SHOULD OPEN AND CLOSE WITH SAME "EFFORT" AS STANDARD, HESITATION SHOULD BE IN SAME POSITION AND MAGNITUDE AS STANDARD

3. CHECK KICK ON EACH BLADE TO MAKE CERTAIN BLADE POINT IS COMPLETELY NESTED IN ASSEMBLY, BLADE SHOULD NOT "BOTTOM" TO POINT WHERE FINGER LIFT IS NOT FUNCTIONAL. BLADE SHOULD NOT "BOTTOM" OUT IN ASSEMBLY
B. IF A KNIFE CANNOT BE ADJUSTED TO MEET FUNCTIONAL STANDARD IT WILL BE REJECTED

IV. APPEARANCE
A. CHECK SURFACE OF KNIFE FOR FOLLOWING:

1. SURFACE OF KNIFE SHOULD BE SANDED IN ACCORDANCE WITH STANDARD
2. NO VISIBLE RIVETS OTHER THAN THOSE DESIGNATED BY STANDARD
3. NO VISIBLE PARTING LINES OTHER THAN THOSE DEEMED STANDARD

4. NO PITS OR HOLES OTHER THAN THOSE DEEMED STANDARD
5. CATCH OR SPRING SHOULD NOT PROTRUDE ABOVE OR BELOW TOP OF ASSEMBLY IN OPEN OR CLOSED POSITION
B. CHECK INLAYS FOR FOLLOWING:
1. NO VISIBLE CRACKS
2. NO SEPARATION OF INLAY AND SIDEPLATE

V. IF KNIFE PASSES ALL TESTS FOR APPEARANCE AND FUNCTION IT WILL BE PROCESSED THROUGH SHARPENING
A. IF APPEARANCE OR FUNCTIONS ARE NOT STANDARD, BUT KNIFE MIGHT BE SHIPPABLE INSPECTOR WILL RECORD KNIFE ON TALLY SHEET AND PLACE IN HOLDING TRAY FOR INSPECTION BY GENERAL FORMAN AND/OR PLANT SUPERINTENDENT

Hand lettered signs in the main assembly area spell out guidelines for maintaining quality and consistency.

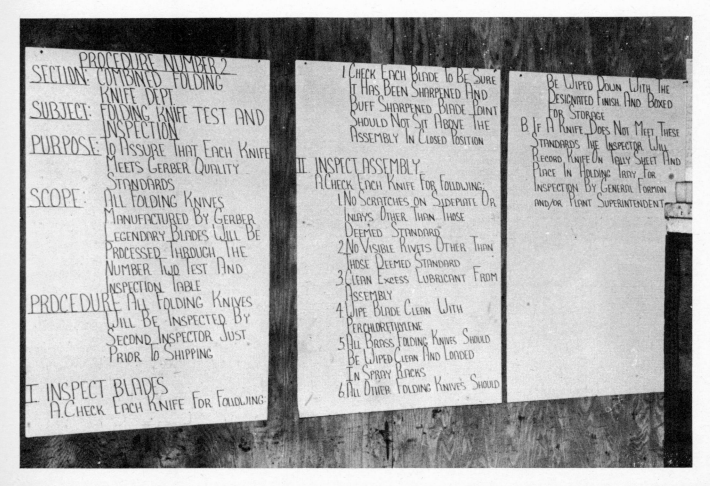

PROCEDURE NUMBER 2

SECTION: COMBINED FOLDING KNIFE DEPT.

SUBJECT: FOLDING KNIFE TEST AND INSPECTION

PURPOSE: TO ASSURE THAT EACH KNIFE MEETS GERBER QUALITY STANDARDS

SCOPE: ALL FOLDING KNIVES MANUFACTURED BY GERBER LEGENDARY BLADES WILL BE PROCESSED THROUGH THE NUMBER TWO TEST AND INSPECTION TABLE

PROCEDURE: ALL FOLDING KNIVES WILL BE INSPECTED BY SECOND INSPECTOR JUST PRIOR TO SHIPPING

I. INSPECT BLADES
A. CHECK EACH KNIFE FOR FOLLOWING:

1. CHECK EACH BLADE TO BE SURE IT HAS BEEN SHARPENED AND BUFF SHARPENED BLADE POINT SHOULD NOT SIT ABOVE THE ASSEMBLY IN CLOSED POSITION

II. INSPECT ASSEMBLY
A. CHECK EACH KNIFE FOR FOLLOWING:
1. NO SCRATCHES ON SIDEPLATE OR INLAYS OTHER THAN THOSE DEEMED STANDARD
2. NO VISIBLE RIVETS OTHER THAN THOSE DEEMED STANDARD
3. CLEAN EXCESS LUBRICANT FROM ASSEMBLY
4. WIPE BLADE CLEAN WITH PERCHLORETHYLENE
5. ALL BRASS FOLDING KNIVES SHOULD BE WIPED CLEAN AND LOADED IN SPRAY RACKS
6. ALL OTHER FOLDING KNIVES SHOULD

BE WIPED DOWN WITH THE DESIGNATED FINISH, AND BOXED FOR STORAGE
B. IF A KNIFE DOES NOT MEET THESE STANDARDS THE INSPECTOR WILL RECORD KNIFE ON TALLY SHEET AND PLACE IN HOLDING TRAY FOR INSPECTION BY GENERAL FORMAN AND/OR PLANT SUPERINTENDENT

To this point, the blade blanks have been left at the customary hardness of the 440C steel and now the blanks are hardened to the final C57-59 figure before bevelling.

Grinding of the bevels is performed on a dual-wheel machine, using liquid-cooled, 60-grit wheels to taper each side of the blade toward the final edge. Blades are not sharpened at this time.

The major components that make up the lock-blade folding knife, in addition to the blade and its pivot pin, consist of the liner, two side plates, locking bar and locking bar spring. In addition, there are the holding rivets and inlaid scales of impregnated tropical hardwood.

The liner and locking bar are of the same thickness as the tang of the blade and, together with the locking bar, comprise the inner framework of the knife. The side plates serve to secure the central components in their correct position and relation to each other.

Depending upon the given model of Gerber folding knife, the side plates may be stamped from brass sheet stock of the appropriate thickness or they may be die-cast, the latter being the case with the larger models. The side plates are held in a precision jig for removal of excess metal from the edges on a vertical-axis grinding wheel, so they will fit the holding jig that positions them for drilling of the holes for the rivets. All of the holes for the rivets are drilled simultaneously on a multiple drill press.

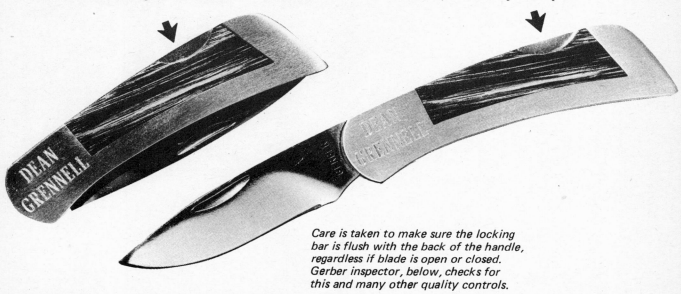

Care is taken to make sure the locking bar is flush with the back of the handle, regardless if blade is open or closed. Gerber inspector, below, checks for this and many other quality controls.

Final detailing is mostly handwork, using progressively finer grinders and polishing wheels. At left, final sharpening consists of stone sharpening and buff sharpening, as being performed here.

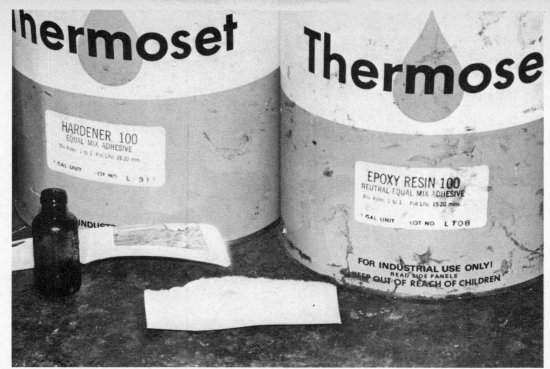

Industrial epoxy cement is used for attaching the handle scales, with curing under controlled time and temperature.

The outer openings of the drilled holes are chamfered or counterbored slightly. This serves the dual purpose of easing the insertion of the rivets and, at the same time, leaving clearance for a secure mushroom expansion of the rivet heads.

Meanwhile, the semifinished blade has been paired to the locking bar, after having the tang area of the blade checked for dimensional tolerances on a dial gauge fixture. In what may be the most critical and exacting phase of the entire production operation, the mating surfaces of the blade notch and the projection on the end of the locking bar are ground to their final fit. This requires patient, highly skilled handwork. Even the most minor discrepancy would result in a knife whose blade would be loose and sloppy or,

With blades partially opened, the joint at the hinge is oiled.

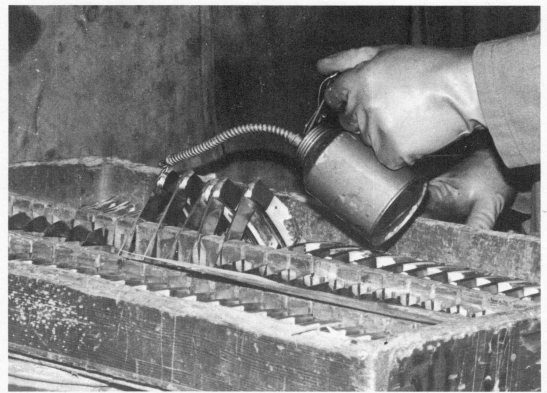

Gerber folding knives are made in many patterns, including one that doubles as a screwdriver.

One of a limited production run, this Gerber folder boasts engraving and colorful scales of Oregon agate.

Another Gerber custom production, featuring scrimshaw by A. Yancey.

possibly, one whose blade would not lock in the open position.

After fitting, the blade and locking bar proceed on through the numerous stages of assembly and inspection as a mated pair. They are assembled to the liner and side plates by delicate, skilled manipulation of ball peen hammers, arbor presses and rivet setters. Both assemblers and intermediate inspectors maintain a rigid and continuous check and quality control effort.

The decorative wooden handle scales are sorted by hand to assure matching color and grain and are fastened to the recess in the assembled knife by clamps with a specialized industrial epoxy cement, followed by curing at 275 degrees for forty-five minutes. The scales are cut precisely to fit the opening in the side plate, but they are thick enough to project above the surface of the metal slightly.

Four knives at a time are fastened to a holding jig for two passes through a machine called the Asher grinder — named for a Gerber employee, Glen Asher, who designed it — and most of the surplus wood is removed from the scale on each side of the handle. The Asher grinder could be set so as to take the wood down, flush with the surface of the surrounding metal. To do so, however, might produce frictional heat sufficient to warp the metal parts, so the last of the wood is sanded dead-flush with the side plate as a hand operation, using equipment that enables excess heat to be avoided.

After finishing of the handle scales, they go to another bench for a step called puttying. The term is misleading, since it does not involve the type of putty used in windows.

A second work by A. Yancey shows two battling elk.

Al Mar is the chief designer
at Gerber's; he offers comments
here to those interested in the field.

Pete Gerber, president of
Gerber Legendary Blades, has
built his plant into one of the largest
by innovative design and highest quality.

The material used is an industrial epoxy resin which, like the adhesive, has been designed and selected for the given purpose. The handles are inspected rigorously and any slight flaw or imperfection in the wood is filled with the epoxy resin putty, cured and finished to a smooth, flat surface or edge.

A fine-grit vertical-axis belt sander is used in conjunction with a holding jig to cut the curved relief opening giving access to the exposed end of the locking bar. The knives move on to the department termed Tycro finish, another hand operation on Tycro machines; trade name for a line of abrasive finishers of appropriate grit count.

After final adjustment and further inspection, the knives go to the sharpening room, to be given the two-stage treatment: stone sharpening and buff sharpening. Another inspection follows the sharpening. Knives with brass handles are coated with a special jeweler's lacquer to prevent corrosion of the brass areas. Naturally, this step is omitted on models with stainless-steel handles. The blades are degreased in a solvent bath and wiped clean. Dust, dirt and foreign matter is wiped and blown out with air hoses and a light application of lubricating oil is made in the area around the tang of the blade or blades.

At this point, the boxes of completed knives are returned to the storage cribs for packaging and shipment.

Al Mar is the chief designer for Gerber Legendary Blades. He had worked in several other fields until, at age 28, he left his native Seattle and enrolled at the Art Center College of Design in Los Angeles. Upon graduation, he went to Gerber originally on a packaging project and ended up behind the drawing board at his present assignment.

"If a person contemplates getting into knife designing — an extremely limited field — he needs some good design background. I'd not advise anyone to put their endeavors into this particular area on a full-time basis. Perhaps if you

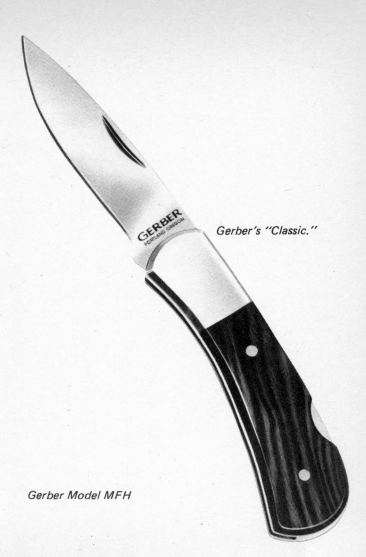

Gerber's "Classic."

Gerber Model MFH

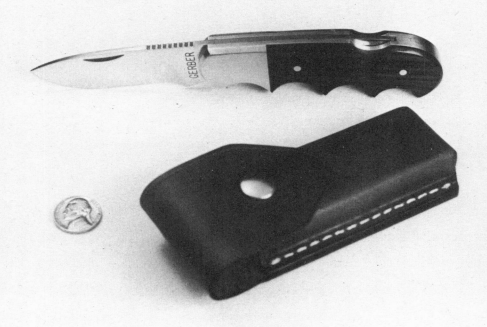

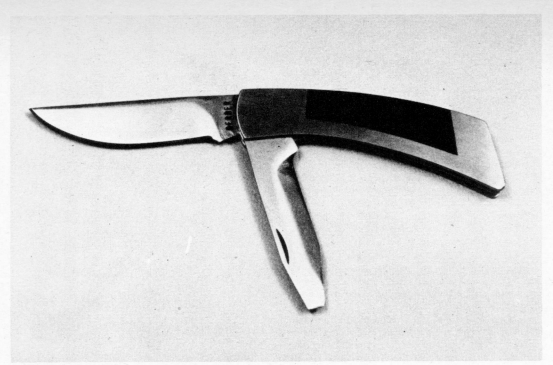

Gerber Model PK3 has second blade serving as a screwdriver.

Gerber Models PK1 and PK2; the latter having nonlocking second blade.

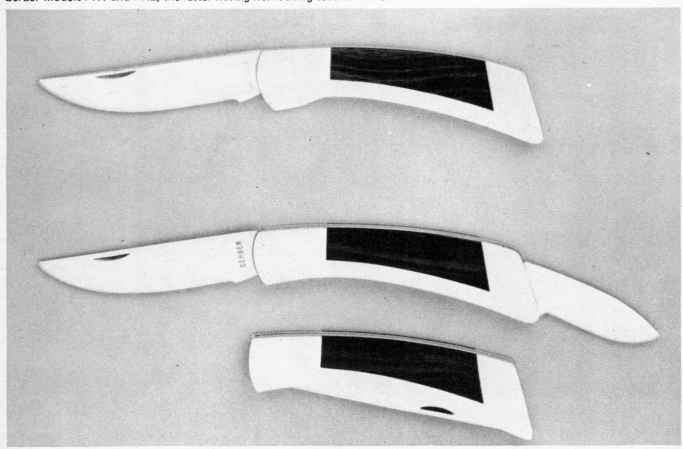

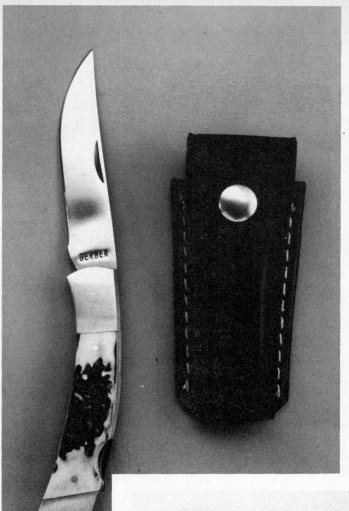

were an industrial designer and had a flair for this particular field, it would be a good sideline.

"I'm one of those lucky people who, purely by chance, has fallen into a vocation that blends with my hobby and it gets damned hard to tell them apart; where one starts and the other ends," Mar comments.

The Gerber Paul Knife was designed by Paul Poehlmann, a research and development employee in the aerospace industry. Poehlmann's axial locking mechanism was painstakingly developed and it is the feature that makes the design unique. There's never a broken nail or a nicked finger because the fingers never touch the blade. The pivot button is depressed and rotated to open or close the blade, which locks solidly in either position.

Originally, Poehlmann made each of his knives entirely by hand and they sold in the price range of $300, available in extremely limited quantities. Production of the Paul Knife at Gerber's will be under the direct personal supervision of Poehlmann and the projected prices will be $55 for the plain satin stainless-steel handle or $60 for the models with hardwood or ivory micarta handles.

"I think the success of this company can be attributed primarily to Pete Gerber. He's got a crew of people working together and the whole outlook of the company is quite positive and aggressive," Al Mar observes. "With this attitude, we've come a long way and we intend to go a lot farther. We're always working on new projects, but a lot of them never get past the paper. My job is particularly challenging: Trying to design one of man's oldest tools into something new and different. It's the tough goal of trying to turn out Cadillac quality at Chevrolet prices, but one of the reasons that Poehlmann chose to let Gerber build the Paul Knife was that he was satisfied we could produce it without compromising its precision and quality."

Below, Gerber Model FSII combines functionality, grace and durability.

Above, Gerber's Folding Sportsman II, with stag handle.

Chapter 16

NEW LOOK FOR BUCK

A portion of the selection of Buck folding knives now on the market, including lock-back and nonlocking blades.

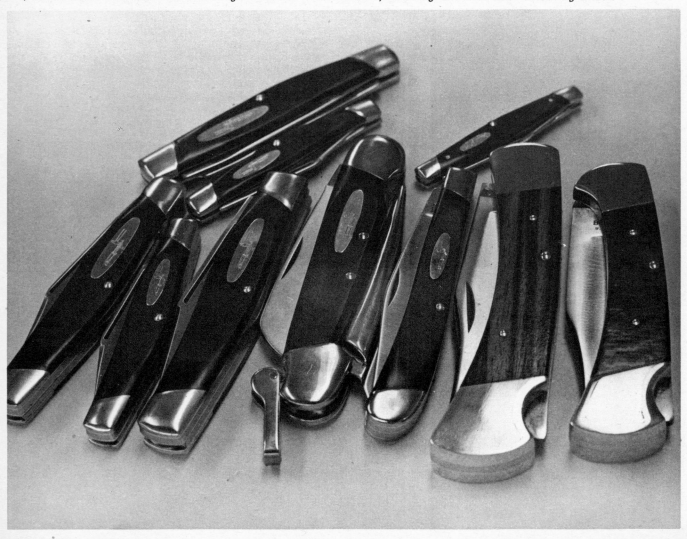

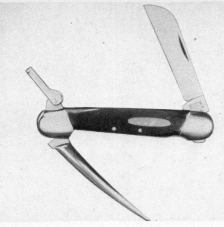

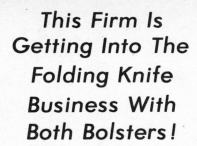

Trailblazer model 317 is 5¼″ folded, complete with sheath, retails for $26.

The folding Buck Yachtsman model (above) features lanyard loop, marlinspike and blade. (Below) Buck's Companion model has two blades.

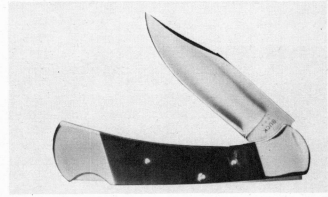

The 112 Ranger (above) with overall length of 4¼″ was second folder introduced by Buck in 1971.

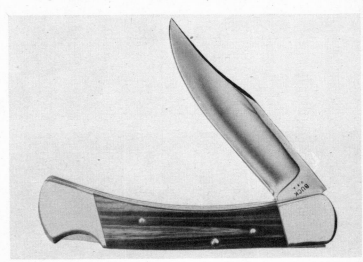

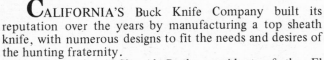

Folding Hunter, Model 110 was first folder produced and sold.

CALIFORNIA'S Buck Knife Company built its reputation over the years by manufacturing a top sheath knife, with numerous designs to fit the needs and desires of the hunting fraternity.

In the early 1960s Al Buck, president of the El Cajon-based company, recognized a need for a quality folding knife for hunters and other outdoorsmen.

"We wanted to design and make a folding knife that would give the horsemen and hunter a knife he could carry safely when riding on horseback or in a vehicle. There is some danger with a fixed blade, if you fall on it, regardless of the sheath design. We wanted a knife big enough for a hunter to be able to field dress big game but small enough to be practical," Buck recalls.

Buck and his design staffers got their heads together and a new folding lock-blade hunter was born, the No. 110 Buck folding hunter. It has a four-inch blade, long enough for any type of field dressing with the possible exception of elk, and the upsweep point popular with many hunters. Safety was incorporated by making the knife what might be termed a large pocketknife, but more properly, it is a sheath blade of folding design. The folding hunter design comes with a leather belt sheath.

This folding lock-blade design has strength, since the liners are made of one-piece brass. The first models were cast but the current method is to place powdered brass in a die, then use a furnace to bring it to the melting point. The cast liners later are restruck with the mould to align and

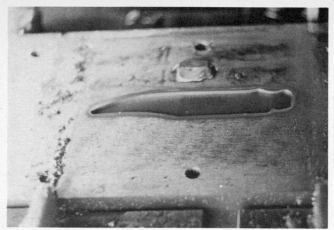

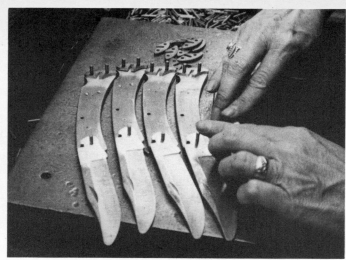

Above, punch press die that turns out blades for folding hunter. A modified 440C steel is used.

Brass pivot is pressed by hand through blade and scale.

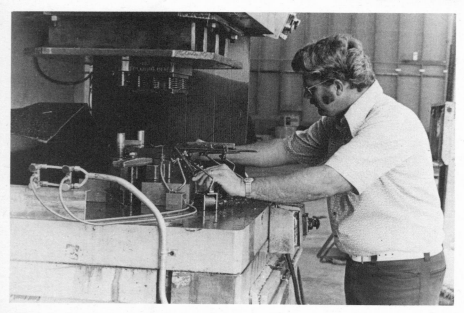

Chuck Buck, grandson of the company's founder, keeps active in plant production.

All Buck folding knives are hand finished and adjusted by factory workers. Each knife is different.

The factory edge begins to take shape with skilled hands on the grinder. Not every step is automated.

Belt sander and steady hands put the finishing touches to bolster and handle.

Workman's gloves protect hands and fingers during final buffing job.

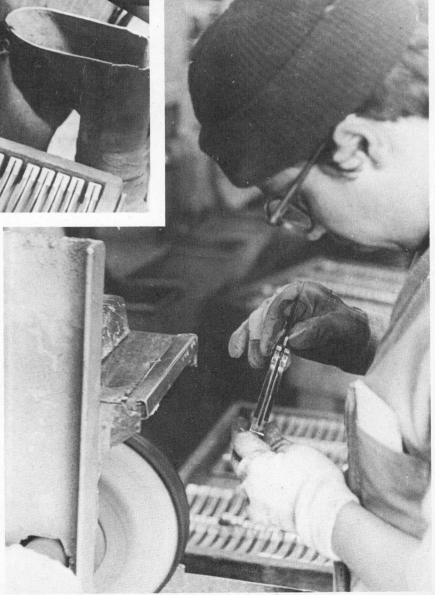

Nearly completed Buck folders (below) await delivery to owners.

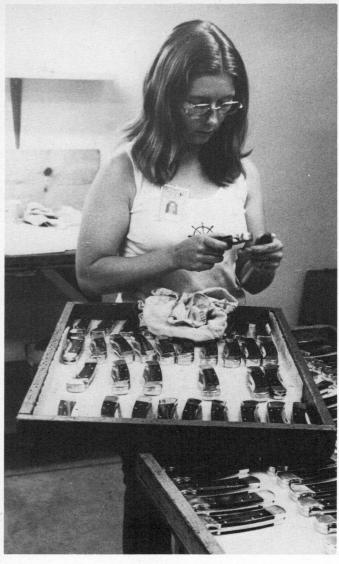

(Above) Orders are carefully checked before shipping.

Each finished knife, folder or otherwise, is
wiped clean of finger prints (left).

Folders large enough for sheaths are shipped with
Buck's own leather protector and boxed (lower left).
Educating the buyer reduces returned knives.

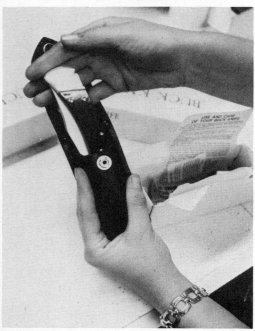

strengthen the metal. The finished product not only takes the high polish associated with a quality brass, but makes a strong one-piece unit.

The handle section is of Macassar ebony. This exotic hardwood is cut, slabbed and mated to the liners with brass rivets before the liners and blade are assembled.

There have been few changes in blade design since the prototype, according to Buck. The first blades may have been a bit more narrow but the basic style has remained the same. Most collectors are aware that the Buck name is just above the blade's opener slot on early models. Now the name is placed at the base of the blade adjoining the pivot section.

Originally the opening slot was struck in the hot steel by pressure but today the slot is milled. Other minor changes are found in the roll-over locking system that is covered by the liners and handles.

From the beginning, blades have been made of a modified 440C steel hardened to 58 to 60 RC. This affords a tough edge and one that will last. Like all Buck knives, they are guaranteed for life.

"When we first marketed the 110 folding hunter models, we started getting returns. Many people abuse a knife badly. Hunters and knife users more familiar with the single-blade styles use them for prying and twisting to cut or move something.

"A folding knife just won't take this kind of abuse, to which no knife should be subjected. Our first folders were opening up at the rivet or pivot section from this abuse. We began to educate buyers with our literature to see if we could prevent this damage," Al Buck reports. Return figures show the educational program has worked for the most part.

The handle section — brass liners and wood scales riveted in place — first is rough polished and cleaned up. Then it is married to the blade by inserting the rocker arm with one brass rivet, and the spacer/stop at the back of the handle. The latter acts as a spacer to maintain proper distance on the liners and also as a stop for the rocker arm, preventing too much travel.

The semifinished blade is inserted on the front with the pivot rivet. At this point, the rocker arm and the blade are hand-fitted. Each knife is a bit different and a skilled cutler works the rocker/blade combination until the knife opens easily and closes firmly.

The fit declared satisfactory, the knife is passed to a finisher who edges the blade and puts a satin finish on the steel. The brass is polished on buffers and final inspection takes place before a final buffing to remove any fingerprints from the brass or steel. A degreaser is used just prior to packaging for the shipping room.

Chuck Buck, executive vice-president, sums up the success of the 110 lock blade: "We have probably sold in excess of two and one-quarter million of these since we went into production thirteen years ago. The idea of making a quality folding knife was a winner. Today, our folding knives equal sheath blade production."

With success of the 110, Buck introduced a smaller version in 1971, calling it the No. 112 Ranger. This knife was similar to its bigger brother but had a smaller blade and a slightly different handle style. The forward bolster was designed for more finger protection with the blade in the open position. It also is a sheath style, a bit bulky for a pocket.

The first models of this style were made with a Buckarta laminated linen and phenolic handle material. The handles now are of wood.

In the same era, Buck introduced a line of pocketknives that now totals ten models from the super-small Cadet designed for the pocket to the Yachtsman with a built-in marlinspike.

Buck knives have to be kept sharpened by the owner/ user. Company sells Washita and hard Arkansas stone as well as special honing oil in kits for customers.

Another useful tool for keeping knife sharp in field is the 5" sharpening steel (above) for $13.

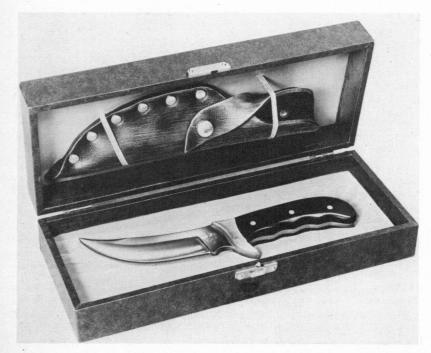

Maintaining the correct blade angle while sharpening a knife is not easy. Buck Honemaster offers help.

Kalinga model Buck sheath knife (left) comes with presentation case and leather sheath for $60.

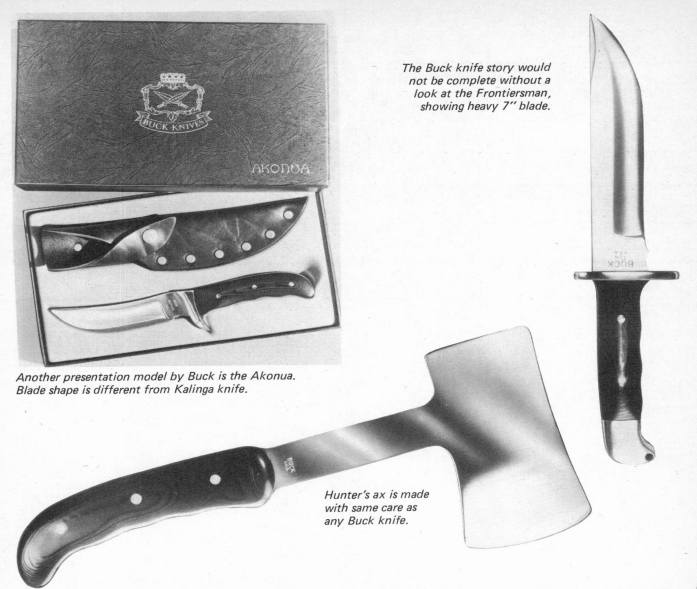

Another presentation model by Buck is the Akonua. Blade shape is different from Kalinga knife.

The Buck knife story would not be complete without a look at the Frontiersman, showing heavy 7″ blade.

Hunter's ax is made with same care as any Buck knife.

If a large folding lock-blade knife that fits a belt sheath was successful, how about one that would ride well in the pocket? To answer that question, in 1975, Buck introduced the first of a new series of folding lock-blade styles they call the Royal line. There will be at least four blades in this new line of knives starting with the first model, the 501 Esquire. This knife is the first drop-point, folding lock-blade made by Buck. The firm makes no other drop-point styles unless one considers their fixed-blade skinner and caper as a drop point.

This first of the new line has a gently flowing curve to the handle and blade when opened. The blade meets the handle in a clean, sharp line. It is designed to fit in the trouser pocket, lying flat, but also is available with a sheath.

The Esquire is of stainless steel primarily, the liner and bolster formed at the same time in the dies. The blade is of 440C steel and the pivot pin, the rocker pin and the base pins all are stainless.

Rivets mate the liner to the red Buckarta, a material made by compressing linen with epoxy under heat and pressure to form a tough, durable handle. The blade is semi-hollow ground.

Newest in this Royal line is the Prince No. 503. This is a smaller version of the Esquire, with no sheath offered.

Still in planning stages at this writing is another Royal lock-blade folder, even smaller than the Prince. After that will be a lock blade of larger design. Both will have the same flowing blade style and drop-point design.

Buck is promising yet another series of executive stainless-steel pocketknives that will be highly polished with small blades for the man who wants a small knife to carry in his daily life. These are still in the design process with no prototypes produced at this time.

Buck now has ten standard folding pocket styles and four folding lock blades. That will be extended to six lock blades when the Royal prototypes are put into production. Technicians continually experiment with current models and, when something better can be incorporated, the idea is phased into production of that particular model.

Don Ham, director of marketing, says, "If we can get people to stop prying, twisting and misusing our knives, we could do away with the repair section. We get knives returned that obviously have been misused. When we see a half-moon break in a blade, the first thing we look at is the top of the blade. Usually we can find hammer marks where someone has banged the top of the blade. We usually repair or replace these knives, but even a good knife must be treated with respect."

Pocketknives, folding hunters and special-use folders are numbered among the hundreds of designs by Case Cutlery.

Chapter 17

A CASE OF NEED

ONE OF THE most familiar trademarks to knife buffs has to be the Case XX marking, but few know how the marking came about.

It started in 1847 in Little Valley, New York, the original site of the Case Brothers Company factory. According to corporate legend, Case Brothers used a method of tempering steel that has been in existence since before the heyday of the Roman Empire.

When a blade first was brought out of the initial hardening furnace, an *x* was marked on the record of that particular batch of metal, according to Robert N. Farquharson, the firm's current executive vice-president. When the blades were returned to the oven for added treatment, another *x* was added to the records after the annealing process was completed. The double cross showed that the blades had been heat-treated properly.

Today, This Old-Line Firm Makes More Than A Hundred Types Of Pocketknives For Every Need Or Want!

"Through the years, different versions of the Case XX have been used," according to Farquharson. "Although exact dates of the various marks are unknown, approximations can be made." This, incidentally, has become a matter of continuing contention among collectors.

"In 1965, Case Cutlery added the lettering *USA* to its stamping die to make obvious the country of origin.

Five years later — in 1970 — Case added ten dots, called measles by the collecting fraternity. These are below the stamped USA and indicate the year the blade was made. As each year passes, one dot is removed. For the decade starting with 1980, according to the vice-president, the firm plans to identify each year in the same fashion but with a redesigned arrangement of the dots.

All of that is fine for collectors, but how did all of this come about? The firm known today as W.R. Case & Sons Cutlery Company was founded more than a century and a half ago in Little Valley, New York, as Case Brothers Cutlery Company. Today, it is another spoke in the corporate wheel of a giant conglomerate, American Brands, having been sold to the firm in 1972.

The founders, in the early 1800s, were Bob Russell Case and his four sons, John, Andrew, Jean and William Russell. As indicated, the brothers adopted the XX as their trademark and, utilizing their talents, the family members soon developed into a fast-growing organization.

Part of Case's Bradford, Pennsylvania, factory called the concave finishing department where a workman is polishing the shoulder side of the guard of a fixed-blade knife on a high-speed buffer.

Hand grinding pocketknife blades is not a thing of the past as these factory workers demonstrate.

Many skilled hands are still needed in the modern Case knife factory. Nonfolding hunting knives also are produced.

Jean Case became the sales manager to function as Case's top salesman for many years. According to company history, he was the first cutlery salesman to offer a complete factory line West of the Mississippi River. At the same time, the firm's ability to produce at what amounted to a wholesale level helped him to fill his orders.

A crimp was put in the firm's fortunes when the factory at Little Valley burned to the ground, but the brothers decided to rebuild their plant, this time in Springville, New York. The firm continued to prosper despite this temporary setback.

The son of William R. Case, J. Russell Case, joined the firm at the turn of the century. As a member of the sales force, he soon found himself in friendly competition with his uncle, Jean, each trying to outdo the other, but in reality making their product one that soon seemed to be found in every household in one form or another.

Perhaps it was only natural that J. Russell Case, the super salesman of the era, should want something more than simply a reputation as a good man with whom to deal. In 1903, his ambitions came to the fore and he left the family business.

Using his savings, he established W.R. Case & Sons Cutlery Company, setting up shop in Bradford, Pennsylvania. Included in the business in the beginning were his father, William Russell Case, for whom the company actually was named, and Harvey Platts — the latter who ultimately was to take a page from Case's book and begin his own firm. Today, the firm that Platts founded is Colorado's Western Cutlery, which still is operated by his descendants.

As the firm grew, they purchased the Case Brothers company, still located in Springville, New York. For undetermined reasons, the older firm was renamed the Robinson Cutlery Company and was redesigned to produce household cutlery. Collectors note, however, that during this period of transition, a number of pocketknives did come out of the purchased plant and were stamped W.R.

Among the hundreds of designs produced by the Case people are several single and double-blade pocketknives.

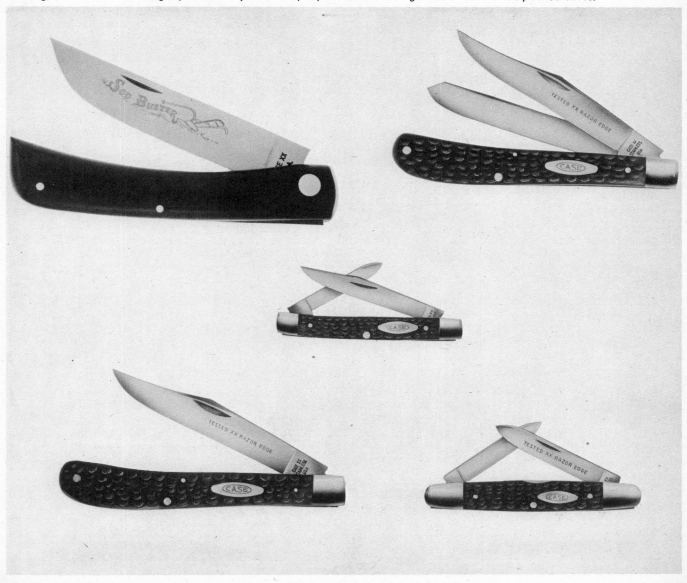

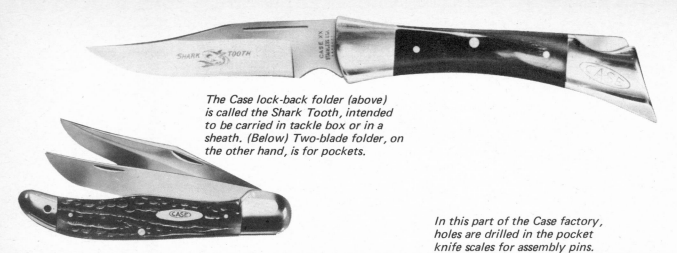

The Case lock-back folder (above) is called the Shark Tooth, intended to be carried in tackle box or in a sheath. (Below) Two-blade folder, on the other hand, is for pockets.

In this part of the Case factory, holes are drilled in the pocket knife scales for assembly pins.

Plastic slabs are snapped into place on folding knife scales. Case uses natural and man-made handle materials.

Folding fishing knife (above) offers hook sharpener on side. (Below) Larger folders may be carried in Case leather sheath.

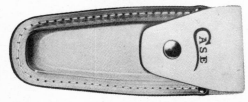

Case & Sons, Springville, New York. The Robinson company was sold in about 1908 and still continues in the manufacture of household cutlery.

As probably has been noted by the reader, most of the cutlery manufacturers of the era all seem to have sprung from the Upstate New York area, which was settled by cutlers migrating from Sheffield, England. It is from these roots that most of today's major cutlery firms originated.

So it is not surprising to learn that, early in this century, W.R. Case & Sons merged with the Crandal Cutlery Company. As might be suspected, this was another family affair; Herbert E. Crandal, founder of the latter firm, was J. Russell Case's brother-in-law. However, the firm continued to be known under the Case name and the XX trademark. Of interest, perhaps, is the fact that the company continued to be family controlled until sold to American Brands in 1972, although J. Russell Case, its founder, had died in 1953.

A "Case pocketknife" is a term known to a large part of the world. Here are samples of some of the standard, smaller styles available. Case uses three kinds of blade steel and dozens of handle slab materials.

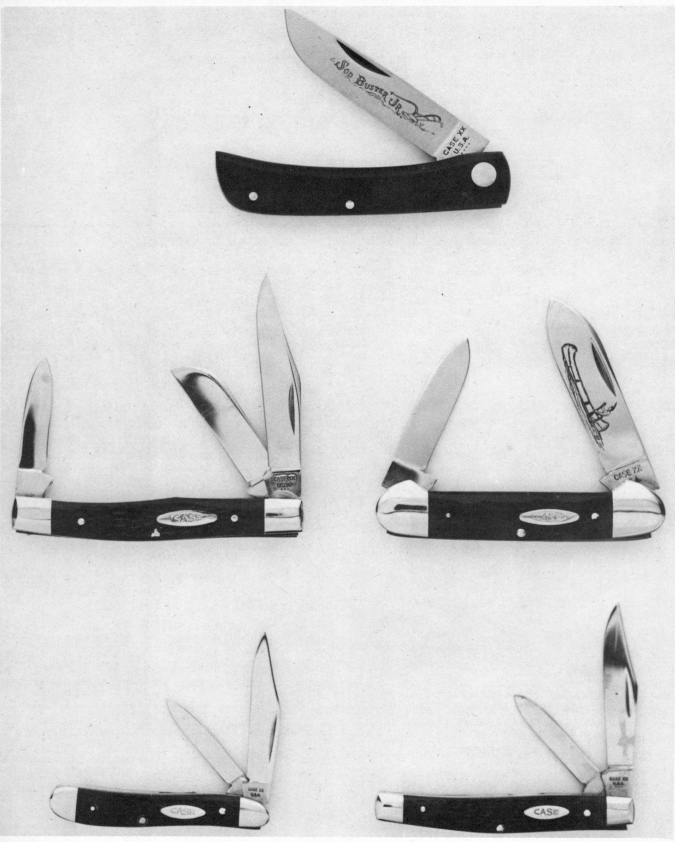

Before packaging and after final assembly, each Case folder is carefully inspected to ensure flawless operation.

According to Bill Derby, who handles advertising and sales promotion for the firm, "We make over two hundred different kinds and models, including more than a hundred pocketknife styles. Each is carefully designed and manufactured for a specific use."

Case now uses three different types of steel: stainless, chrome vanadium and carbon steel. "The higher the carbon content, the harder the steel is to work, but it will hold an edge longer," Derby says.

Originally, Case craftsmen hand-forged their blades. The impurities in the raw steel were literally beaten out of the metal as the grain was compacted. Theory was that the finer the grain, produced through such beatings, the tougher the resulting steel.

In this modern age, however, Case purchases knife steel

either in coils or flat strips. Which type of steel is used depends on the knife pattern and the type of equipment to be used in stamping out the blades.

"Because of the vastly improved mechanical and metallurgical techniques of today's steel mills, there is little difference in a blade that is forged and one that comes from this mill stock," Derby insists.

"The strip stock is cut into lengths and fed by hand into the press. It goes through several other stages that result in the necessary holes, the nail mark and the trademark."

Some of the coil stock is blanked in what is called a Feinblanking press. A relatively new method of stamping out blades that was developed in Switzerland, Case was the first United States firm to use it for pocketknives, according to Derby, who adds that, "It leaves a cleaner and smoother edge on the blade than the conventional methods."

At this point, the blades are ready to be heat-treated. Other than the type of steel that is used, this step is probably the most important factor in coming up with a quality blade.

First, the blades are heated to a temperature of 1400 to 2000F, the temperature varying with the type of steel that is being processed.

The blades are quenched in water, oil or salt to harden the steel, but this results in a too brittle blade. The answer is tempering, which is accomplished at Case in salt baths or by slowly reheating the blades at lower temperatures in draw furnaces.

"We used to drop the blades into the quench tank by hand," Derby reports, "but this never did enable us to get an even quench. In our newest plant, we have two new batch-type hardening furnaces. These each have an integral quenching unit that handles the job automatically. Recently, we have begun using temperating furnaces

exclusively rather than the liquid salt baths that were used in the past."

Case technicians feel that the result is finer grain for the steel, resulting in a better blade.

When the heat-treating step is completed, the blades are ready for grinding. Each blade will be given either a flat or concave grind, depending upon the type of knife and its ultimate use.

"The flat ground blade is tapered from the back to the edge of the blade, producing a thin edge," Derby says. "As the blade wears, the edge becomes thicker. The concave ground knife has a concave area on each side of the blade which starts near the back of the blade and becomes exceedingly thin before it reaches the edge. Thus, this type of knife can be sharpened many times before the blade starts to thicken."

Today, in the new plant, both types of grinding are accomplished on semiautomatic equipment, but during the hand-grinding stage, a swedge is put on the blades.

"On a pocketknife, this swedge actually is the rounding

The final step prior to shipment to dealers' shelves is wrapping and packaging. Each knife is individually boxed.

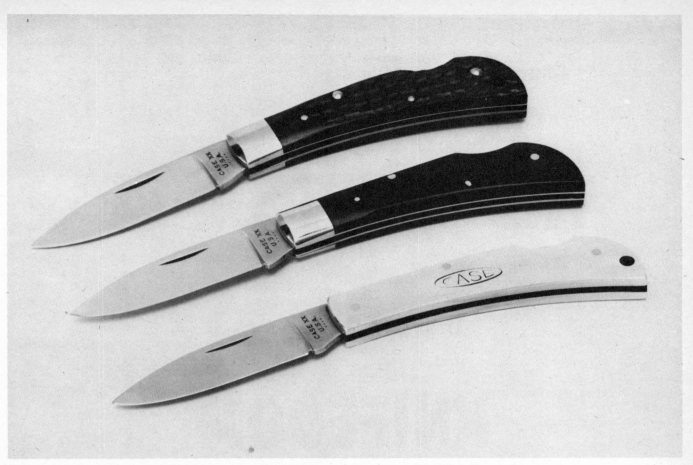

In its manufacture of lock-back folders and pocketknife styles, Case uses solid nickel silver bolsters and nickel silver or brass for the liners. Many of the Case designs of the past have become collectors' items.

of the edges on the backs of the blades. It's done for safety and so that the blades will fall past one another easily when the knife is being closed," according to Bill Derby.

Once the grinding phase is completed, finishing is done on a double-header machine, which has two wheels opposite each other and turning towards each other.

"These wheels are headed with felt and covered with layers of emery dust, wax and glue," according to Derby. "The swedges are finished on a single wheel, which allows the operator to work in small, difficult areas. With the rough-grind marks removed in this manner, the blade is ready to be polished."

Polishing is done on machines that are equipped with large, cotton buff rolls. When the blades have been polished to a high-mirror finish and pass inspection on this phase, they are ready for assembly.

Pocketknives are assembled by hand, placing the center scales, springs, liners and handles, as well as the bolsters to cover the end rivets that form the blade hinges.

"Many manufacturers use stamped sheet metal bolsters that are simply crimped into the lining," Derby says. "Case uses solid nickel silver bolsters that are die-pressed to shape. Whether they are riveted or spot-welded depends on the knife model being assembled.

"We also give the liners an extra rigidity by stamping a slight crease along the center length of each one. These liners are either of nickel silver or of brass."

Any knife buff knows that the springs that go into a pocketknife play an important part in its construction. These springs must be the exact shape, thickness and temper to afford the proper tension for each blade.

"At Case, these springs are hand ground in a special jig, then heat-treated to the proper temperature for the correct degree of tempering."

Handles used at Case cover a broad spectrum of materials, including wood, laminated wood, shin bone from cattle, stag horns and mother-of-pearl, as well as plastics. With all of these components together, the knife is hafted to be sure it has the proper shape and that parts are smooth and flush.

"The cutler makes the final adjustments for fit, grinds where necessary and puts the finishing touch to the cutting edge by hand-holding it on a grinding wheel," Derby reports. "After final cleaning and inspection, the knife is ready for packaging. By that time, a pocketknife has undergone more than two hundred hand operations in its manufacture."

Knife repairs used to be handled in the Case factory, but more recently, the firm has authorized a number of repair stations throughout the country. John Carlson operates such a repair center in Temple, Texas, where he repaired some 5000 Case knives over a three-year period.

Many, he reports, are family heirlooms that have been mistreated over the years. Others are from knife collectors who want their prizes put in top shape, thus reclaiming their value.

Chapter 18

THE QUIET GIANT
OF
KNIFEDOM

*Moving Into Its
Second Century, Camillus
Maintains Founders'
Old World Cutlery Skills*

CAMILLUS CUTLERY COMPANY gets its name from its location situated on the banks of Nine Mile Creek in Camillus, New York, just west of Syracuse. More than 350 full-time employees turn out tens of thousands of knives each month for the consumer trade, for the government and under various private brands. Camillus Cutlery Company has been the quiet giant of the industry.

In 1976, when the United States celebrated its Bicentennial, Camillus Cutlery Company observed its one hundredth year as suppliers of pocket, hunting, household and government fighting knives.

According to the company's official historian, the origin of Camillus Cutlery Company is really a composite story of two men: A German-born immigrant named Adolph Kastor and, to a lesser extent, an American named Charles Sherwood. Adolph Kastor was born on April 14, 1856. In the Summer of 1870, at the age of 14, he emigrated to the United States and immediately went to work in his uncle's

The Camillus Cutlery Company factory, as it appears in 1977, is located in Camillus, New York, on the banks of the Nine Mile Creek, west of Syracuse. Several new buildings have expanded plant capacity in recent years.

Nilo M. Miori has been with Camillus since 1932. In 1977 Miori was elected president of American Cutlery Manufacturers Association and has headed Camillus since 1964.

hardware store. He soon found himself managing the cutlery department where he became thoroughly exposed to all aspects of the cutlery business.

In 1876, he started on his own as a hardware wholesaler, specializing in cutlery. He eventually became the largest importer of pocketknives in the United States.

However, politics came into play, and the McKinley protective tariff of 1890 was passed to encourage domestic production. Imports became too costly and forced Kastor to seek out a domestic source of knives in order to remain competitive. His search led him to Camillus, New York, where Charles Sherwood owned a knife manufacturing operation that employed twenty cutlers, schooled in the Sheffield tradition, that laboriously turned out each knife by hand. This became his domestic source and Kastor bought the factory outright in 1902.

As the years passed, the factory grew — new buildings, greater production, more employees, more machines and the company was blessed with greater sales.

When World War I began the company, according to all

Brass linings, blades, center scales are stamped out by machine from coils of metal materials.

Above, knife blades are heat hardened in hot lead bath, then quenched in oil solution.

Another step in blade heat treatment uses electric furnaces.

Camillus factory hands are used to operate automatic machine that rivets knife bolsters and linings together, ready for cover.

reports and records, was in excellent financial position. Production was stepped up as imports ceased. The United States and allied governments bought military knives by the thousands. From the time the United States entered the war in 1917 until the cessation of hostilities, less than a year later, knife production for the services numbered 1,400,000. The return to peace brought a brief postwar national recession, but the upcurve of prosperity soon swung high.

In about ten years, however, the swing drastically went downward as the world plunged into the Great Depression. Through the difficult depression years of the 1930s many businesses floundered. Even great companies such as Winchester and Remington discontinued their knife operations. Camillus, however, remained sound.

According to reports, the relationship between the townspeople, labor and Camillus Cutlery Company continued to excel. Mechanization and methods that

Folding knife cover slabs and blade liners are united in this step of factory operation.

King-size belt sander grinds dozens of springs and blade backs mounted in jig. Factory workman ensures each part is in contact with abrasive belt.

Skilled hands are required for final assembly of Camillus folders prior to riveting and finishing.

Machine performs two operations at once: rivet pins are cut to correct length and riveted in position.

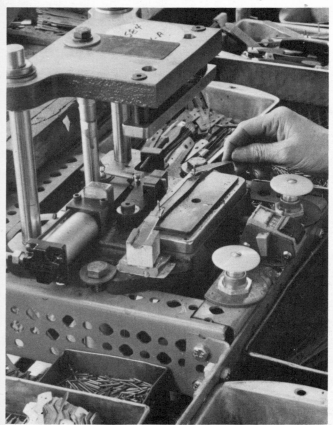

Machine uses spinning action to draw knife parts together for accurate fit and improved appearance.

Completely assembled knives are loaded into device that grinds and polishes spring backs.

seemed to be so modern at the time gave way to even more sophisticated equipment and systems.

Then came World War II. Camillus Cutlery Company produced nearly 15,000,000 knives, for the Army, Navy, Marine Corps and Coast Guard. During those war years, the government required knives to be manufactured with much closer tolerances. Camillus' history notes that the company changed its methods of making dies, rebuilt many of the automatic grinding machines and installed new ones during the war. The experience acquired during those years imbedded itself in the production structure in future years. Camillus is still the manufacturer of the pilot's survival knife used by the Air Force, the Marine Corps' seven-inch blade, push-button knives for paratroopers and other general purpose pocketknives.

When the conflict ended, it appeared to take little time for Camillus to get back to peace-time production. Three months after V-J Day, the first consumer catalogs were

Sharpening wheel and skilled hands are the ingredients of the factory edge placed on completed Camillus knives.

Each knife receives final inspection and buffing. Note protective gloves and tape on worker.

rolling off the presses, followed shortly thereafter by the knives themselves. Production and expansion increased dramatically in the years after WWII.

Nilo M. Miori assumed the presidency in January 1964. In the decade that followed, the new administration, production and sales according to a company spokesman, more than tripled and employment doubled. Manufacturing facilities were further expanded and mechanized to accommodate a growing demand for Camillus' output.

The Sixties and Seventies have been boom years for Camillus Cutlery. Although they produce some nonfolding hunting and survival knives, most of their business is in pocket folders. Following are a few of the latest:

The No. 26 Big Jack is just what its name implies: a massive two-bladed jack knife. Closed, Big Jack measures 5¼ inches with saber-ground clip and flat-ground skinner blades. The No. 6 is similar in size and construction except that it has only the clip blade.

The No. 7 Cam-Lok is a simple, safe sliding-lock folding knife. Closed, it measures 4¾ inches with a 3½-inch stainless-steel blade, Indian stag handles, leather wrist loop and a cowhide pouch.

The No. 88 Lok-Rancher features Indian stag handles, stainless-steel clip, sheepfoot and spey blades. It's made with a lock on the clip blade and its size when closed is 4¼ inches.

Roughness on completed knives is removed during hand glazing, scouring and final buffing.

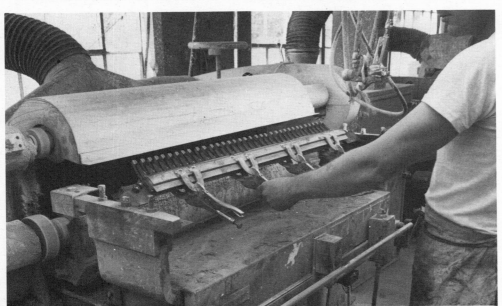

Bolsters, shields and handles are gang-polished by machine depicted at left.

Excess oil, dust or other foreign matter is removed before packaging.

Final step before leaving factory is packaging each knife in distinctive box.

The finished product. Camillus' American Wildlife series features wildlife sculpture on handle.

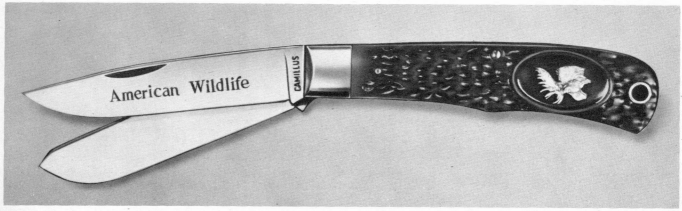

Camillus, as do most other knife factories, supports its dealer organization with various product displays.

Camillus' latest offering to the public is its contemporary Lok-Backs designed for the modern sportsman who demands a rugged knife with blades of high-carbon 440A stainless steel, and a recessed lock that secures the blade in the open position. Camillus Lok-Backs come in three sizes: No. 2 with two-inch clip blade, when closed size is 3-1/8 inches; No. 3 with a 2¾-inch Turkish clip blade, when closed size is 4-1/8 inches; and No. 4 with a 3¼-inch clip blade, when closed size is 4¾ inches. No. 2 bolsters are made of solid nickel silver while Nos. 3 and 4 are solid brass.

In 1976, to correspond with America's Bicentennial, Camillus introduced its American Wildlife Series which has proven to be the most successful knife series in the history of the company. All knives in this series are made with 440A stainless-steel blades, nickel silver bolsters and delrin handles. Inset into each handle is a sculptured figure struck in pewter from original masterpieces by wildlife engraver, Sid Bell. Following is a listing of some of the editions offered.

Edition No. 1 — No. 10 folding hunting knives, two blades (clip and long spey), 4½ inches closed, with sharpening steel. Wildlife: buck deer, coyote, running deer, bear.

Edition No. 2 — No. 10 (Same as Edition 1). Wildlife: elk, mountain sheep, moose, antelope.

Edition No. 3 — No. 17 wildfowler knives with Turkish clip blade and gut hook, 3-7/8 inches closed. Game birds: duck, goose, turkey, pheasant.

Edition No. 4 — No. 32 angler's folding knife, two blades (serrated tip sabre clip and flexible filet blade). Size when closed is five inches. No. 1006 — Filet knife, six-inch blade, overall length is eleven inches.

The knife collector hasn't been forgotten either. Almost all firms who have contracted pocketknives manufactured under their own private trade name, at one time or another have had Camillus handle their contract, says the company historian. Some of the most cherished knives were

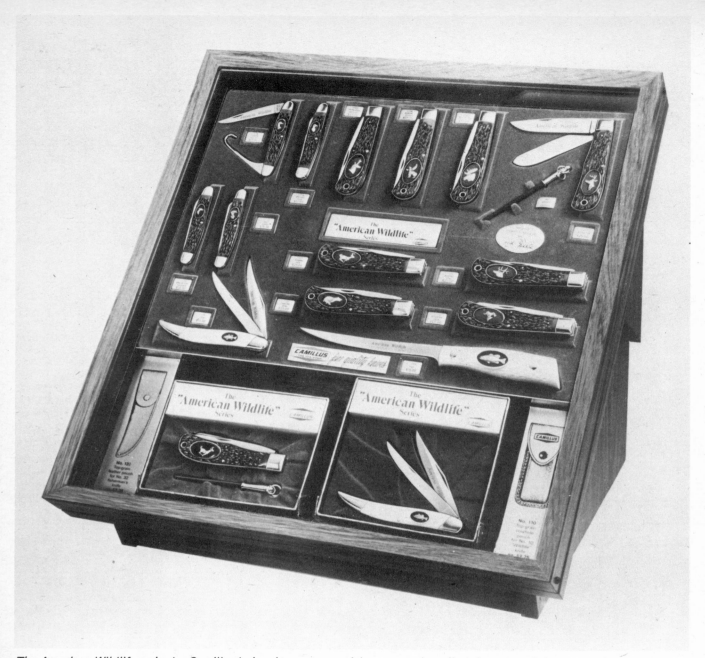

The American Wildlife series by Camillus knives is a common sight at several retail outlets around the country. Many of these knives (above) are sold with a sharpening steel and carrying sheath. The model below is designed with the wildfowler in mind, has a Turkish clip blade and gut hook. Blade is 440A steel.

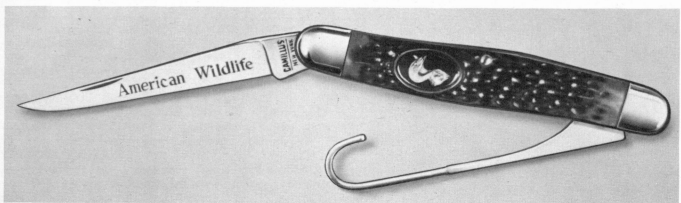

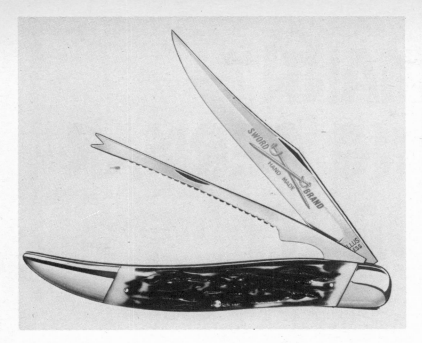

The fisherman is not forgotten by Camillus as this angler's knife features saber clip blade of stainless steel and combination hook disgorger/fish scaler blade.

manufactured by Camillus, for instance the Hibbard Spencer Bartlett, OVB, Keen-Kutter, Diamond Edge, Circle Van Camp, America's Best and Henry Sears 1865 to mention a few.

Even with today's mechanization, it takes 120 hand operations to make a Camillus knife. Each operation is carefully executed and put through a rigid quality-control procedure to help insure top-quality knives for the customer.

Camillus uses both high-carbon and stainless-steel alloys for their knives, depending on the specific and intended use for which it is designed. All Camillus knife blades maintain a Rockwell C scale hardness of 57-58, which has proven ideal, according to the company.

In Syracuse, the one-story white wood building where Sherwood began his manufacturing operation still stands, and is still part of Camillus Cutlery Company. A brick building was constructed in 1925 and another addition completed in 1940. In 1972 to 1973 an additional 25,000 square feet was incorporated into the complex and in 1976 to 1977 another 7000 square feet was added. The historian told us that Camillus Cutlery Company's operations cover more than 130,000 square feet of manufacturing facilities that produce nearly 3,000,000 knives yearly. Production is still on the rise.

Camillus has three model sizes of locking blade folders. The smaller model has bolsters of nickel silver, while larger two bolsters are brass.

Chapter 19

GUTMANN — IMPORTING GERMAN QUALITY

During 1977, Mr. and Mrs. Kurt Gutmann observed the 30th anniversary of their company which imports some of the best Solingen knives from Germany. Tom Palmer, right, presents plaque from employees to the Gutmanns.

For Thirty Years, The Gutmann's Of Mount Vernon, New York, Have Been Successful At Marketing Solingen-Made Knives

GUTMANN CUTLERY, currently headquartered in Mount Vernon, New York, contends that the firm is the largest importer and distributor of cutlery in the United States today.

April 11, 1977, marked the thirtieth year in business for this firm which was founded by Kurt and Ruth Gutmann, who began to import knives shortly after the end of World War II. The company originally was located in New York City, but space for the ever-growing lines became a problem and the firm moved to new headquarters in Mount Vernon in 1972.

"We've continued to grow since then," declares Kurt Gutmann, who continues as president. "Only recently, we have increased our office and warehousing space by an additional fifty percent." Tom Palmer, incidentally, functions as executive vice-president for the import firm.

The points on the world map from which Gutmann imports its growing line of folding, hunting and filet knives covers a wide net to include Germany, Japan, England, Ireland, Switzerland, Sweden, Italy and even Brazil and Pakistan.

As an example of its place in the cutlery sun, Gutmann currently is the largest distributor in the United States of the familiar Victorinox Swiss Army knife. Other leading brands finding their way to the firm's warehouses for reshipment to dealers across the nation are Puma, Edgemark, Bullet and Hen and Rooster.

According to Tom Palmer, the Puma line of custom knives currently consists of forty-three models ranging in retail prices from $16.50 to $250, while the Edgemark Explorer lineup has forty-four styles with a price range from $5 to $50.

"Our Puma knives are made in Solingen, West Germany," says Palmer, "which has long been recognized as the cutlery capital of the world. Puma quality and craftsmanship are unchallenged and represent the best of a two-hundred-year-old tradition.

"Perseverance and adherence to long-established standards are the prime force behind the consistent superiority of Puma knives," the executive adds, "and the reason they have won worldwide acclaim as the ultimate achievement of the cutler's art."

Among the Gutmann company's best sellers has been the Puma line of lock-back folders. Selling for less than $100, Puma 4-Star models feature drop-point stainless-steel blades.

Gutmann's Adventurer (top), Explorer (center) and Explorer Silver model lock-back folders are each available in three, four or five-inch lengths. Retail prices are in the $9.50 to $16 range.

Admittedly there are others who might argue the point with Tom Palmer, but there is little doubt that he respects his product.

Investigation shows that many direct descendents of the artisans who established the Puma standards more than two centuries ago continue to work in the constantly updated Puma factory in Western Germany. Their skills are being applied on a daily basis to turning out sporting knives that are meant to meet the acceptance standards of America's demanding hunter, camper, backpacker and fisherman.

"Their achievements are the result of meticulous attention to every detail from the forging of the steel to the final hand-polishing operation," according to Palmer, who has spent a good deal of time in the West German factory.

The Puma knives currently are being fashioned from two

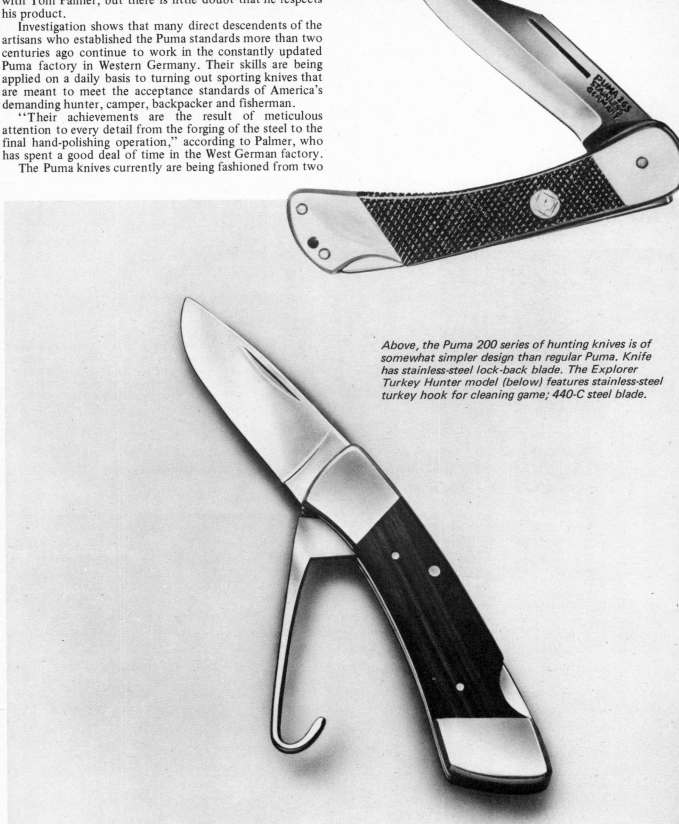

Above, the Puma 200 series of hunting knives is of somewhat simpler design than regular Puma. Knife has stainless-steel lock-back blade. The Explorer Turkey Hunter model (below) features stainless-steel turkey hook for cleaning game; 440-C steel blade.

Each Puma knife blade is drop forged and hot tempered.

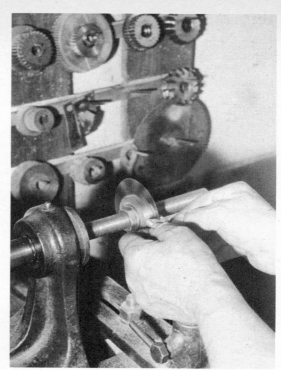

Hollow grinding knife blades is accomplished with special dual-wheel grinder, left. Above, metal parts are hand trimmed for close fit. Company is said to pay premium price for top-quality stag horn to be used as handles. Photograph below illustrates how sections of stag horn are sawed before softening.

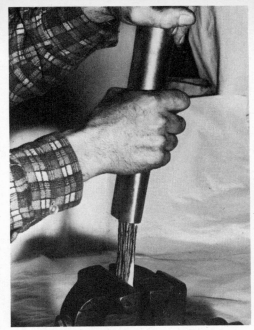

Antler horn material is boiled
and softened before being bent.

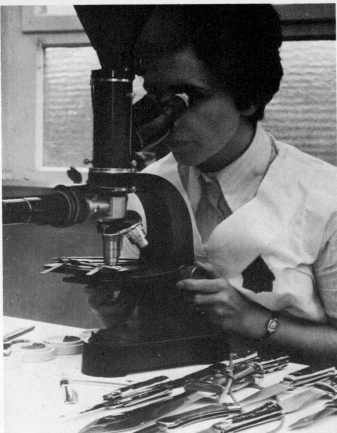

Skilled German hands (left) place rivets through
handle of nonfolding hunting knife. During final
inspection, blades are microscopically examined.

types of steel. One is something called Pumaster steel, a high-grade carbon material that is drop forged and tempered for top cutting qualities. Also used is stainless cutting steel, a special stainless alloy with high-grade carbon, chrome, molybdenum and other selected components incorporated in the final product.

Each blade is hammer forged and hot tempered to provide the precise characteristics the artisans have found essential for a quality knife's intended use. Measured on the Rockwell C scale, Puma steel generally rates at 61, which tends to be a bit harder and perhaps more brittle than some American-made knife steel.

"The actual cost of producing such steel is as much as three times that of most other sporting knife steels," the executive vice-president insists.

After the initial forging, tempering and the all-important step of pregrinding, the blade is hand ground through twenty-two different stages. Each of these steps employs increasingly fine lubricants, oil coolants and special polishing grease. The resulting top-quality blue blades go through at least one inspection during each of the twenty-two stages, with twenty-six quality control measures being used in all.

"Not only is the finished blade subjected to microscopic examination, but one blade out of each hundred is broken intentionally. It then is placed under a microscope to double-check the composition of the steel and to assure there is a complete absence of flaws," according to Tom Palmer.

Factory sources also claim that each year Puma pays premium prices for its supply of hand-selected stag antlers. These antlers are boiled in a special formula, then stretched and dried for a period of several weeks. The handle scales of genuine stag or of exotic jacaranda wood are hand fitted to the blade. The handle edges then are rounded for comfort to the user. The guards also are rounded smoothly and nickel-silver rivets are used as a guard against rust.

After the correct temper of the blade is tested for hardness by impressing it with a diamond-pointed needle, a control number is stamped on each knife. The same number appears on the Puma certificate of guarantee which is included with each knife, attests Palmer.

Chapter 20

A.G. Russell Has Made
A Sharp Career Out Of
A Rock Quarry!

The A.G. Russell Company display booth at the 1976 Knife Expo in Dallas was a popular gathering place for knifemakers and buyers. Stones and knives were shown.

ONE DAY IN early 1968, A.G. Russell walked into a hardware store in Fayetteville, Arkansas, and asked for a first-quality sharpening stone. The clerk explained that there were none in stock, but he would be happy to place an order if Russell would buy three stones; that was the minimum number that could be ordered.

Andy Russell didn't want three stones; he wanted one, so he declined the offer. That might have been the end of

Well-known knifemaker Bob Dozier and A.G. Russell discuss the state of the art during the 1973 Knifemaker's Guild Show, Kansas City. Thus, Russell has helped many cutlers.

Looking back a few years at a somewhat younger and clean-shaven Russell in his Springdale, Arkansas, shop.

the story, but Russell reasoned that he couldn't be the only man who wanted a good sharpening stone. The result was that he started his own sharpening stone business!

Today, his stones, marketed as Russell's Arkansas Oilstones, are recognized by most makers and fanciers of handmade knives as possibly the best available. The stones are made of novaculite, a hard, extremely fine-grained siliceous rock, quarried near Hot Springs, Arkansas.

Russell went at the stone business with zest and enthusiasm, and quickly reasoned that, if the small number of custom knifemakers in business in the late 1960s prospered, his business would benefit. So he began to promote handmade cutlery. His advertisements carried pictures of custom cutlery, together with the maker's name and address, plugging the makers' work as well as his own stones.

Listing the now well-known makers who owe much of their fame to Russell's efforts would be an impossible task, but this roster would include Bob Loveless, Lloyd Hale, Don Zaccagnino, Ron Lake, Buster Warenski, Bill Davis, Bob Dozier, Bob Ogg, Dwight Towell, Corbet Sigman and numerous others.

Late in 1971, Russell purchased the honored old knifemaking firm of Morseth, and moved that operation to Springdale, Arkansas. Some knife fans feel the Morseth knives made in Springdale are the finest that have carried this proud name in the company's history, which dates back to the 1930s. The latest Morseth effort, a Russell design, is a folding lock-back hunter.

Russell designed this recently introduced Morseth locked-back folder. Russell moved his operation to the Morseth firm site after buying it in 1971.

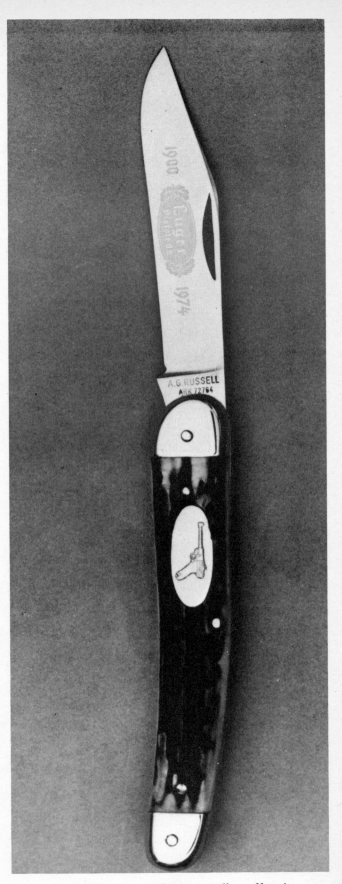

The limited edition Luger folder was first offered in 1974. Knife is serial numbered for collectors.

Russell, at left, takes over the grinding wheel at the Morseth knife factory. Below, a Russell employee clamps a chunk of valuable novaculite prior to diamond-edge sawing process.

As many as eight diamond-edge saws, such as the one above, may be in operation at one time at the stone cutting factory in Hot Springs. Stone is cut and transported from quarry in nearby Arkansas hills.

Along with the Morseth models, Andy Russell also stocks in his shop knives made by most contemporary cutlers. This is primarily a service to his customers, and Russell also serves as a clearing house for collectors who desire to dispose of duplicates or knives that no longer fit into their collections. The small fee Russell charges for taking these knives on consignment is more than made up by the vast exposure that his newsletters of available hand-made models provide. This widespread publicity virtually guarantees the seller that he will receive a fair, current market price for his knife or knives.

Recognizing the vast popularity of folding knives, Russell purchased several from Ron Lake for resale, and these moved so well that Russell decided there was a market for folding knives that were collectible. The result was a series of limited edition knives such as the Grand Daddy Barlow and the Luger. These sold well, and they are increasing almost daily in value.

Russell brings out one new commemorative folder per year on the average, and most of the news of these issues is distributed by a newsletter that goes out to the members of the Knife Collectors Club. Russell, of course, is the president of this organization, which extends such benefits as

opportunities to purchase low serial numbered knives, special collectors' sets and discounts on many desirable items. One of Russell's first limited editions now sells — when available — for approximately five times its original purchase price, which strikes us as a particularly sound investment!

All the while, Andy Russell continued to assist fledgling knifemakers, and on numerous occasions he would suggest

Getting the maximum use from each rough-sawn cake of novaculite stone requires considerable skill and training. Note the outlines of future sharpening stones as drawn. Stones may be discarded at any point.

B.R. Hughes' daughter, Lee Ann, appears impressed by this stack of novaculite cakes awaiting a trip to the saws.

to one journalist or another that "so-and-so is really doing excellent work. He's really deserving of publicity. Why don't you give him a call?"

Russell never has charged a nickel for promoting any maker's work.

Not content with his activities, which included writing an occasional article for some periodical, Russell took control of the Hen and Rooster Knife Company in Germany in 1975. Under his guidance this firm, one of the most respected in the world, has regained its share of the market and has been put on a sound financial footing. The name Hen and Rooster has been synonymous with quality in the knife world for over fifty years, and through Russell they now are available to the American knife buyer.

It was his sharpening stones, however, that first brought Russell to the forefront of American cutlery, and they are still one of his major interests. Having said that Russell

stones are noted for their quality, a person might be justified in asking, "Why are Russell's oilstones superior to novaculite stones of other dealers and suppliers?" The answer is deceptively simple: Russell's stones must be virtually perfect before they are offered for sale. They undergo two critical examinations, and, if a stone is considered of less than top quality, it is rejected. A.G. Russell estimates that approximately two-thirds of the stones that are completely finished in Hot Springs are rejected for one reason or another. To the best of our knowledge, no other supplier has a quality control program to match this.

Although there doesn't appear to be much to a stone when you examine it in its finished state, a great many operations go into each stone.

In its rough state, the material is shipped via truck to the plant from the quarry. The chunks then are inspected visually and those which pass this preliminary examination

At this step in the manufacture, the workman is cutting the novaculite cake to the outline drawn. The cutting operation requires considerable skill as each edge and angle of cut must be precisely done or stone is discarded.

are cut with a circular toothless saw that has an edge of crushed diamonds. Next, a workman examines each cake and draws out the exact shape and size of the stones that will be cut from that slab. Another workman cuts out the stones with another saw, and still another employee shapes them on a revolving wheel. This last operation requires considerable skill, as all corners and edges of the stones should be at right angles to each other.

The stones then are submerged in a mild solution of hydrochloric acid for several days. This does a first-class job of cleaning the stones. The solution, incidentally, is so mild that one can easily reach into a vat for stones without injury to the skin.

After their bath, the stones are washed individually and inspected. It is at this point that Russell selects most of his rejects, as more than fifty percent of the finished stones flunk the test. Those that pass are shipped from Hot Springs to Springdale, Arkansas, where Russell puts them through still another inspection before they are packaged and shipped to the consumer.

After final shaping, each stone is bathed for several days in a bath of mild hydrochloric acid solution.

Russell stones have been shipped over most of the free world, and a number of his oilstones have been purchased by professional hunters in Africa and Asia.

Unlike some stone suppliers, who suggest that three different stones are needed for proper sharpening, Russell maintains that only one — a soft Arkansas — can produce a perfect working edge, and that such a stone, used in conjunction with a hard Arkansas type, will result in a shaving edge.

One of the most important points concerning a Russell stone is the accompanying guarantee. Many promise satisfaction, but he guarantees "Russell's oilstones to be the best sharpening stone you have ever used."

When asked why a natural oilstone would do a better job of sharpening than an aluminum oxide stone, Russell replies, "Mother Nature has done a better job of making a material well suited to sharpening knives than man has been able to up to this point.

"One of my goals when I started this business was to offer stones of consistent quality, so that if a man loses a stone, he can buy another of the same size secure in the knowledge that it will perform in an identical manner."

Each finished stone is bathed in a mild acid solution to remove sawdust, dirt and other impurities from novaculite pores.

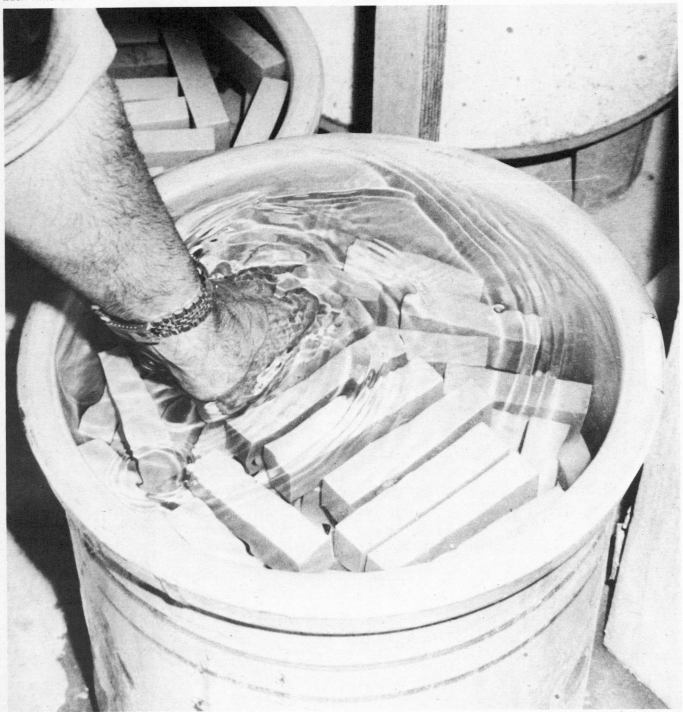

Completed and inspected, the Russell soft Arkansas oilstone has passed every test and is not among the two-thirds which are rejected for one reason or another. The stone is ready for packaging and shipment to customers throughout the world.

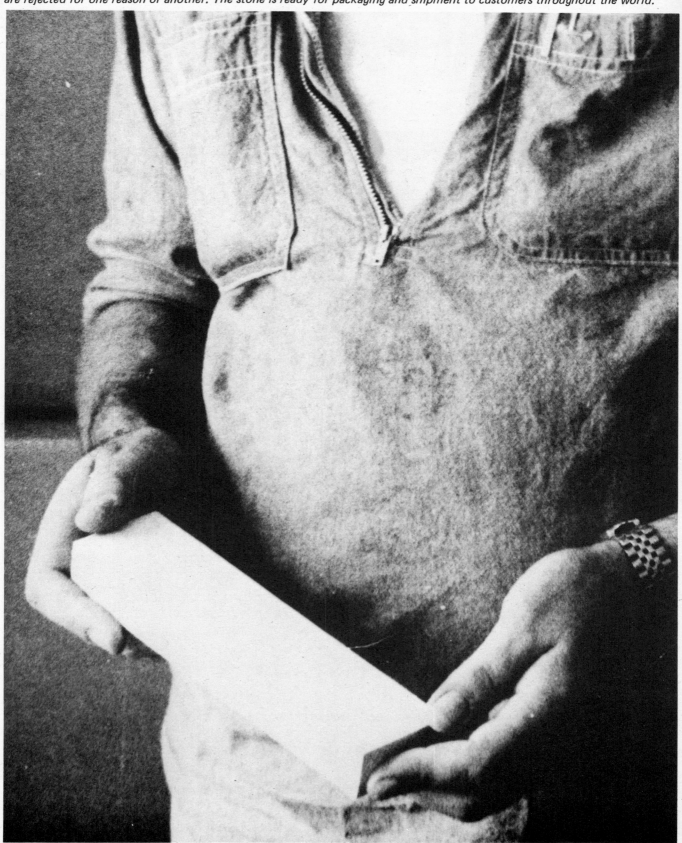

Chapter 21

ALL ABOUT KNIFE STEELS

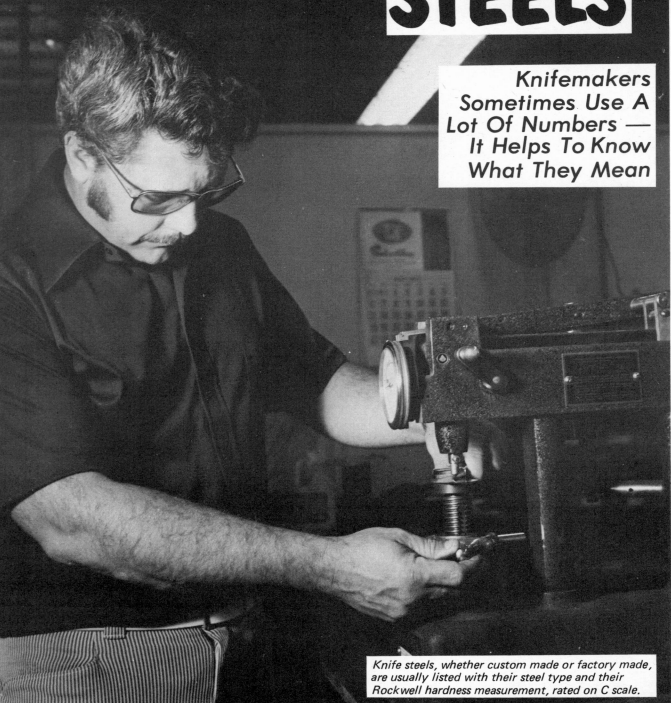

Knifemakers Sometimes Use A Lot Of Numbers — It Helps To Know What They Mean

Knife steels, whether custom made or factory made, are usually listed with their steel type and their Rockwell hardness measurement, rated on C scale.

The knife blade to be tested is first placed upon the base of the Rockwell testing machine in contact with the Brale point, a precisely designed diamond point in steel mount. Scale readout is direct.

SOMETIMES, so many numbers and terms may be confusing. Or at least not fully understood. Terms such as RC-58, Rockwell C 60-61, about 60 to 62 on the Rockwell scale, 440-C, 154-CM, D-2, O-1 and on and on are commonly seen throughout this book as in any other knife literature. They each have a specific meaning and some knowledge of these meanings will help the collector or the knife buyer obtain the knife that will best suit his needs.

Perhaps the place to start is with the metal of the knife blade itself — the steel. Let us state at the outset that each knifemaker has his own one or two favorites in the steel he uses and there is not, never has been and most likely never will be any such thing as the perfect steel for a knife blade — or for any other use for that matter.

Steel alloy is a mixture of iron and certain elements. In every case, a certain amount of carbon is added to the iron refining process, plus varying percentages of other elements such as manganese, phosphorous, sulfur, silicon, chromium, molybdenum, nickel, tungsten, vanadium and occasionally some others. Arriving at the exact percentages and elements to be added is a difficult and exacting science itself and much too complicated and comprehensive to go into in any great detail here.

Nobody knows for sure how steel first came to be made from iron. The formulas for adding or subtracting the carbon and other elements to iron ore were originally painstakingly worked out through literally hundreds of years of trial and error.

Different steels are designed for different uses and each has specific characteristics of its own. Some are hard and brittle, some soft and pliable, some nearly impervious to penetration, some resist corrosion and stains, while others do not. Some may be rolled, bent, pounded, stretched, heated, cooled, filed and pounded again, and the end result often is a material with entirely different properties than the original.

Some of the numbers and letters we started to talk about are the designations arrived at and agreed upon to describe some of these steels in their varying elemental compounds. Most custom makers and many of the factories will list 440-C as their most common blade material. This steel is one of the so-called stainlesss varieties and therefore is popular with knifemakers. There may or may not be a completely stainless steel in existence but it would most likely not be suitable for knife blades. The 440-C comes rather close but the owner/user of a knife of that material will find that, if he abuses or ignores common rules in the care of his knife, the blade will stain and eventually corrode, which may ruin what was once a work of art.

Bob Loveless of Riverside, California, is generally credited with discovering — or at least pioneering — the second most popular blade steel, designated 154-CM. The story told is that Loveless, in his seemingly never-ending

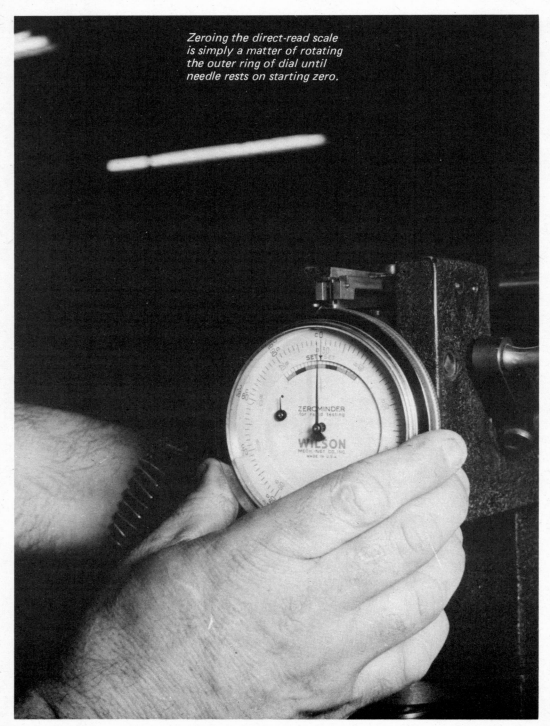

Zeroing the direct-read scale is simply a matter of rotating the outer ring of dial until needle rests on starting zero.

search for the best knife steel, was told about a new steel which was developed for the Boeing Airplane Company of Seattle for use in jet engines. This steel, 154-CM, was reputed to maintain its strength even at operating temperatures in the 700-degree Fahrenheit range. In 1971, Loveless took delivery on a quantity of the new steel and immediately began experimenting with it. He produced a number of his knives from the steel and put them out for testing.

The new material seems to fill most of the knife steel requirements. It certainly is stain and corrosion resistant; even to salt water. Blood, snow, water, sweat and other commonly encountered foreign substances don't seem to bother it. It seems to be no more difficult to work with than most other knife steels and Loveless is able to produce

blades and tangs which are thinner yet maintain their strength.

Not every knifemaker — custom or factory — agrees that 154-CM is the ultimate blade material. Others swear that 440-C, W-2 and O-2 contain many more desirable features for steel blades than does 154-CM.

Perhaps this is the point at which to do some research and quote a bit from the Encyclopedia Britannica in its section on alloy steels. Generally speaking, the addition of various elements to carbon steel allow the metal, after heating, to be cooled more slowly and harden more deeply than if the steel was only iron and carbon.

The encyclopedia says that an alloy bar will harden much more deeply upon heat treatment than will a simple carbon steel bar. It has been found that when steel is heated above 750 degrees Centigrade there is an actual crystal change within the metal. As the metal cools, the substance forms a hard, 'molecular structure called martensite. The speed of cooling and the cooling medium — substances such as air, oil bath, brine, water — have a marked effect on the hardness and brittleness of the martensite. The addition of different alloys to the carbon steel affects the hardness, brittleness, impact resistance and other properties. Different alloys heat-treated the same way will end up with different properties. Different heat treatments on the same steel also will result in different properties.

The scale of measurement for steel hardness is known as the Rockwell scale. As the numbers are quoted, it should be noted that generally the higher the number, the harder the steel. There may be other differences between steels, such as stain resistance, but if the Rockwell number is the same, they will be tested to the same hardness.

Just as there is no agreement on the types of steel to be used in knife blades, there is no agreement among makers or users as to what degree of hardness the blades should be. Some prefer a blade fairly soft, which may be sharpened easily, but often, while in use; others prefer a hard steel blade that will hold its edge throughout a job but will not be so easy to sharpen. Some users go so far as to insist on the hardest of steel blades and return the knife to the maker or a professional sharpener when the edge becomes dull.

Commercial knife factories, some custom knifemakers

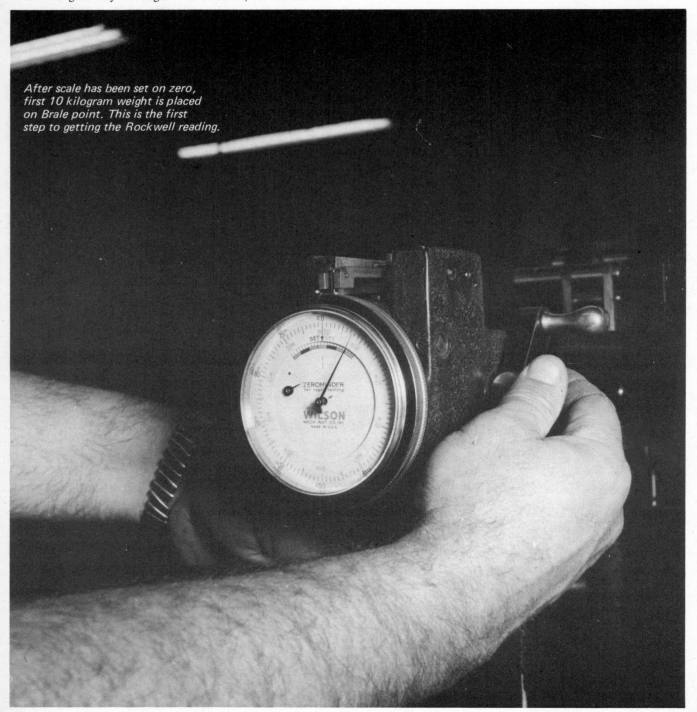

After scale has been set on zero, first 10 kilogram weight is placed on Brale point. This is the first step to getting the Rockwell reading.

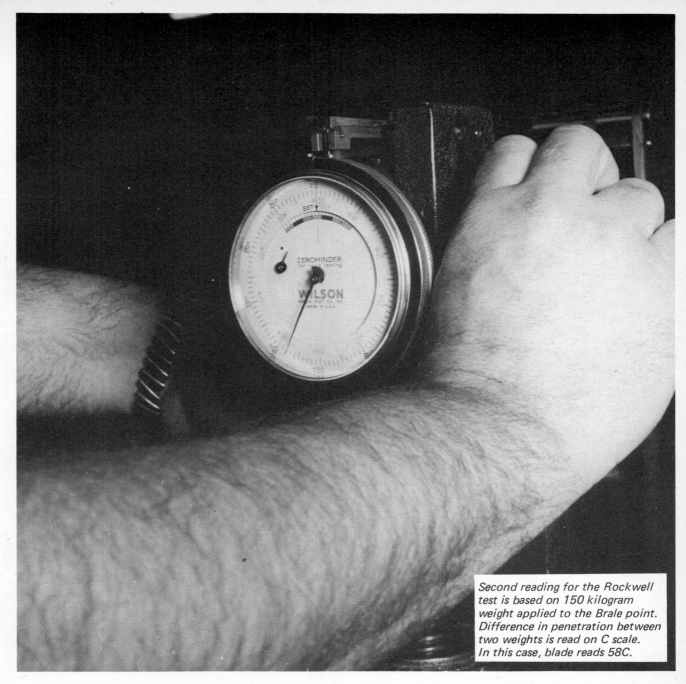

Second reading for the Rockwell test is based on 150 kilogram weight applied to the Brale point. Difference in penetration between two weights is read on C scale. In this case, blade reads 58C.

and heat-treating plants have a Rockwell testing machine to test the metal used or treated to ensure it meets the prescribed hardness. The Rockwell machine, incidentally, may give readings on a number of scales but for the purposes of knifemaking, the C scale is universally accepted.

The readings and results with which we have become familiar, are a measurement of difference between two known penetration attempts by a diamond-tipped point, known as a Brale Penetrator.

The steel — knife blade or otherwise — is placed on the level bed of the Rockwell testing machine. The blade may, in fact, be tested at more than one spot.

The Brale penetrator tip is lowered to the steel with a force of precisely ten kilograms. The second step is to force the penetrator down, by use of the machine's lever

arrangement, with a weight force of 150 kilograms. A scale on the Rockwell machine then measures the difference between the first and second penetration depths.

The steel to be tested by the penetrator is not moved under the diamond point. It is held in exactly the same position through the two penetration attempts. Reading is automatic. The point is lowered for the first ten kilogram load and then the lever is rotated further until a 150-kilogram load is indicated. The difference is simply read off the dial.

The design and shape of the Brale diamond penetrator holds the key. The tip is carefully selected, carefully machined into a spheroconical shape that is ground to mathematical precision with microscopic accuracy. Each point on the Rockwell scale represents a depth of 0.00008-inch. Fifty-seven times as deep would give us the Rockwell reading of RC-57.

Obviously, on blades such as we are used to, the penetration is slight. It takes a sharp, trained eye to detect the point at which the metal was tested. Often, it cannot be seen at all with the naked eye. It may be done on the tang or on a portion of the blade otherwise covered with the handle or bolster of a folding knife.

The actual test takes but a few seconds and the tester reads the results directly from the scale. Most custom builders test or have their blades one hundred percent tested. Some commercial heat-treaters insist upon it as proof of their competency. Some makers spot-check only a certain percentage of the knife blades passing through.

The typical folding knife blade is hardened to a Rockwell C of 58-60. This would seem to produce a blade with fairly good edge-holding characteristics but not so hard as to be brittle. As mentioned, steel hardness is not entirely a function of the Rockwell reading results. Some steels are allowed to be relatively hard without becoming brittle. With the most common blade materials, a hardness rating much in excess of 60 or 61 might prove to be too brittle for most knife uses. True, it will take and hold an edge keen enough to shave the hair off a man's forearm, but who wants to shave arm hair all day?

On the other end, if one is going to use a folder with a four-inch blade around the campsite to split firewood or trim branches, then a Rockwell reading of around 45 to 50 is in order. A camp hatchet or axe would read in this zone and with such a low reading, the user should have a pocket sharpening stone handy to touch up the edge. It won't hold a keen edge long but it won't be brittle and it will take impact.

A buyer about to lay out considerable bucks for a factory-made or custom knife is entitled to know at least two things about the tool he is acquiring: what the composition of the steel in the blade is, and its hardness. Most makers include that basic information in their sales catalogs and other literature. Many custom makers offer the buyer a choice of two or more steels. Some will recommend the most appropriate steel and hardness after determining the primary use of the knife.

Remember that each type of steel alloy has several specific properties that make it unique, and each may act differently at the same hardness factor. The higher the Rockwell C scale reading, the harder the steel has been made. Hard steels will hold an edge longer in use but will be more difficult to sharpen. Softer blades are easier to sharpen but need to be honed more often. The choice is up to the user.

The weights employed in the Rockwell tester are shown at rear of machine. Tester may be adjusted to read different scales, depending on materials.

Overall side view of Rockwell testing machine shows weights and leverage system used to set two loads on knife that is to be tested.

Reading the outer, or C scale on the dial at left reveals a 60. Different areas of the same blade may test out at different readings.

Chapter 22

THE CUSTOM CRAFTSMEN

The When And Why Of Custom Folders And The Men Who Make Them!

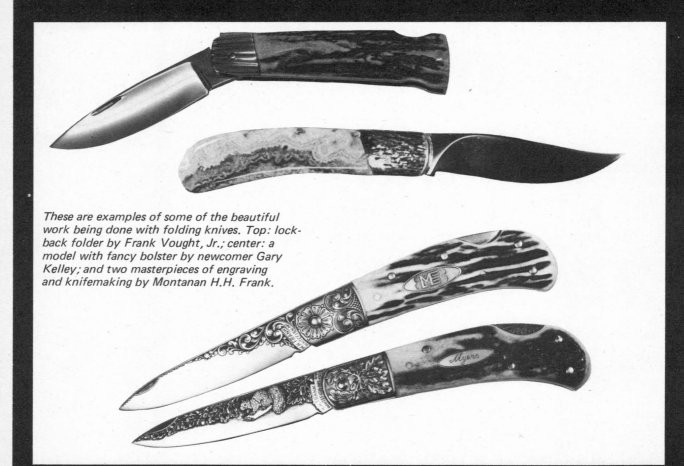

These are examples of some of the beautiful work being done with folding knives. Top: lock-back folder by Frank Vought, Jr.; center: a model with fancy bolster by newcomer Gary Kelley; and two masterpieces of engraving and knifemaking by Montanan H.H. Frank.

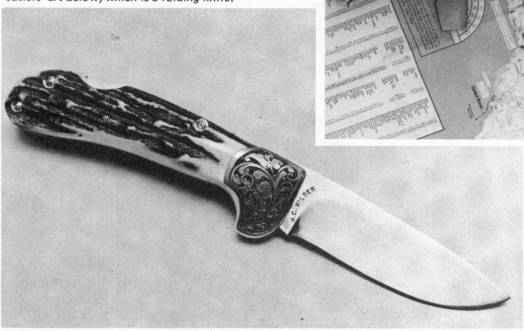

Two Barry Wood creations now out of production and sought by collectors. Right model was made for Colt, while knife at left features Loveless blade.

W.C. "Bill" Wilber, of Spartanburg, South Carolina, produced the superb piece of the cutlers' art below, which is a folding knife.

AS FAR AS the Twentieth Century is concerned, handmade cutlery was born between 1900 and 1910 when Bill Scagel first began turning out a limited number of handcrafted knives that were well-made by that day's standards. These hand-forged blades would hold an edge and Scagel's work was avidly sought by better-heeled sportsmen of the 1910 to 1940 era.

The majority of Scagel's knives were fixed-blade models, but he did make a few folders, and the prices that these knives will fetch today is a positive caution! Scagel even made a few sheath knives with small folding blades in the handles. Being rarer than the standard folders, these knives are even more expensive today.

In the 1920s, Rudy Ruana and John Nelson Cooper began to turn out a few handmade knives, but few if any folders. In the 1930s along came Harry Morseth and Bo Randall, but these men made their reputations via the sheath knife route.

During the 1940s and 1950s, other custom makers entered the field, including Bill Moran, Dan Dennehy, Ralph Bone, Pete Heath, Merle Seguine, R.W. Loveless and a handful of others. Moran and Bone did and do offer folders, but the fixed-blade knife still was very much the kingpin in the world of handmade cutlery.

Then, in the late 1960s, the market for handmade knives doubled, tripled and quadrupled! Such men as Lloyd Hale,

Ted Dowell, D.E. Henry, Gil Hibben, G.W. Stone, Jimmy Lile, Clyde Fischer, H.H. Frank, Joe Martin, Chubby Hueske, Bernard Sparks, Walt Kneubuhler, George Herron and many others began to attract regional and national attention.

Even so, the market for handmade folders remained small. Frank specialized in such knives, as did Robert Ludwig of Port Author, Texas. These were perhaps the first two American cutlers to offer only handmade folders, although others did make folders, but in most cases these models played second fiddle to sheath knives.

The handmade knife boom, which had started in the late 1960s, gathered momentum in the early 1970s, and some of today's more famous makers first jumped into the national limelight during these years — men such as Corbet Sigman, Buster Warenski, Dwight Towell, Herman Schneider and Ron Lake. Mark that last name well, because in the annals of handcrafted knives, only a few cutlers have had an overpowering impact on the entire profession — Bo Randall, Bill Moran, Bob Loveless and Ron Lake.

The story has been told elsewhere, but suffice to say that when Lake walked into the 1971 Knifemakers Guild Show at Houston with the first of his magnificent folders, he literally turned the knife world upside down! The crowd

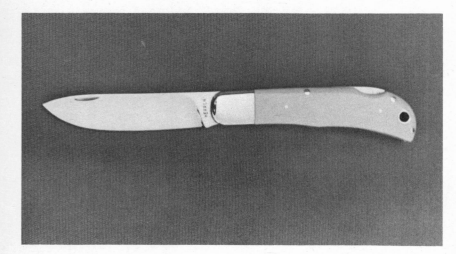

Veteran cutler George Herron offers a number of handsome folders, such as the lock-blade model (left) with ivory handle slabs and lanyard hole.

Many contemporary American custom knifemakers offer acid etching as an extra option for their customers; most of it done by Shaw-Leibowitz. The firm's booths at the annual Knifemakers Guild shows are always popular.

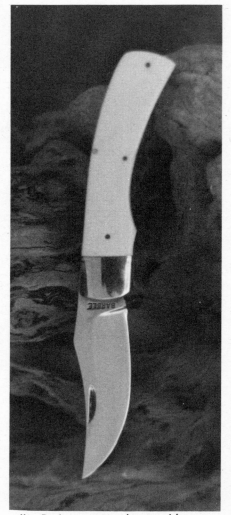

Jim Barbee, veteran hunter, big-game guide and knifemaker, recently introduced his folding knife model.

that gathered around his table, placing orders by the score for a Lake folder, proved there was a market for well-made custom folders, even at prices, which in 1971, were fairly stiff!

Highly skilled makers rushed home after the show to see what they could develop in the folding line. Within a few months, literally dozens of makers were offering handsome folders, and this brought to light an interesting development. In bygone years there were a significant number of collectors who specialized in folding knives, but who had no interest in fixed-bladed models. Consequently, such collectors had heretofore largely ignored custom knives, but now, almost overnight, there were handmade folders by the score available, and a vast new group of buyers became buffs of handcrafted knives.

The handmade folders of that period were, for the most part, primarily utilitarian models, but slowly many such knives became veritable works of art. In addition to Lake, Moran and Frank, newcomers such as Harvey McBurnette, the Nolen Brothers, Billy Imel, Russ Andrews, Jess Horn and W.T. Fuller began offering magnificent folders that were in truth *objets d'art*. Many of these knives featured engraving, etching, inlay work, scrimshaw, file work on the exposed metal parts, and handles made of ivory and silver.

This ultra-rare folding knife was made by the first great knifemaker of the twentieth century — Bill Scagel.

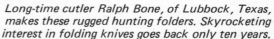

Long-time cutler Ralph Bone, of Lubbock, Texas, makes these rugged hunting folders. Skyrocketing interest in folding knives goes back only ten years.

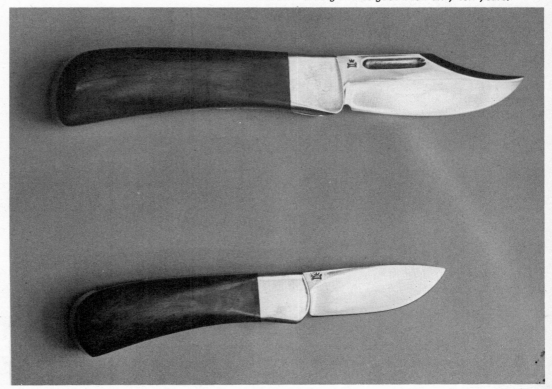

Sixty dollars would still purchase a sound working folder, but something special might easily set the buyer back $400 or more. Add a blade of Damascus, such as those offered by Moran, and you have a folder that is a solid investment at $1500!

To appreciate the fantastic growth pattern of the handmade folding knife, consider that in 1968 there were perhaps eighteen cutlers actively seeking orders in this country. Today, there are more than two hundred! If this growth seems phenomenal, and it is, consider that in 1970 there were only about six makers of handmade folding knives, but today that clan has increased to more than one hundred!

The current folding knife market is a buyer's delight. There are so many excellent craftsmen of similar ability vying for the customers' dollars that the person who attends a large knife show and does a little shopping can easily come up with an excellent buy that will surely increase in value muy pronto!

In the face of this evidence, it would take a person very oblivious of the facts to argue that the handmade knife of the future is not the folder.

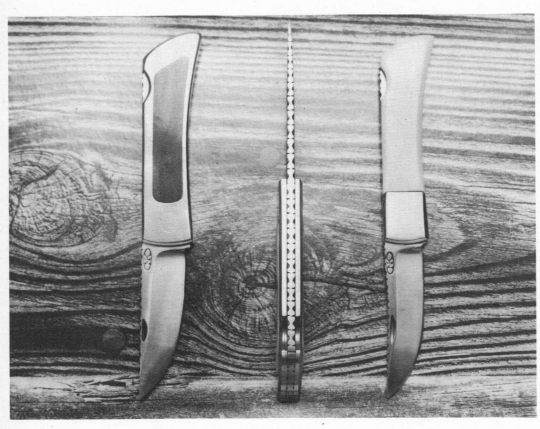

Three fine folders by the Nolen brothers of Texas, with file work on all three models.

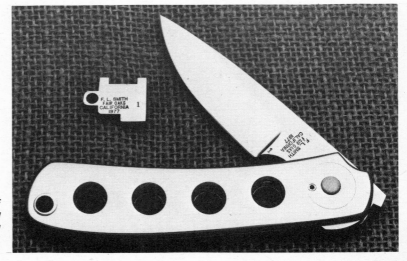

A most unusual folding knife from the shop of Californian Fred Smith. The blade may be opened or closed with one hand and by using the special tool, the blade may be removed for cleaning.

It would, obviously, be impossible to publish biographical studies of the many cutlers currently engaged in producing excellent folding knives. Therefore, we have selected only a few for inclusion in this book. These, however, may be considered representative.

Each is a craftsman in his own right — a person to whom the quality of the finished product is more important than the income it may represent. Some are veterans; Bill Moran has been at it for more than thirty years. Others are newcomers; Bill Davis has been engaged in knifemaking for less than one-sixth this period of time.

These are rare men, totally dedicated, tremendously talented. Of the millions upon millions of men and women gainfully employed in the United States at this time, only one hundred or so can offer a genuinely professional quality handmade folding knife. The following pages will tell you something of just a few of them. They are not machines; they are human beings who experience the same joys and heartaches that all of us undergo.

Theirs is a path not often traveled, and that makes them all the more interesting.

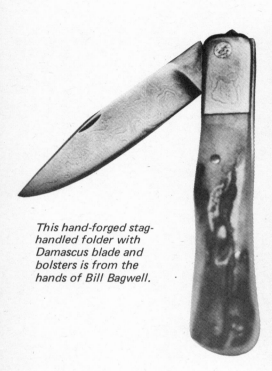

This hand-forged stag-handled folder with Damascus blade and bolsters is from the hands of Bill Bagwell.

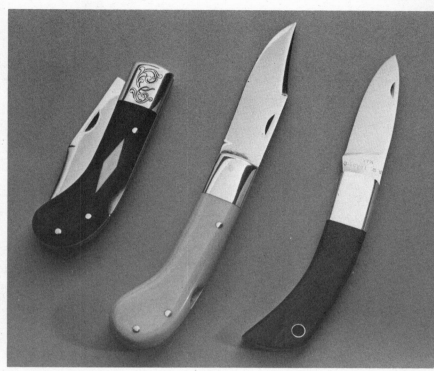

Three specimens of the cutlers' workmanship by R.W. Trabbie.

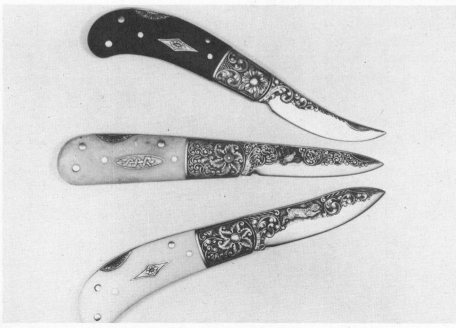

Many consider the work of H.H. Frank as examples of masterpieces in cutlery.

Knifemaker Russ Andrews hard at work in his small, well-equipped Harrisonville, Missouri, shop.

RUSS ANDREWS:

He Created A New Era Down Missouri Way

WHEN RUSS Andrews was 8 years old, his parents gave him his first knife — a folding Scout model — and the first use to which young Andrews put his prize was cutting up the family garden hose!

This promptly brought about the confiscation of the new knife, and it was not until several months later that it was again presented to Andrews, together with a long list of dos and don'ts.

"I might add," comments Andrews, "that I cut no more hoses."

Born in Rochester, New York, in 1947, Andrews' father was in the military, and the list of places where he has lived reads like a geography lesson: Washington, D.C.; Biloxi, Mississippi; Fairbanks, Alaska; Denver, Colorado; Salina, Kansas; Phoenix, Arizona; San Antonio, Texas; Tachikawa Air Force Base, Japan; McGuire Air Force Base, New Jersey; and his present home, Harrisonville, Missouri.

The Andrewses settled in Harrisonville following the

Andrews built this 3" blade folder as an experimental model. Blade is of 3/16" stock with fiddleback walnut handle slabs. He made his first folder in 1976.

senior Andrews' retirement as a light colonel in 1963, and young Russ Andrews graduated from high school there in 1966. Immediately following graduation, Andrews, following in his dad's footsteps, joined the Army and requested paratroop training. After basic training at Ft. Leonard Wood, Missouri, he underwent infantry training at Ft. Ord, California, and then went to jump school at Ft. Benning, Georgia.

While in training, Andrews listed Vietnam as his first choice of duty and Panama as his second preference. After receiving his silver wings, it should come as no surprise to those familiar with the military to learn that he was assigned to Alaska.

In 1967, Russ Andrews reenlisted in order to be sent to Vietnam, and prior to his departure, visited friends in Orlando, Florida. It was, perhaps, fate that took him to the shop of W.D. "Bo" Randall, probably the most famous name in American handmade cutlery.

"After I explained that I was about to go overseas, they agreed to sell me a Randall Model 14. That knife was, without question, the finest that I had owned. One thing that impressed me was that Mr. Randall, himself, insisted upon polishing it up a bit before allowing it to leave his shop.

"I lost that knife during the battle for Hill 875 in November 1967, and immediately I ordered another just like it. Both knives saw a great deal of genuine abuse, and they held up quite well. They also taught me a lot about knives. All in all, I've purchased seven Randall's, and I still have three of them."

Finally, after twenty months of duty in 'Nam — followed by fifteen months at Ft. Bragg, North Carolina — Andrews was discharged.

Having discovered an interest in knives and motivated in part by a number of articles he had read about knifemaking, Andrews decided to try his hand at the craft.

"Having done some forging and heat-treating of basic tool steels in high school shop classes, I thought I knew a little about what it would take to make a decent blade," he recalls. "Files seemed to make fair blades, as long as the spine was spring tempered, but they were not what I really wanted. So, in the Fall of 1970, I began a study of tool steels.

"I purchased some 01 steel and made up some blades. Some were forged, others were not. While there seemed to be little difference in the actual performance of the forged blades, I found that there was a difference in the feel of the steel. Call it character if you will, but there is a definite difference — one that has to be felt to be understood."

At this stage, Andrews was operating with minimum equipment. He owned a small electric grinder, an electric hand drill, and a makeshift forge.

"The blades were roughed out on the grinder, heat-treated in the forge, and the grind was trued up using the drill and small abrasive wheels which I wrapped with electrician's tape and varying grits of sandpaper. I then tried to

Andrews no longer uses the mark on upper knife. He has switched to the ERA II mark for folders and sheaths.

polish the blades using pieces of leather and buffing compound," Andrews recalls.

"The first knife I made is still in use in our kitchen," he told us. "Those early knives weren't much to look at, but they worked well. Most of them are still in use."

The first knife that Andrews sold was purchased by his foreman at the telephone cable plant where the aspiring maker was employed as an inspector. The foreman wanted a knife that could be used to butcher cattle, and Andrews and the customer drew several patterns before both were satisfied.

"That knife had a five-inch blade of quarter-inch stock," he remembers, "with a narrow tang, walnut handle, and brass guard and butt cap. He paid me $30 for it, and I was tremendously pleased that he seemed so impressed with it. Sad to say, he didn't use it, but put it on a wall plaque.

"Most of the early ERAII knives were primarily copies of the Randall's that I owned. In 1972 I heard of the Knifemakers Guild, and in the Summer of 1973 I arrived at the site of the Kansas City meeting, knives in hand, and introduced myself to Bill Moran, who was secretary that year. The actual show began the next day, and when I showed my knives to the members of the technical com-

mittee, they were not exactly impressed. I was actually embarrassed when I talked with Corbet Sigman and looked at his work. No comparison! I came away from that show feeling like an amateur, and I began to wonder if I were capable of anything more than second-class workmanship."

Russ Andrews went home and started working. He studied steels. "I used nine or ten steels other than 01, including D2, F8, D5, F2, M2, 06, 154CM and two types of Stellite. As with most such testing, the results were loaded with a multitude of ifs and buts. I had to consider what heat-treating process was used or specified, and how closely these specifications were followed. Possibly the single most important question that was asked was 'What am I looking for?' and my conclusions had to be based on the answer to that question. Even so, my conclusion in regard to steels is that there is no single conclusion — there are only qualified answers and tendencies."

More important, Andrews began to develop his own style. By 1974, when accepted as a probationary member of the Guild, his knives — still all sheath models — incorporated full tangs and dropped points. By this time, Andrews was using D5 and D2 for blade material, and his work was much slicker. "I shared a table with Bill Davis at the '74 show," he recalls, "and I sold one knife."

Slowly, Andrews began to drift back to the narrow tang design, and dropped D5 in favor of 154CM. He currently offers blades made of D2, 154CM and Stellite 6-B.

"Each of these materials," Andrews says, "excel in one or more areas, but they all have their shortcomings. Stellite offers best edge retention, and for all practical purposes, it is corrosion proof. But, it does not stand up well under stress or impact. The D2 has excellent edge retention properties, and adequate strength and flexibility, but offers only moderate resistance to corrosion. I find 154CM retains a cutting edge quite well; though, in my opinion, not as well as D2. It does, however, exhibit greater strength, flexibility and resistance to corrosion than does D2."

Looking at one of his ERAII folders, it seems virtually impossible to believe that Andrews' first attempt at making a folder occurred in January 1976.

"Perhaps the reason it took me so long to get around to folders is that I felt they were not worth the prices that I would have to get for the additional work," he explains. "Well, that wasn't the first time that I had been wrong! It took a while, but I now realize that folding knives are more personal and far more useful on a daily basis than are fixed-blade knives. Folders are practical in the field, and if made and used properly, generally can be used instead of a standard knife."

After existing orders are completed, Andrews hopes to incorporate a new style, which will be lighter and more compact. Brass is not used on any ERAII folder, as this maker believes it is soft and wears much more rapidly in use than does nickel silver. The ERA II folding hunter incorporates a stainless bolt as the blade pivots, and a stainless lock-bar pivot. Structural pins are of nickel silver, and a variety of handle materials are available.

"I make every knife as if it were to be my own, and I make them one at a time. I've tried doing batches of knives, and I found that it not only feels wrong, but it does not work as well. If my workmanship is to be at its best, I have to live with the knife, not for simply a few minutes at a time, but for hours for as long as it takes me to make it right.

"Though my customers express great satisfaction in my work, I am quite critical of it. I still can pick out flaws, and frequently after a knife is completed, I'll go back and touch up something that doesn't seem quite right. I have no illusions of how my work stacks up against other makes. Mine is better than most, I believe, but not as good as others, and I am tremendously impressed with the excellence which has been achieved by Corbet Sigman, Buster Warenski and Herman Schneider. To be better than those three would probably require the hand of someone devoid of human imperfections, and that won't happen. I hope that eventually I'll achieve a similar degree of excellence in my own way."

Perhaps the personality of Russ Andrews can best be explained by the guarantee he puts on his knives: *Should you ever have a legitimate complaint about your ERAII knife, I'll make it right.*

Andrews' classic lock-blade hunter is notable for its purity of line and obvious outstanding workmanship.

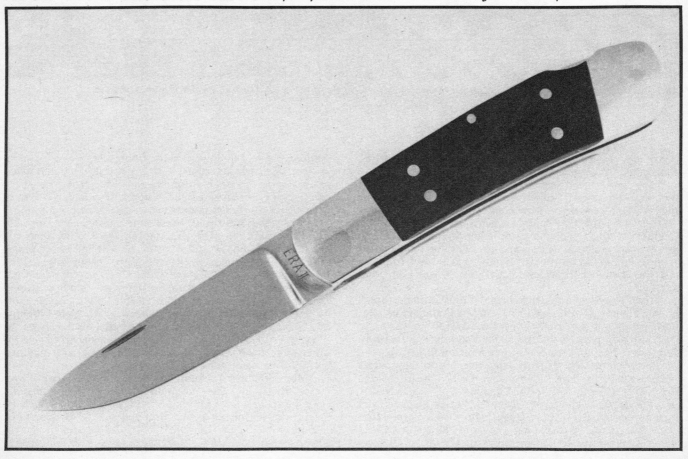

The knifemaker says this is the proper fit of lock and blade before treating.

The Custom Craftsmen:

JIM BARBEE

Not a folder, but this hunting knife proves that Barbee's work is not only functional, but is worthy of the collector.

From West Texas With Skill

Knifemaker/Hunter/Guide Jim Barbee Gives His Folders A Thorough Test Before He Puts Them On The Market

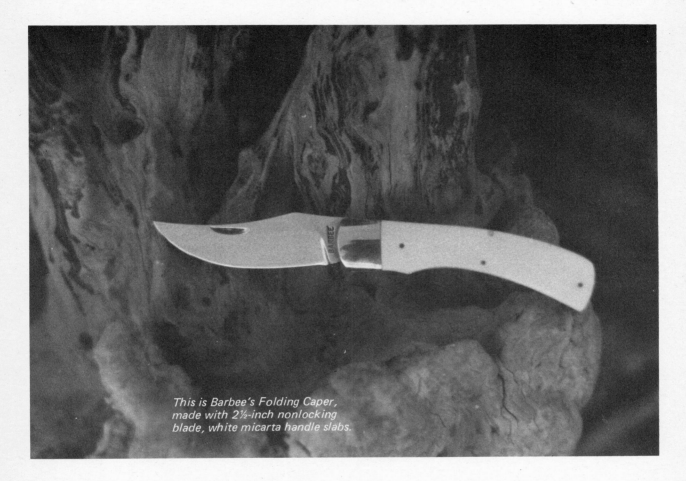

This is Barbee's Folding Caper, made with 2½-inch nonlocking blade, white micarta handle slabs.

WHEN B.R. HUGHES went on an African Safari in 1976, he took four handmade knives with him. One of them was made by Jim Barbee of Fort Stockton, Texas, and while Barbee may not be as famous in the knife world as, say, Bo Randall, this personable West Texan has hundreds of satisfied customers, including Slim Pickens, the well-known movie and television personality.

Hughes' first personal contact with Barbee occurred in the Fall of 1974, when he went on an antelope hunt near Van Horn, Texas, and his guide was none other than Barbee, who is a professional big-game outfitter and guide. That hunt resulted in a trophy antelope for Hughes and during the evenings there was plenty of time to sit around and talk about knives.

As a result of that hunt, Hughes booked a December 1975 outing for mule deer with Barbee. Hughes had to settle for a so-so mulie, although it was through no fault of his trusty guide.

Barbee, who is listed with the National Rifle Association as a guide, has been in the hunting business for approximately fourteen years. It was through his guiding that he first became interested in handmade knives.

"To put it bluntly," he once told us, "I wanted a better knife than it was possible to purchase in hardware and sporting goods stores. When you have to dress out literally dozens of head of game each Fall, you quickly become interested in a knife that will hold an edge under hard usage. Moreover, the blade had to be tough and reasonably easy to sharpen."

In an effort to find such a knife, Barbee first purchased some ready-made blades and fitted his own handles. "They weren't bad," he recalls, "but then they weren't much better than what I had been using."

In his quest for a superior blade, Barbee purchased some equipment and started making his own blades. "As well as I can remember, that was in the late 1960s," he told us. "Those first knives may not have been much for looks, but they were tough," he explained. "I knew that I was on the right track. Finally, by 1969 or so they not only held an edge pretty well but also were good-looking knives."

Jim Barbee, professional guide and hunter of West Texas, with his favorite rifle, a pre-1964 .243 Model 70 Winchester.

Barbee's antelope camp near Van Horn, Texas, features many of the comforts of home. Barbee, right background, checks his binoculars as hunters enjoy early morning pre-hunt coffee.

Author B.R. Hughes (left) with the West Texas mule deer is congratulated by knifemaker/guide Jim Barbee. Barbee has made it a habit for years of trying out his new knife models on at least a season of game animals.

Naturally, Barbee used a knife of his own making on his guided hunts, and so did the men who worked for him. "It wasn't long," he remembers, "before our hunters began asking where they could buy similar knives. Of course, I told them, and pretty soon I found myself backlogged with orders."

Thus encouraged, Barbee opened a sporting goods shop in Fort Stockton in 1971 where his knives as well as guns, fishing tackle, et cetera may be purchased. It might not be remiss at this point to add that Barbee's charming wife Pat does custom leather work, such as belts and slings, and her handmade fishing rods are indeed items of beauty.

It would be altogether correct to describe the average Barbee knife as a lesson in functionality. There is, however, a danger here, as all too often, a person gets the impression that such knives cannot be useful and beautiful at the same time. Such is not the case with a Barbee knife, but they were designed to be used.

"When you have to go through the pelvis of a mature mulie or antelope," states Barbee, "or get through the brisket of a big buck, maybe in temperatures hovering around 10 below zero, you want a knife that can do the job neatly and quickly, and this is no time or place for a

delicately ground blade that looks more like a razor than a hunting knife. Such blades may be great for slicing bacon, trimming the fat off a roast or even skinning, but that's not what I want in the field, and I believe that I have dressed out as much game as any living knifemaker."

Hughes has watched Barbee dress out several head of game and, as he puts it, "Each time I see Barbee in action I am literally amazed. I believe he can field dress a buck in a matter of seconds, and I have seen him skin and dress out an antelope in well under ten minutes."

The steel used in most Barbee knives is 440C, which was the first so-called stainless to win general approval among handmade knife fanciers. Occasionally, a Barbee knife will be delivered with a 154CM blade, if the customer so specifies, but Barbee strongly favors 440C.

"Properly heat-treated, I doubt that there is a better blade material among modern steels than 440C. The catch is, most of the men who make their knives from 440C don't have their blades treated properly. My electronically controlled oven was designed and made by a scientist at NASA in Houston, and I do my own heat-treating and, if you'll pardon me for saying so, I do it right!"

Each knife in Barbee's brochure, which may be yours for

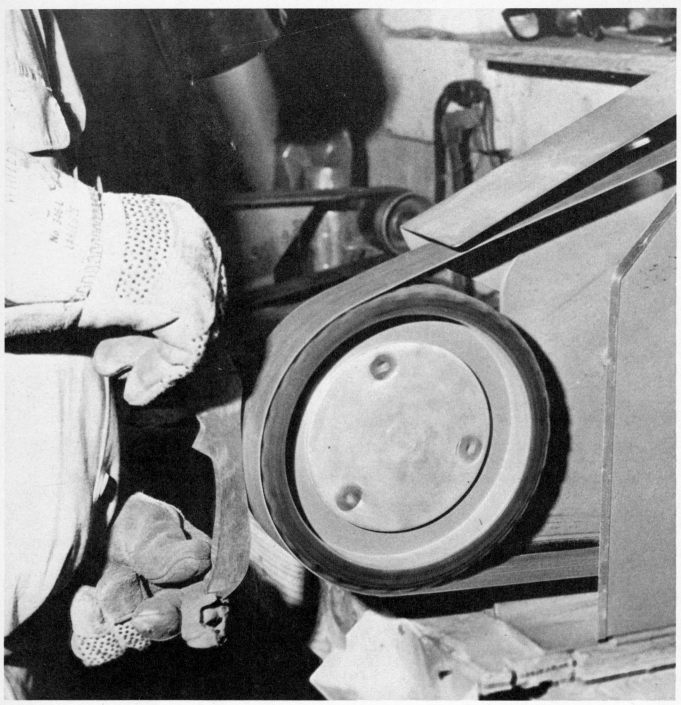

The skilled hands of knifemaker Barbee at work in his Fort Stockton, Texas, workshop. Barbee does his own heat-treating on an oven designed by a NASA space scientist. Barbee expresses preference for 440C steel.

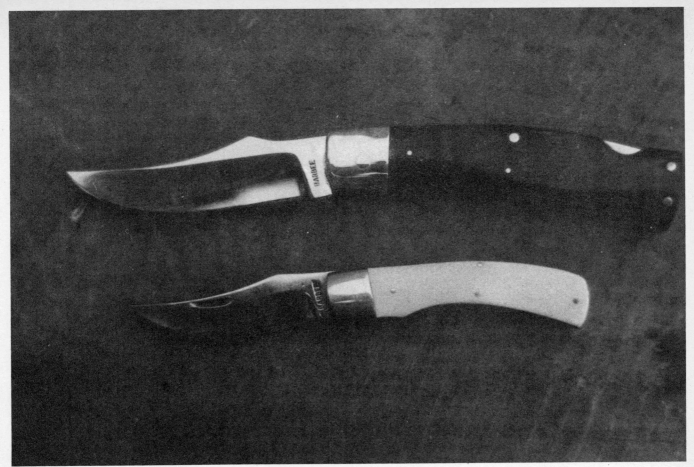

Folding hunter model (above) features 3½-inch locking blade. Folding caper model is somewhat smaller and is offered without locking blade. Prices start at $125 and $100 respectively with micarta handles.

$1, was designed by the maker himself. Before placing it in his brochure, Barbee uses it for at least a year to see if it is functional. He will work to the customer's design, of course, but for all-around usage he favors what he calls his A-1 Personal.

Barbee first showed me the prototypes for his two folding models in 1974, but he didn't unveil them until 1976. His Model 2100 Folding Hunters come with 3½-inch blades made from one-eighth-inch stock. Closed, this knife measures 4½ inches overall, which makes it just a tad large for packing around in your pant pocket. His Model 2200 Folding Caper is an inch shorter overall with the blade closed, and this one isn't bad for carrying in your jeans. The 2200 has a 2½-inch blade and the larger version is ordinarily delivered with a belt sheath.

The Folding Hunter has a blade lock, while the Folding Caper does not. Both feature micarta handle slabs and the customer may select from white, rosewood, red, black, wood grain and zebra. The Folding Hunter lists for $125, while the Folding Caper is an even $100. If the buyer is so inclined, he may request such handle materials as sambar stag, water buffalo, ivory or ox horn, all at extra cost.

As far as Barbee's sheaths are concerned, it should be noted that in all probability no current maker offers better leather work than does Jim Barbee. Made from nine to ten ounce top-grade leather, his sheaths are first-rate in every respect; basket weaving is available at no extra cost. Also available are sheaths that are made to be worn parallel to the belt. Packed in a cross draw fashion, many hunters now swear by this arrangement.

Getting back to Barbee's folding knives, the maker himself has this to say about them: "My Folding Hunter is big enough and tough enough to handle just about any chore. It can do anything that a 3½-inch bladed sheath knife can do. In the same vein, if a 2½-inch blade can get the job done, my Folding Caper can handle it. Let's face it. If a folder can't do what a sportsman desires, a sheath knife should be selected. There is no wisdom in choosing a knife that can at best turn in an unsatisfactory performance. I didn't put my folders on the market until I was convinced that they could measure up. They do."

Most of Jim Barbee's hunting clients are repeat customers. The same can be said about many of his knife buyers. But the best testimonial to his knives is the one that he provides himself. When a man has dressed out several hundred head of game and prefers one make above all others, that speaks highly of that brand of knife. Jim Barbee likes Barbee knives.

The Custom Craftsmen:

THE LUXURIOUS BLADES OF LEW BOOTH

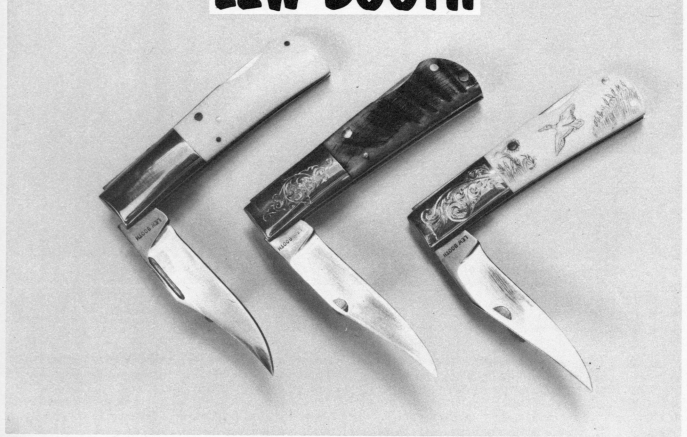

Booth's Barlow model folding knife has proven to be a popular seller for the maker. Three grades are offered, ranging from the standard model, left, through more elaborate types. Barlows are consecutively numbered.

Folding Knives Are This New Jersey Cutler's Specialty, Though He'll Make Anything A Customer Fancies

THE NAME, BOOTH, is of Welsh origin and in one family with this surname, it is a tradition to call the first male son Llewellyn. Thus, there lives today in Boonton, New Jersey, knifemaker Llewellyn Hardin Booth, better known to cutlery buffs as Lew.

Born in Cincinatti, Ohio, in 1941, Lew attended school in West Palm Beach, Florida, and Ocean View, Virginia. The senior Booth's construction business was responsible for these moves and, at seventeen, Lew Booth did a little moving on his own, joining the United States Air Force, serving six years in the States and the Pacific. During those years,

Booth turned out perhaps two hundred knives for his fellow servicemen.

"My first knife was made while I was in my early teens," he remembers, "using Dad's power tools in the family garage. I've always been interested in knives."

Following discharge from the Air Force, he opened a knife shop in Albuquerque, New Mexico, but after six years, was hit by wanderlust and drifted through the West and Southwest, holding down such jobs as lumberjack, trucker; anything that would guarantee a day's pay.

He recalls his days as a drifter with something akin to

Custom knifemaker Lew Booth displays one of his nonfolders with some of the awards and prizes he has won.

nostalgia. "For example, once while mountain climbing in New Mexico I placed my hand on a rock and almost put it on top of a rattler! I guess I was faster than the snake!"

Booth also had a short but memorable experience in the coal mines. "First day on the job, the lift took us down. Down was more like three decks below hell. The next day, I was chopping cord wood for a paper mill."

In 1966, Booth married an Italian girl from East Hanover, New Jersey. At that time, Paula was a health and physical education instructor; today she is a guidance counselor in a New Jersey high school.

"Paula is my number one brochure editor, shipping clerk and hostess. We have an 8-year-old son and a wire-haired terrier."

In 1967, the Booths finally settled in Jersey. He launched a trucking business, which was purchased in 1971 by a larger firm. With time on his hands, Lew Booth again turned to knifemaking. Since then he has been a full-time maker. Initially, he mainly produced sheath knives, but in the past two years, has stressed folders.

"I think the greatest day I've had yet at knifemaking came when I finished my first two-bladed Barlow," Booth relates.

"Just about anyone can make an acceptable sheath knife, but the folding knives represent a genuine challenge. You might say that it separates the men from the boys. It seems to me that the market is almost flooded with shoddy workmanship.

"Too, a few are offering so-called handmade knives at low prices. The eye of an expert, however, can tell the difference quickly in workmanship. One customer told me that my folding Barlow is akin to the Purdey shotgun, but I can't see how. They don't even look alike."

Essentially, this model features one-piece bolsters and liners of 303 stainless steel. The blades are made from D2, one of today's most admired cutlery steels. A blade stop is employed to prevent the cutting edge from touching the handle center as the blade snaps into the closed position. Nic-a-loy stainless pins are used to hold all the pieces together. The handle slabs are made from a variety of micarta.

The blades are flat ground and are approximately 3¼ inches long. All Barlow knives are consecutively numbered. The current base price of a Booth Barlow is $250.

Booth still offers a number of fixed-blade models, including a boot knife, three hunting models, an all-steel utility knife and two hatchets. Prices begin at $50 and go up to $150, with a number of extra-cost items available, such as nickel silver guards, ivory handles, scrimshaw work and hand-tooled sheaths.

"My worst day as a knifemaker came last Fall," Booth remembers. "My left hand was mangled by the belt sander and took three months to heal. Fortunately, there is virtually no scar. At that point, I decided to get some specialized insurance, a move that I would recommend to any aspiring knifemaker. Freak accidents can occur. On several occasions the buffer has grabbed the blade and driven it point

Sheath knife below is called the Positive Grip Hunter, and is made with either 3½" or 4" blade. Booth offers etching and scrimshaw by master craftsmen at extra cost.

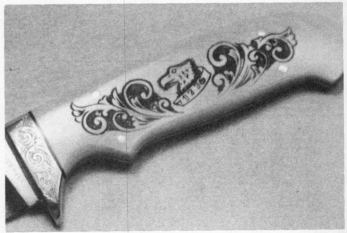

first into the concrete floor. This could be dangerous, even though some may regard it as a good test for the steel.

"As for my injury, it is almost impossible for me to believe at this point that I actually made more than thirty knives with one hand. Three of these were Barlows and two were integral-guard boot knives. I received many letters from impatient customers, but after I explained the delay, I had no problems and all were well pleased with their knives."

An average working day for Booth is approximately twelve hours, frequently seven days a week. "There are days I get going on a project and work through the next day until I'm finished," he explains. "Working alone, I completely make and ship out perhaps twenty knives each month."

At present, he is working with a steel that heretofore has received little attention in the world of knives: BG-42. He is pleased with the initial results, but is waiting before making any rash promises. However, he believes it will offer the edge-holding ability of M2, will be stain resistant and will offer more strength than M2.

"My feeling is that a blade is designed to do a job. Regardless of how fancy it may be, it is nonetheless a working tool. If it is not properly heat treated, it is no better, if as good, as a mass-produced factory blade.

"I suppose it is in my nature to try to do one better — better than factory knives, better than other knifemakers, but, more important, better than my last knife. I gain considerable satisfaction in analyzing and improving upon my own work as well as what is currently available on today's market. I expect some major changes in my shop and my offerings and these should be announced soon."

Booth prizes the complimentary letters he has received from satisfied customers, including hunters, guides and collectors from all parts of the world.

"It makes me feel proud — my wife says too proud — and gives me greater determination to keep trying to improve. When a man writes and describes how he skinned a

Booth working in his New Jersey shop on belt grinder.

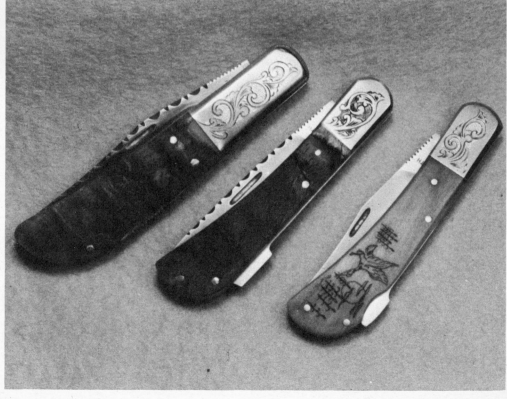

Most of the Barlow folders Booth makes are of the lock-open design. Note the fancy file work on back of two blades.

Kodiak bear, a moose and an elk without having to sharpen his Booth knife, then I feel that I must be doing what I originally attempted to achieve. I intend to keep on working towards perfection, until the Booth knife is proved the finest of them all."

One of the latest features offered knife buffs by the Booth shop is an engraving service. "I have enlisted some of the finest talent in the country to satisfy the demand for all types of engraving," he declares. "We will engrave any knife — the maker does not matter — and no knife is too large or too small. We will engrave one knife or one hundred." A customer writes Booth, explaining exactly what is desired in the way of decoration, and receives a quotation.

Booth produced a bicentennial commemorative series, which included a sheath knife and a Barlow appropriately engraved and scrimshawed. Only seventy-six of each model were offered, with prices beginning at $400 for the sheath knife and $100 more for the folder.

Booth's wife, Paula, is advertising and brochure designer. Literature below is typical of what many custom knifemakers use to respond to customer inquiries.

Lew Booth ----------
KNIFEMAKER

16 Cypress Terrace
Boonton, N.J. 07005
(201) 335-9817

I am only one. But I am one. I can't do everything. But I can do something. And what I ought to do. By the grace of God I shall do. Amen.

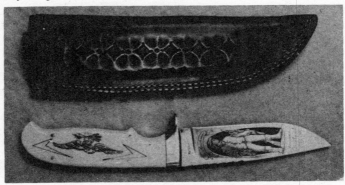

Bi Centennial Commemorative Hunting Knife
1776 to 1976

A 4 inch stainless blade. A 4½ inch ivory micarta handle. A nickle silver guard. Near side is engraved and scrimshawed and numbered 1/76 to 76/76. Off side is plain. I am only going to make 76 hunter commemoratives. Cost as pictured $400.00 each. Ivory and other extras are available upon request.

Bi Centennial Commemorative Barlow
1776 to 1976

The Barlow folding knife to accompany the above hunter. 3¼ inch blade. 4 inch ivory micarta handle. The near side of Barlow is engraved and scrimshawed. The off side is plain. Only 76 commemorative Barlows will be made and so numbered. Cost $500.00 each. Ivory and other extras are available upon request.

A fancy walnut box will hold one or both knives and sheath. Among other features, it has an ivory micarta shield. 2 x 4 scrimshawed eagle and glass cover, etc., Cost $125.00 each. Order a boxed set and receive matching numbers.

The Custom Craftsmen:

BILL DAVIS:

Inspired Afield

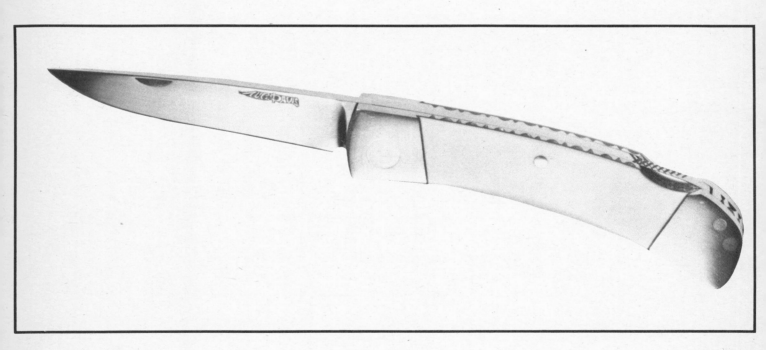

A Tough Buck Deer And A Not-So-Good Blade

Put Him In The Handcrafted Knife Business

The middle three knives are folders made by W.C. Davis and feature a variety of sizes and shapes available from the midwestern craftsman. At top is Davis' four-inch bladed sheath knife, while a petite boot knife is at bottom.

IN NOVEMBER 1972, a Missouri sportsman dropped a nice buck and, in the process of dressing it out, became so disgruntled with his mass-produced knife that he resolved he'd get a better cutting instrument, even if he had to make it himself!

"That wasn't my first deer by any means," recalls W.C. "Bill" Davis, "but I had been reading a lot of articles on handmade knives and how well they would hold an edge. That made me even more dissatisfied with the low-priced special that I had been using."

Davis went home, and before that month was over, he had made a sheath knife using a broken saw blade as the blade material.

"That did it!" he admits. "I decided I wanted to be a knifemaker, and my wife thought my work was pretty good. So I switched over to 01 tool steel and made a few more that were even better. Then I made the big plunge: I borrowed $1000 to buy supplies and equipment — and soon discovered that this was insufficient funding. With the help of my wife and God, I managed to scrape up enough to get us through."

Davis paused for a moment in telling us this, then added: "Understand, I had never actually seen a handmade knife until I showed up at the 1973 Kansas City Knifemakers Guild Show. I kept my knives in my case and, in fact, hid them under my table. I had never seen so many beautiful knives. All of a sudden, mine didn't look so good anymore. Bob Loveless gave me some encouragement and I finally put my knives out on the display table. I even sold one!

"For months, I would work on my knives during the evenings and weekends, and every cent I made on them was put into a savings account. I was looking ahead to being a full-time knifemaker."

Then Davis got a break. A friend, Jerry Criswell, showed some of his work to A.G. Russell, president of the Morseth Knife Company. Russell, who always has an eye out for unheralded talent, was impressed. He ordered two dozen Davis knives, chipped in some advice, and even loaned Davis some equipment.

"I'll always be indebted to A.G. Russell," Davis vows. "He gave me encouragement when I needed it most."

Gradually, Davis developed a decided preference for folding knives, although he will make virtually anything the customer desires.

His work first came to our attention at the 1976 Knife Expo in Dallas. Strange to say, the thing about his knives that caught our fancy was the light weight of his folders. Davis uses aluminum for many of his bolsters.

"I would like to use aluminum as my standard bolster material," he explains, "but my customers need to be convinced that it makes a satisfactory knife."

Satisfactory is hardly the word. Imagine a full-sized

folder, with lock, weighing no more than 1½ ounces! Actual usage confirms that the resulting knife is rough and tough, but a real looker!

Davis uses 440C as a standard blade material, although he will furnish D2 and A2 if the customer so specifies. He has his 440C blades treated cryogenically.

"So treated," he maintains, "a 440C blade has superior edge-holding ability. It is as good as any modern steel and better than most." For quite some time many have felt that 440C, properly treated, is a far better blade material than normally is believed, but few users have it heat-treated properly.

the overall knife is only five-sixteenths-inch thick! Davis expects this one to be his most popular model, with a price of $65.

Another good everyday knife is his No. 1, which comes with a 2-7/8-inch blade. Perhaps his most unusual model is his Mule Deer Special, a sheath knife with a four-inch dropped point blade plus a 2¾-inch folding blade located in the handle. Neat! This knife lists at $150.

For handle materials, Davis prefers one of the many micartas "for durability," but likes stag "for beauty." He charges $8 extra for stag when available but, at no additional charge, the customer may select from rosewood,

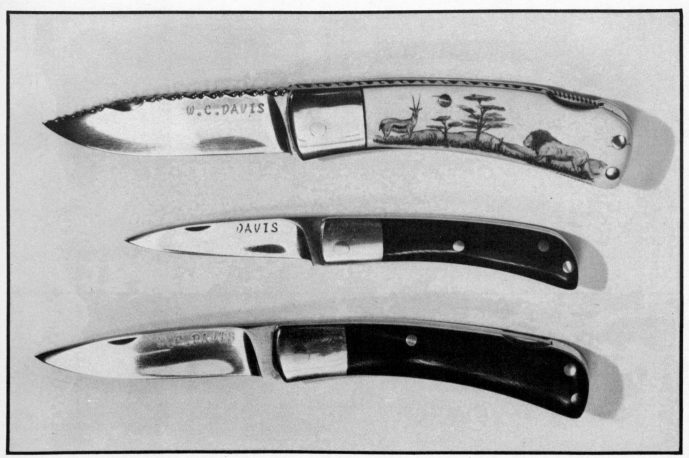

Of these three folders by Bill Davis, the one at the top is a collector's item that probably never is going to see any serious use; the knife at bottom is designed for hunting and the folder in the center is for everyday carrying.

Davis' current prices are reasonable by any standard. His nonlocking models begin at $65, while those with locks are $10 higher. Unlike most makers, Davis prefers to turn out models with locks. "I make the nonlockers only on special order," he told us.

For hunting, we favor Davis' No. 5 lock-back folder, which comes with a 3-1/8-inch blade. With aluminum bolsters, this full-sized hunter weighs only two ounces! This was the model that originally caught our attention at the Dallas show.

His latest knife is his "everyday" model, which is just what the name implies: a knife made for packing in your pants pocket 365 days a year. This new folder has a 2½-inch blade made of three-thirty-seconds-inch steel, and

vermillion, cocobolo, walnut, and black, maroon, green or wood grain micarta. Ivory micarta is an extra-cost item for $5.

Asked why he feels a customer should consider his knives instead of those made by another maker, Davis is quick to reply: "Because of my knives' quality, combined with my prices, which are reasonable for handmade work."

He adds, "My idea is to make a good knife, but at the same time to keep the prices as low as possible, so that the man who wants a good working knife can afford one."

Davis also caters to the collector market, and the buyer who wants something a little fancier may request custom scrimshaw work performed for Davis by Ron Legendre, who, like Davis, lives in Raymore, Missouri.

(Left) W.C. Davis looks thoughtful during a formal moment away from his shop. (Center) The style that Davis calls his everyday folder weighs less than an ounce and is one of his all-time best sellers. Blade is 2½ inches long. (Bottom) This fancy folder has a worked back, a sterling silver liner and bolsters. Handle work by Ron Legendre.

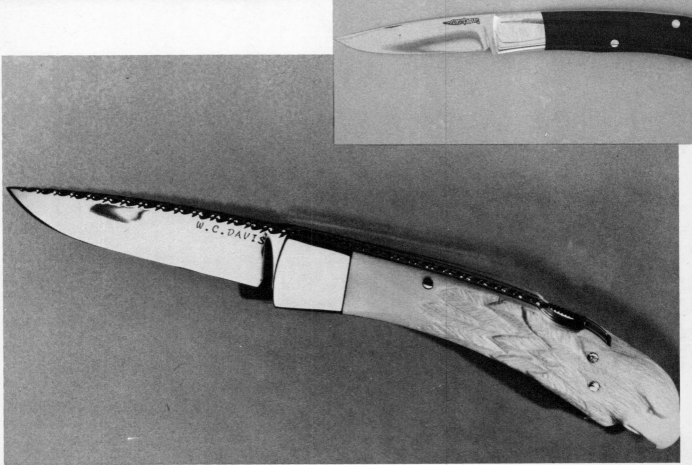

The Custom Craftsmen:

W.T. FULLER
One-Hand Folder

This Alabama Knifemaker Makes One-Hand Folders —
And He Makes Them With But One Hand!

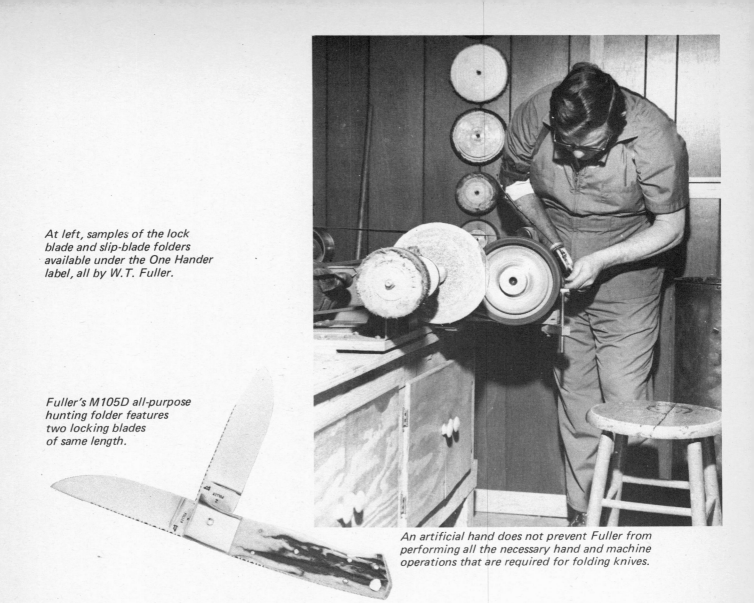

At left, samples of the lock blade and slip-blade folders available under the One Hander label, all by W.T. Fuller.

Fuller's M105D all-purpose hunting folder features two locking blades of same length.

An artificial hand does not prevent Fuller from performing all the necessary hand and machine operations that are required for folding knives.

THE FIRST TIME that we saw W.T. Fuller, Jr., of Gadsden, Alabama, and his beautiful handmade folding knives was at the 1976 Dallas Expo. There were literally dozens upon dozens of makers there, and it would have required something very much out of the ordinary to attract our attention. Fuller's knives did just that.

After looking critically at the various folders arrayed on the table, we glanced at the maker, who was sitting behind his display, to ask his permission to examine the knives, and right there we experienced something of a surprise.

Fuller dubs his knives "One Hander," and one might be forgiven for thinking that this is due to the fact that these knives are so easy to open and close that such a feat may be accomplished with a single paw. To be sure, this is perfectly correct, but there is much more to it than that: W.T. Fuller himself has only one hand!

Let us hasten to add that Fuller doesn't expect you to buy his knives because they were made by a one-handed cutler; he hopes you will purchase one because they can withstand the most critical scrutiny and still compare favorably with most any folding knife that you may care to name.

Just for the record, Fuller lost his right hand in an industrial accident several years ago, when a large cutting machine that was turned "off," made a sudden revolution, severely cutting Fuller's lower arm. He is still employed by that firm, but he is looking forward to retirement when he can devote his full workday to turning out knives.

Addressing the obvious, we asked Fuller if he felt the loss of a hand adversely affects the quality of his knives. "Not at all," he replied. "I feel that my product is as good, if not better, than it would be if I had two hands." He then added with a smile, "That other hand might get in my way."

His knifemaking career goes back several years, but only since 1974 has he taken it very seriously. Those early knives were either given away to friends or sold for the cost of materials. Then, as his work improved, so did the demand, and he decided to attend a few national knife shows and see how his work compared with the professionals. The comparison proved satisfactory, and today Fuller's knives simply have to be ranked among the better handmade folders on the market.

"I got into knifemaking quite by accident," he told us.

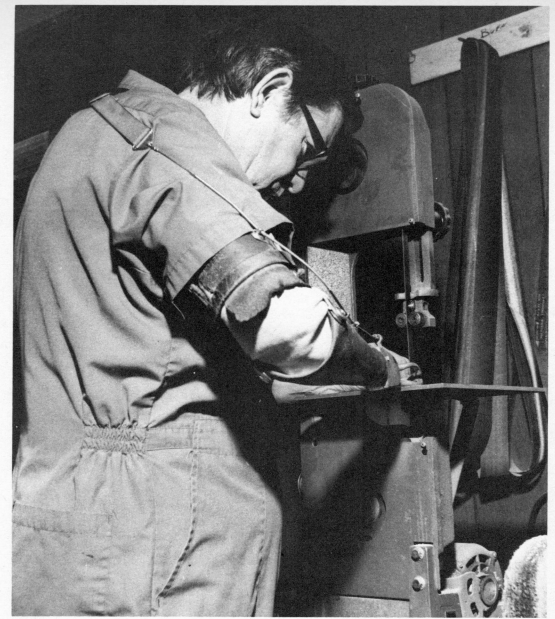

Fuller's workshop, in Gadsden, Alabama, has a full complement of power machines.

"One day I was looking at a knife — I forget the brand — and I said something to the effect that I could make a knife as good as that one." Fuller says that one thing led to another, so he decided to try his hand at knifemaking.

For many years Fuller had been a professional machinist, and this, of course, was a tremendous advantage to him when he began turning out knives. He has even made some of the equipment in his shop, including a grinder and a buffer.

In his brief career as a serious cutler, he has sold knives to customers from all over the world, and many of his orders come from satisfied customers who desire another One Hander or two for their collections.

At the present time Fuller is approximately eight months behind in filling his orders, but with retirement coming on rapidly, Fuller hopes to cut that down to no more than three to four months.

The base price for a One Hander folder is $100, but he

offers several models that go up to $300. Fuller's standard blade material is D2 steel, although he will furnish 440C if the customer so desires.

All bolsters are made from nickel silver and he uses stainless-steel liners. Basic handle materials include exotic woods and either maroon or ivory micarta. Most of Fuller's knives possess blade locks, with these located high on the back of the handles. He does, however, offer several models sans locks. Should you desire decorative file work on the back of the blade this will set you back an extra $20; such handle materials as ivory, stag or sheephorn also are added cost items.

The model that Fuller is probably most proud of is his Model 105D All-Purpose Hunting Folder. This beauty features two blades, both of which lock, with one having a point located in line with the back of the blade, while the other is a dropped point. Both are 3-5/16 inches in length and are made of one-eighth-inch stock. File work decorates

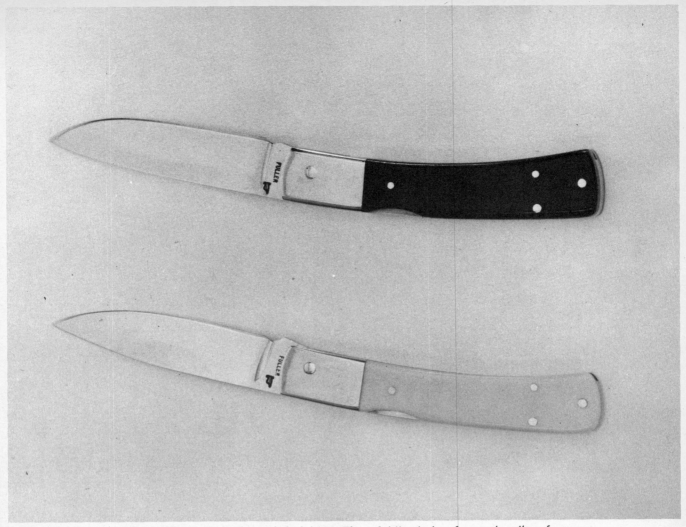

Two of W.T. Fuller's standard One Hander lock-blade folders. These folding knives feature handles of maroon and ivory micarta, with prices starting at $125. Fuller heat-treats his own blades, offers lifetime guarantee.

both blades and the handle slabs are made from sambar stag. All in all, it is difficult to conceive of a better-designed or better-executed folder. The price for this knife, as described, is $300. If you desire only one blade, the same basic model may be yours for $200.

For the gent desiring something to carry on an everyday basis, cast an eye on Fuller's Mini-101 Folder, which comes with a two-inch blade and an overall length of only 2½ inches. With a blade lock, this baby carries a price tag of $125 with either micarta or hardwood handle slabs.

"Although I exhibit my work at a number of shows," Fuller explained, "most of my orders arrive through the mail. It helps if the customer will tell me exactly what he wants. I have just about every type of wood imaginable, but if I were making a knife for myself, it would have stag slabs."

Fuller does his own heat-treating, and, as he puts it, "Since I make everything in my knives from beginning to end, I can guarantee my knives for life. I believe this is to the mutual benefit of both myself and the customer. I know what goes into every knife and I am completely, one-hundred percent responsible for any knife that bears my name. If it's good I don't have to share the credit with anyone, and if it's not good, it's my fault."

When we visited Fuller at the 1977 Dallas Expo, he seemed to be doing good business from his table, and he reported that by the time you read this he probably will be retired from his machinist's job and will be a full-time knifemaker. If anything, the knives seemed to have improved from one year to the next and there wasn't much room for improvement to begin with!

When the men and women who prepare the television advertisements beseeching employers to hire the handicapped give some thought to future productions, they might give some thought to using W.T. Fuller as a prime example of a man who can get the job done in spite of having only one hand. There's only one thing wrong with this thinking: One Hander doesn't consider himself handicapped.

He did tell us, however, that if something should happen to his left hand, his delivery dates probably will have to be pushed back several months!

Eager and impatient buyers lined up an hour before the opening bell at Dallas 1976 Knifemaker Show to await their turn to purchase a Horn knife. Horn sold 83 of his knives in less than a minute at the knifemaker show.

The Custom Craftsmen:

THE HORN OF PLENTY

Horn finds his replica of Remington Bullet pocketknives popular.

One Of The Rapidly Rising Stars Of The Custom Knife World Specializes In Folders

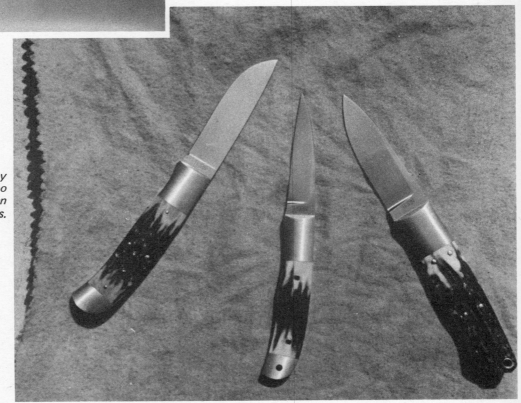

Sheath knives by Jess Horn are no less popular than his folders.

"THE SMALLER they get, the more popular they become," says Jess Horn, a custom knifemaker from Redding, California.

"My specialty has become custom folders," says Horn. "Almost every year, I introduce a new model, each one smaller than the last. And I can't turn them out fast enough to satisfy my buyers."

In 1977, Horn introduced his smallest pocket folder yet. It has a blade which is 2-5/8 inches long. He calls it the Baby Horn and its popularity should match or exceed that of his famous Little Horn model.

Horn sees considerable demand for smaller and smaller knives, especially folders, but is of the opinion that knifemakers may hit a physical or at least a practical limit to how small they may become. The amount of work which a custom knifesmith must put into smaller knives goes up in direct proportion to the reduction in knife size. "Smaller

knives take a great deal more careful handling and work, just because of their size," says Horn.

How popular are Horn's knives? This may be judged in a number of ways. For one thing, there is and has been almost since he began making knives, a four-year delay from order to delivery of a Horn knife. Not the longest known in the business, but it does say something about how much demand exists for these fine knives.

An anecdote may further illustrate the Horn knife popularity. In the Summer of 1976, Horn, who has been a full-time custom knifemaker since December 1975, attended the knifemaker show in Dallas, Texas. He must have had some sort of inkling as to what was going to happen because he brought with him a fair number and sample of his craft; namely, upwards of ninety custom knives for display and sale, if anybody was interested.

To say the collectors were interested may be an

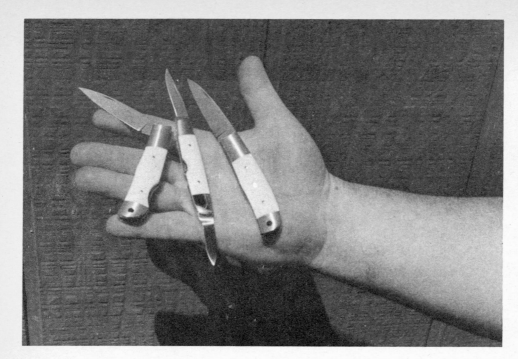

Three models of Horn folders: single blade with locking system, twin blade with slip joint, and single blade slip joint.

Knifemaker Jess Horn in his small but well-equipped shop in Redding, California. Horn has been a full-time custom cutler since December 1975. Demand for his work has brought delivery time to four years.

The maker calls this model his Dropped Horn. The folder has stag handle slabs and features a 3-3/16" blade of 154 CM steel, 1/8" thick. This lock-blade knife was designed for Horn by Bob Loveless.

understatement. Horn's display area was surrounded by avid collectors an hour before the official opening time for the show. The crowd kept pushing forward to see each knife as he carefully laid it out on display. Horn had devised a rather simple method to aid him and his wife when it came time to take orders and make receipts. He placed a number tag beside each knife and had identical tags — much like taking a number at the butcher shop in the old days — on pegs atop his display case. This allowed the would-be buyers to view the knives without handling them and allowing each to make a selection before the opening gong.

At the minute of the official opening time, Horn announced he was open to take orders. In less than a minute, Horn relates with some astonishment, eighty-three out of the ninety numbered tags he had brought, were in the hands of collectors and they waited their turn to hand over their money as Horn and his wife wrote out receipts as fast as they could. Some of the buyers realized Horn's potential plight and agreed to leave the knives they had purchased at the booth so that Horn would have something to display during the remainder of the show. He continued to take additional orders for the displayed models as fast as he would be able to build them.

What about the remaining seven knives that year? Five of them, Horn says, were purchased by a collector who came by after the initial rush and said he would take them all, regardless of price. And he did. The last two were sold later. That's popularity!

As mentioned, Horn has been a full-time knifemaker since December 1975, which means he is able to support his family in a modest but comfortable manner from his custom knife earnings.

Horn finds the demand for smaller knives increasing and he introduces new models almost yearly. However, he says that working on smaller knives requires more time and care. Here he belt-sands folding blade back.

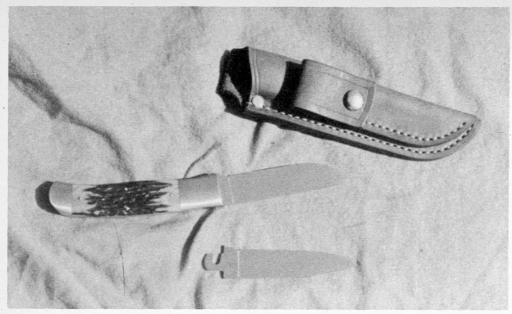

The Twin Horn features two blades and a special sheath by Jerry Ashton.

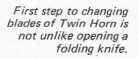

First step to changing blades of Twin Horn is not unlike opening a folding knife.

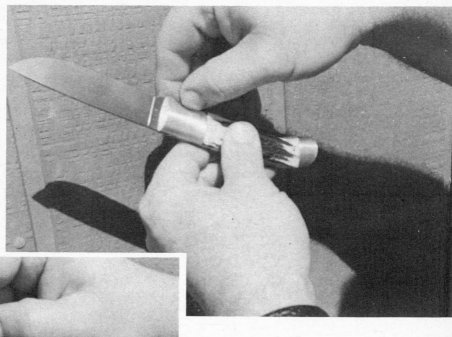

The locking bar begins to pivot out of the case similar to a folding knife.

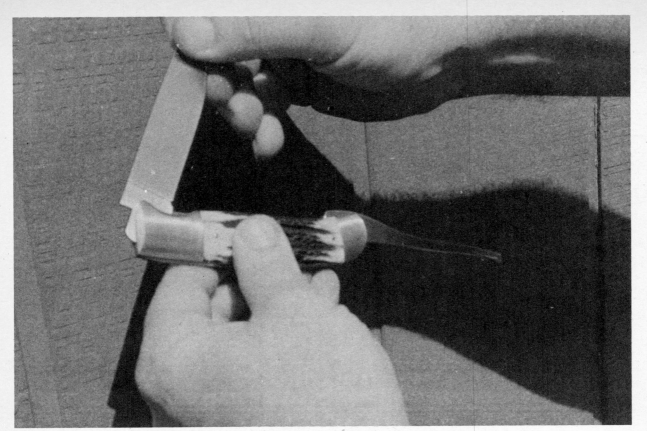

With the locking bar completely open, the blade may be pivoted down toward handle as if closing a folder.

Blade slips out of knife as locking bar remains open. Second blade may now be inserted and locked.

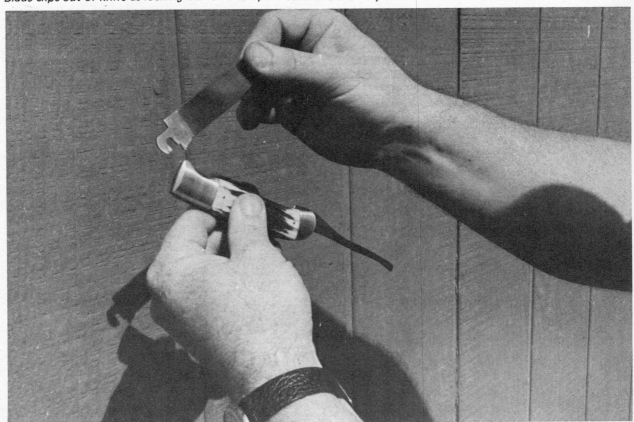

He tells how in the late Sixties, he was working in the construction engineering field and there seemed to be an inordinate amount of chain-saw bars which were not holding up. Always mechanically inclined, Horn was determined to devise a way to repair or make a better bar. To do so, he found he had to build his own heat-treating furnace to produce the right metal for a strong chain-saw bar. Along the way, a friend asked him to heat-treat a knife blade he had made. That was the start.

He made up a few sheath knives in his spare time and began to gain a reputation for his skills at a few local shows. Bill Loveless of Riverside, California, discussed folding models with Horn. In fact, Loveless is credited by Horn with the design of most of his folders. Horn so states in his catalog. He began making folders, although still on a part-time basis.

A number of years of experience as a part-timer had indicated to Horn that the month of December was traditionally one of the worst for knife orders. For a reason he cannot explain, in December 1975 Horn was inundated with more orders in one month than he had received ever before.

Horn puts it this way: "We're a Christian family. We always have been. At a time in my life when I was at a crossroad, I believe the Lord was saying to go into the custom knifemaking business full time." Horn has not been sorry he made the move.

Horn loves doing what he's doing. "Knifemaking is one of the few occupations left that lets you do your own thing and make a living at it. I'm doing what I like to do. I work at home. I have no commuting problems and I can live in a beautiful part of the country to enjoy all the outdoor activities I want."

Most of the knives Horn makes and sells are of standard design which he illustrates in his catalog. He has eleven or twelve folding models — his most popular — a half-dozen sheath knives and a special Bowie knife which he offers in two sizes. One of his sheath knives, called the Twin Horn, features two interchangeable blades of different profile. Both blades have a length of 3-5/16 inches with an overall length of 7-11/16 inches. The blades may be dropped point, skinner, semi-skinner or whatever the customer orders. Once the interchangeable blade has been inserted, the locking mechanism is nearly invisible. The Twin Horn is in great demand.

Horn produces most of his knives, folding or sheath type, from 154CM steel. Virtually the only exceptions to this are his Bowies, which he produces from O2 steel that he himself heat-treats.

Horn sends out the blades of 154CM to a custom heat-treating firm for hardening. Horn specifies that the blades are hardened to a Rockwell C reading of 60-61 and the spring locking parts to 55-56. The heat-treater hardens and tests each and every blade and part, says Horn, and he feels this is the only way to go. Horn likes the 154CM because of its stain resistance and ability to hold an edge. He credits Loveless with discovering the attributes of 154CM for custom knives.

About ninety percent of the custom knife output by the Redding maker is folders. Most of them are lock-back models with several of his designs available in either lock blade or slip joint. His smallest knife, the Baby Horn, was mentioned earlier. His largest folder is a replica of the famous Remington Bullet pocketknife with a 4-5/16-inch blade.

Jess Horn believes that most of his output is being snapped up by custom knife collectors rather than the users in the field. His correspondence and face-to-face meetings with customers at shows leads him to this conclusion. His buyers are from all over the world, as well as the United States. He gets many orders from Canada and Japan. Japan has a leading gun publication which has featured his knives. As he doesn't do any commercial advertising, Horn says that virtually all his business comes from knife shows

Horn has found that sambar stag is the most sought-after handle material for folders and fixed blades. This is his replica of the Remington Bullet No. 1256.

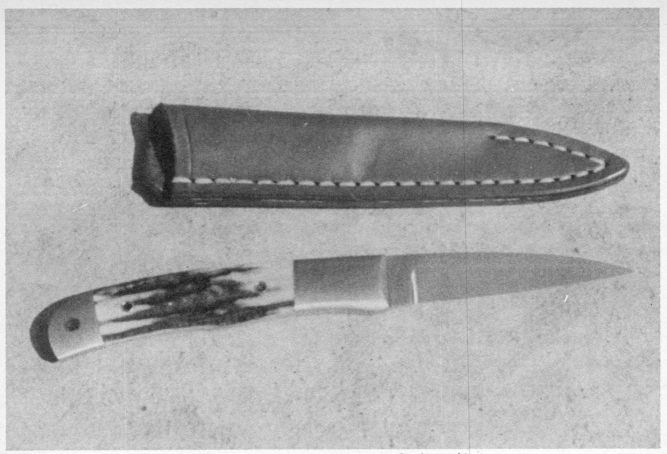

Horn sheath knives, as well as his folders, are popular with collectors all over the world. Horn works at his craft on full-time basis and finds himself pleased with his new vocation.

(which he feels are most valuable for exposure), various magazines and other publications, and word of mouth among his customers. He is well aware that four years is a long time to wait for an order for anything to be filled and he appreciates the patience of his customers. But, says Horn, he will not compromise quality for speed and quantity. He works as many hours a day as he is able to work carefully, but does not take shortcuts or reduce quality.

Horn finds the most popular handle material for folders or sheath knives is sambar stag. It is difficult to obtain and there is considerable waste and culling because of the inferior quality of much of the stag available in the United States. Horn says that the micarta materials are easily available, are stronger and are of more consistent quality. Nevertheless, most of his customers prefer the natural handle materials. Also popular for Horn are mother-of-pearl and natural ivory. Both are hard to get and ivory will become more dear as a ban on ivory import into California has been in effect since the middle of 1977.

There have been times, early in the cutler's career, when certain handle materials, rivets and springs were difficult to obtain. Now, however, Horn has built up his own sources and inventory to the point that he is able to satisfy most any request.

As material costs have risen in recent years, Horn feels he cannot accept any money on deposit from people who wish to order one of his knives. With continuing inflation he is forced to write the person who has placed an order,

perhaps four years previous, and notify him of the current price. As with all craftsmen who cannot control the cost of their material input, he must pass on the increased costs to his customers. His system apparently causes him no problems. Horn even maintains a list of people who wish to be notified in case of an order cancellation. That list is growing all the time.

He makes no warranty or guarantee statement about his knives but states that if any legitimate problem should arise with any of his knives, he will make it right.

Ten percent of his output is sheath knives, which includes the interchangeable blade model. The sheaths are handmade by Jerry Ashton of Denver, Colorado, from high-quality leather. Because each knife is custom made and each will vary slightly from the next and the latest, Horn sends one of each eight or ten sheath knives he builds to Ashton who cuts, stitches and wet-fits several sheaths to that model knife. Horn feels that after about ten knives, the sheath must be redesigned and constructed to fit.

Horn's folding knives start in price in the $150 to $200 range. If optional special handle or bolster materials are specified, the price goes up. The two-knife Bowie set starts in the $650 range.

If a collector cannot wait four years for a Horn, there are some brokers, such as A.G. Russell of Springdale, Arkansas, who often have previously owned models for sale, albeit at somewhat higher prices.

Will Horn come up with an even smaller folding model? He won't answer, but there is a twinkle in his eye as he refuses comment.

The Custom Craftsmen

THE FOLDING KNIVES OF RON LAKE

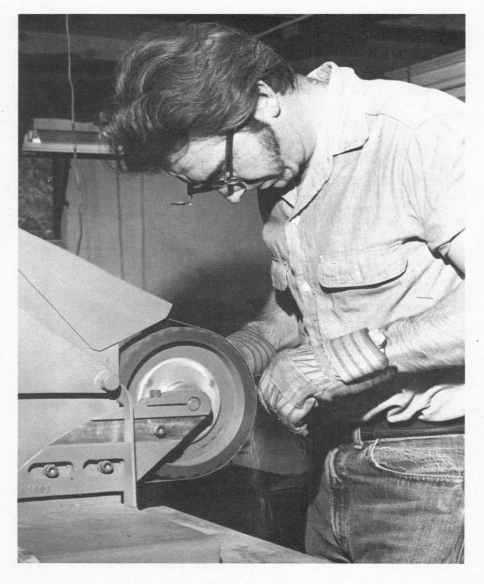

Entirely Self-Taught, This Folding Knife Maker Has Gained Many Fans In A Few Years

RON LAKE makes folding knives. He has been making folders as a professional since 1971. He is very good at his trade. There are those folder fans and collectors who refer to Ron Lake as Mr. Folding Knife. Over the years, Lake has developed a number of unique and patentable techniques of handle construction and blade locking systems.

It was the Summer of 1971 and, as I walked down the aisles of the Houston Gun Show at which the Knifemakers Guild was holding its second annual meeting, I was surrounded by the many tables containing nothing but handmade knives.

I was perhaps more interested in seeing such old friends as Bob Loveless, Chubby Hueske, Bill Moran, Ted Dowell, Bucker Gascon and many others than I was in looking at knives.

Then, as I passed a table behind which sat a slight young man whom I had never seen before, I spotted it! I looked at it a second time. Yes, there was no mistake. On the table was the finest folding knife I had ever seen.

"May I look at this?" I asked.

"Certainly," replied the young man, whose name tag proclaimed him to be one Ron Lake.

A close, critical examination revealed that the locked-blade folder was even better than the first impression had suggested.

That show was the first time that anyone in the knife world had heard of Ron Lake, but today he is generally accepted as one of the finest makers of folding knives in America. Perhaps some measure of his ability can be

gathered by the fact that at the present time he is approximately two years behind in filling his orders.

Lake first became interested in knives about seven years ago, when he assisted a friend in redressing a German dagger brought home as a war souvenir. At that time he was employed as a model pattern maker. His work consisted primarily of building electromechanical devices, working models, prototype samples, and mold and die work. Lake enjoyed working with the dagger, so he decided to try his hand at making a knife from scratch. The result was a Bowie with a 10½-inch blade.

"For the final polish I used my bare fingers and 800 grit diamond paste with light oil," he remembers. "I didn't count the hours involved, but there were many." The knife was given to a friend as a Christmas present.

Lake made a number of other knives in the next few

Blade and spring are so precisely fitted that without partially folded blade, joining surface is almost invisible.

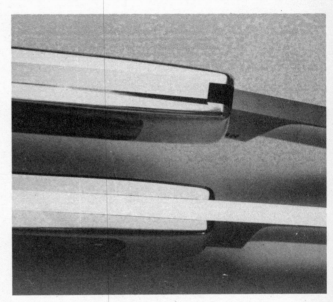

Working alone, Lake developed his patented locking system for folding knives. Using a variety of handle materials, he frames inserts in solid aluminum or steel case.

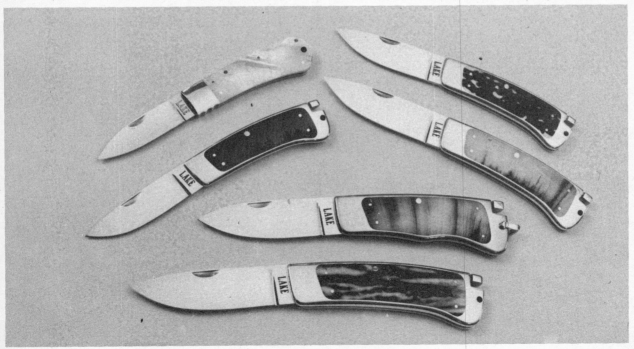

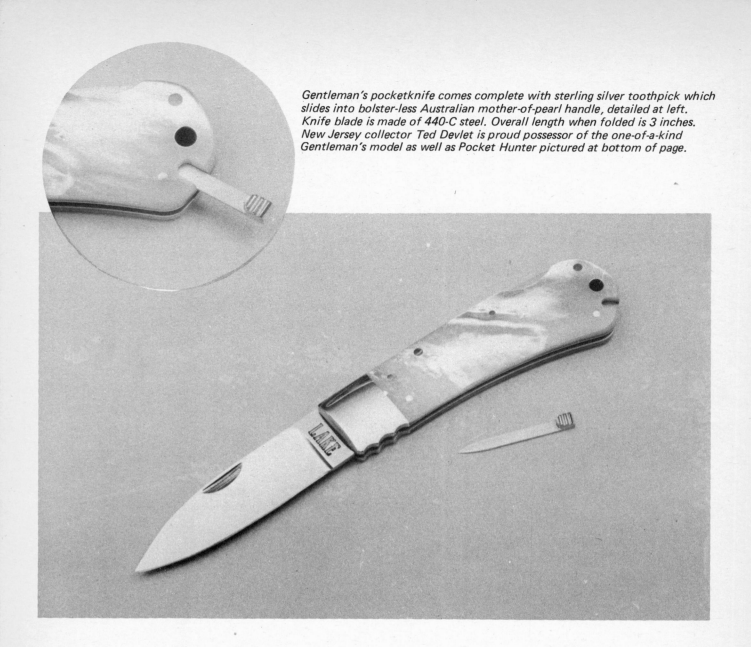

Gentleman's pocketknife comes complete with sterling silver toothpick which slides into bolster-less Australian mother-of-pearl handle, detailed at left. Knife blade is made of 440-C steel. Overall length when folded is 3 inches. New Jersey collector Ted Devlet is proud possessor of the one-of-a-kind Gentleman's model as well as Pocket Hunter pictured at bottom of page.

Lake Pocket Hunter features 440-C stainless-steel blade, titanium case, special belt loop on bolster and handle of big horn sheep horn.

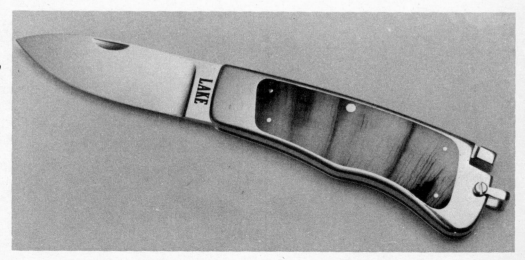

Three Lake folding hunters show coco bolo handle on top knife, ivory handles on other two.

months, but ended up giving most of them away. "People in this area looked at me like I was crazy when I asked $30 to $35 for a hunting knife," he recollects.

In those early days, Lake recalls, he had no problem finding good blade steels, but he did have trouble finding handle materials.

"I taught myself all of the rudiments of knifemaking over a year and a half period, and things got pretty discouraging at times. Buying needed equipment and materials is only part of knifemaking; a lot of midnight oil and a lot of research are involved. For many it would be too high a price to pay. I paid my dues, and I'm still paying them."

The basic idea for Lake's folder came about when a friend brought a famous brand factory folder to Lake's shop. The knife was difficult to open and close, and the owner asked Lake if he could do something about it.

"I had a few ideas before I saw this knife," comments Lake, "but I felt that, if this was typical of the stuff being produced, it was time to get with it."

Lake wanted a folding knife that would be easy to open for either a right or left-hander, so he put deep finger notches on both sides of the blade and precision-fit a bushing for the pivot.

"I wanted it to close easily, but with plenty of spring pressure, so I extended the lock lever for a mechanical advantage over the spring, then added a tab for more pressure surface," Lake explains. It is noteworthy that a Lake folder is wear adjusting. He tested one of his knives for 9000 cycles and there was little if any wear.

One of the first things a person notices about a Lake folder is that the handle inlays seem to have grown out of the brass body. This requires a considerable amount of skill and time, but there is a practical reason for this design.

"In the past, I noticed a lot of pocketknives with the handle edges splintered or chipped and I felt containing the material would solve or at least help considerably this problem. I developed the inlaying process, and I use it on all my folding knife designs." It might be added that whereas Lake's original design featured cocobolo inlays, then micarta, he now offers stag, when available, at extra cost. In addition to the standard brass frame, customers interested in saving a bit of weight may specify an aluminum frame at extra cost.

"When I walked into the motel room of Bob Loveless and introduced myself the evening before the 1971 Houston show opened," Lake recalls, "I had no idea my folding knife design was something new. In fact, I had never

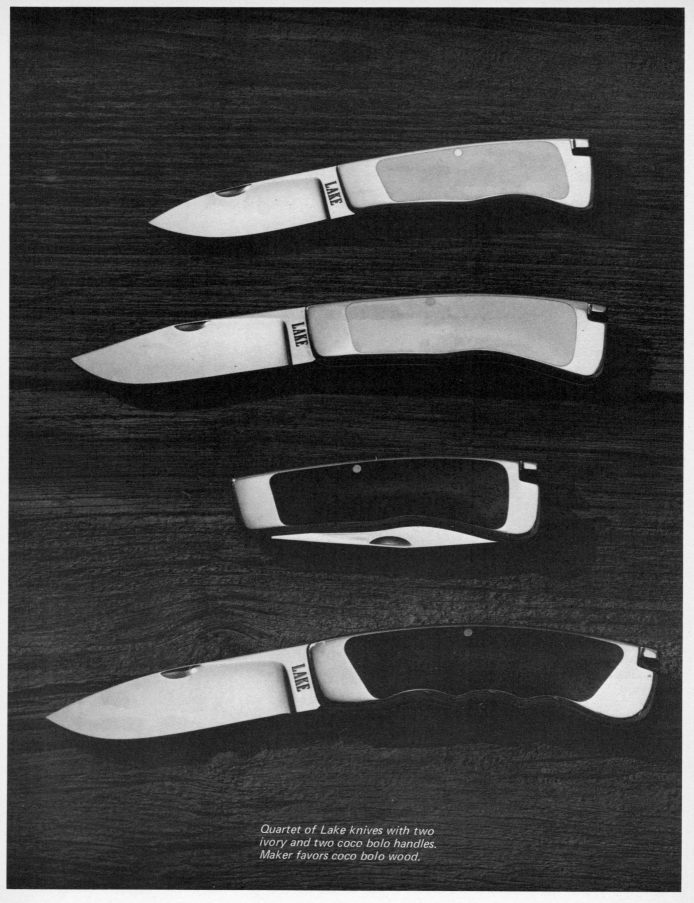

Quartet of Lake knives with two
ivory and two coco bolo handles.
Maker favors coco bolo wood.

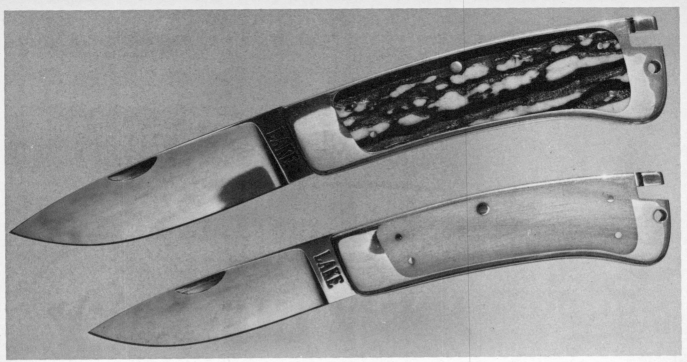

The two Lake knives above feature blades of 154-CM steel with frames of hard aluminum producing minimum weight. Top handle insert is India stag, other is Stone sheep.

seen a custom knife other than those I had made. I'd never met another knifemaker before. The room was crowded with makers and a coffee table was two-feet deep in knives.

"Loveless had praise for my folding knife and suggested I attempt to patent it. His comments gave me quite a boost. With a lot of effort, money and a patent attorney, I now hold a patent on my folding knife."

At present, Lake has settled on A2 for his blades, "I feel it is a good balance between edge-holding qualities and toughness. True, the steel will tarnish and rust even with five percent chrome, but so will a gun if it isn't cared for in a proper way," Lake explains.

"Although a few of the cutlers use the forging process and think highly of it," he says, "I feel just as strongly about the stock removal process. I feel the controlled rolling at the steel mill is the best way of aligning the grain structure and it cannot be surpassed by eyeballing the temperature and hammering the steel."

As intimated earlier, Lake has paid the price for success by teaching himself to make knives. Thus, he has scant sympathy for those who seek shortcuts.

"Not long ago a man from St. Louis called me," he recalls, "He said he was interested in making knives. He informed me he had a little shop experience, but no knowledge of knife construction and asked that I teach him to make knives.

"I explained that his request was one of many that I had received, and that I had a very busy schedule, so I would have to decline. He replied very sharply, 'How do you guild members expect people like me to learn how to make knives if you don't teach us?' With that remark he hung up. What can you say?"

If you'd like to learn more of this talented cutler, send $1 for Ron Lake's brochure to Lake Knives, 904 W. England, Dept. GW, Taylorville, Illinois 62568.

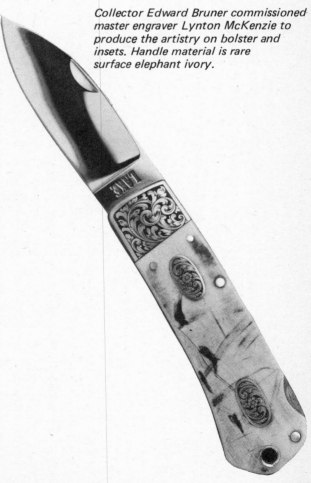

Collector Edward Bruner commissioned master engraver Lynton McKenzie to produce the artistry on bolster and insets. Handle material is rare surface elephant ivory.

The Custom Craftsmen:

JIMMY LILE:
The Arkansas Style

From Bowies To Folders Isn't As Long A Step As One Might Think!

JIMMY LILE has made knives for governors, generals, movie stars, a vice-president, senators, presidents and kings, but he takes great pride in the fact that the majority of his knives are sold to sportsmen.

When you walk into Lile's attractive shop located on Route 1, Russellville, Arkansas, it is impossible not to notice the many handsome knives featuring engraving, scrimshaw, inlays, carved ivory handles and other adornments. Many of these knives are either one-of-a-kind specimens or else pieces from limited editions. There are,

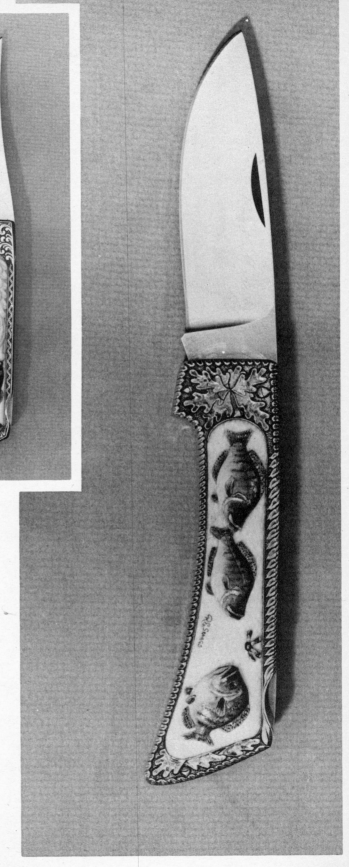

The folding knife, by custom maker Jimmy Lile, at right has handle slabs of elephant ivory, carved and scrimshawed into a work of art. The knife at far right is decorated by R.E. Skaggs.

however, a profusion of functional using knives made for the deer hunter who desires a handmade knife.

At the present time, Lile's output is about equally divided between fixed-blade models and folders, but he feels that the latter is rapidly gaining in popularity. "A few years ago I had very few calls for handmade folders," he reflects, "but today such models are among my best sellers." The personable Arkansan is particularly proud of his latest folding model which features a push-button release for his patented lock. Lile is planning to soon offer a smaller version and a choice of one or two-blade models in either size.

In 1970, it was Lile who was selected by Arkansas Senator John McClellan to build an elaborately engraved ivory-handled Bowie knife for Richard Nixon, then President.

Lile, born in 1933, has been making knives since he was 8 years old. "Those first knives," he remembers with a smile, "weren't bad for an 8-year-old knifemaker, but I doubt that they would stand up too well by today's standards."

Selling knives helped to pay Lile's way through college, where he met his wife Marilyn. After spending a few years teaching and coaching basketball, Lile decided he would go into the construction contracting business. Finally, in

Jimmy Lile and his wife have become familiar faces at knife shows in the
Arkansas-Oklahoma-Texas area. Maker feels such shows are boon to business.

Jimmy Lile's own words, "I went broke." That was in 1965, and for the next few years he worked a full workweek as a construction supervisor and made knives during his spare moments. The money that came in from knife sales went to pay off the debts he had incurred as a building contractor.

Finally, in 1969, Lile reached a turning point in his life — he became a full-time knifemaker. By that time he had made literally hundreds of knives and had established a wide-spread reputation as a first-class cutler.

It was about this time that we first met Lile, whom we found to be a large man, possessed of a keen sense of humor and a ready wit. He was one of the first professional cutlers who regularly made most, if not all, of the major gun and crafts shows throughout the South and Southwest.

It was and is rare to walk into a major show in this area and not see the beaming face of Jimmy Lile. He made friends virtually everywhere he went, and today it is difficult to locate a knife buff who does not remember Lile and look forward to seeing him again.

These days, Lile has to spend less time promoting. In fact, it is a facet of the business to which he wishes he could devote more time. Instead, he is constantly laboring to catch up with promised orders.

In his days of displaying, one observer noted that Lile might sell as many as twenty knives at a show, while makers with names far more famous were selling a half dozen or less, although the price range was roughly the same. The reason, when explained by Lile, sounds quite simple.

"I think the major reason why I sell more knives is that I

In addition to the lock-blade models, Lile also offers a profusion of nonlocking folders for the man or woman who wants to carry something different for everyday use. He believes in producing enough knives to satisfy customers.

Dedication of the Washington, Arkansas, Bowie knife museum (above) saw the gathering of Mrs. James Lile, author B.R. Hughes, Jimmy Lile, Bob Riley, Lt. Governor of Arkansas, and Kelly Bryant, Arkansas Secretary of State. Lower right, knifemaker Jimmy Lile at work on the replica of original James Black smithy at Washington, Arkansas.

have more knives to sell," is his explanation. "When I go to a show, I take selling knives, not samples. The other makers are selling orders, while I'm selling a knife that the buyer can put in his briefcase and take home with him. Most of the others sell a knife from a display sample, then the purchaser has to wait months to get what he's ordered.

"It seems to me that most people tend to buy knives on impulse. Then there's the pretty basic philosophy that, if a man pays a good price for a handmade knife, he wants to be able to take it home with him then to show his friends and let them admire it. It's pretty tough to show off an order receipt and not be able to say exactly when you're going to get the knife."

The first knives that Lile made were forged, and he continued to use this method until customers began to

request knives with sophisticated modern steels such as D2 or 440C. Since these steels do not lend themselves to forging, Lile used the stock removal process when working with such metals. He still, however, forges a few blades each year and is a member of the board of directors of the American Bladesmiths' Society.

Lile made his first folders around 1970, and since then such knives have been in great demand among both sportsmen and collectors alike. D2 is the standard blade material for folders, although other steels are available on special order.

In both his fixed-blade knives and the custom folders which he has introduced recently, the Arkansas craftsman tends to prefer steel, which he has heat-treated commercially to Rockwell 60-C. He notes that, if a customer wants a blade harder than that, it can be accomplished at an additional charge. This knifemaker, though, feels that 60-C is hard enough for any practical knife use.

Jimmy Lile isn't hard to deal with, though. He realizes that his customers have preferences. He also will make a blade of 440C steel, if that's what the paying customer says he wants. He is one of today's few knifemakers who will either forge or grind the blade, depending upon what his customer requests. The blades of his folding knives, however, are not forged.

In his fixed-blade knives, Jimmy Lile tends to favor stag, Osage orange, mesquite, purpleheart, rosewood, ironwood, micarta, ebony, walnut and several other woods, as well as tough leather washers for his handle materials. His own favorite in these versions is walnut, since he feels this particular wood is traditional for American cutlery, coming down from the factories of New York State where the workers migrated from England.

There is reason to feel that Jimmy Lile has a particular affection for the Bowie knife. In addition to the one made for President Nixon, he made some twenty-five others, listing them as the James Black Commemorative. He announced these in June 1971, at the formal dedication of a collection of contemporary Bowie knives at Washington, Arkansas, where Black is supposed to have made Jim Bowie's original model. Needless to say, these knives were gobbled up in a hurry by collectors. Less than a decade ago, the price for these was $250 each, considered a more than respectable sum in that era. Today, each of these knives is worth several times that amount among avid collectors.

When he first began making folding knives, Jimmy Lile tended to favor the Barlow pattern, using ivory for the handles, although mother-of-pearl is incorporated in some of his pen knives, which feature long bolsters.

As his expertise in folders developed, Jimmy Lile began to turn out what amounts to one-of-a-kind models, which have brought a great deal of interest, as well as numerous orders.

This is the small shop near Russellville, Arkansas, where Jimmy Lile makes and sells his custom knives. Although he enjoys a certain amount of business from his shop, most of Lile's customers deal through the mail or directly at knife shows.

He has developed a small folding hunter that is available with engraved metal handles, which are inlaid with ivory. Artworks are incorporated in some of the ivory insets, giving each of the knives an exclusive appearance.

In developing this approach to his work, Jimmy Lile has enlisted the help and talents of Ronnie Skaggs, an expert engraver and ivory carver, who introduces what amounts to a three-dimensional look to his ivory work.

Currently, Lile is assisted in his shop by Louie Evans and Gary Goree, while Sherry Goree works in the showroom. Frequently, during rush periods, such as the Christmas season, Evans and Gary Goree will put in eighteen-hour days.

Among Lile's more famous customers may be listed such names as Peter Fonda, Buddy Hackett, Hank Williams, Jr., Richard Nixon, Gerald Ford, Nelson Rockefeller, Senator Dale Bumpers and Governor David Pryor.

In late 1975, Lile, who was then a member of the board of directors of the Knifemakers Guild, was asked by the Guild to take over the presidency after Ted Dowell was forced, due to personal problems, to resign that post. At the Guild meeting in 1976 held in Dallas, Lile was formally elected president, and there is little doubt in anyone's mind that had he cared to accept the post, he could have been reelected in 1977. Instead, he decided to step down, although he continues to serve on the board. Several cutlers have said that they felt Lile served with great distinction

Lile tries out the Arkansas governor's chair while one of his fans, Governor David Pryor, stands at left. Lile has produced knives for presidents, many entertainers, senators, governors and knife fanciers the world over.

Using one of his hand-held files, Lile concentrates on the finishing touches to one of his fine blades.

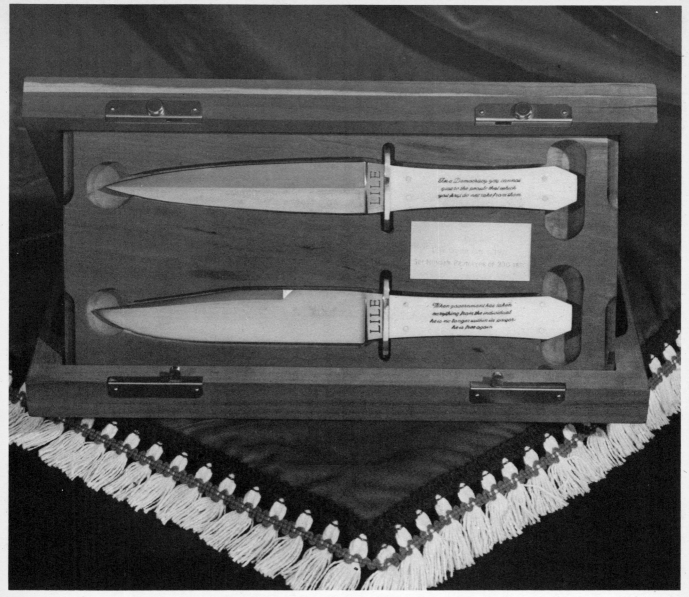

These limited edition sets of special Bicentennial Bowie knives certainly are not folders, but they do represent the meticulous work of Lile. The pair shown was the prototype for 200 similar sets made by the Arkansas Knifesmith.

and they credit him with eliminating to a large extent the internal bickering that had gone on between many Guild members in bygone years.

Our observation was that Lile served with dignity and used a great deal of wit and wisdom in his twenty-one months as president, and future presidents' tasks will be much easier due to the efforts of Lile.

At the Second Knife Expo held in Dallas in June 1977, we chatted with Lile and he expounded on some of his views concerning knives and knifemakers.

"I believe knifemaking as a profession is entering a plateau. The number of makers will decrease dramatically during the coming years. The makers who price their work reasonably, do a competent job and treat their customers with quality and respect will survive as makers, while those who do not will weed themselves out of the picture."

Lile then added, "I have seen the process begin during

my tenure as president of the Guild, and I have no reason to believe that this trend will change."

In the same vein, Lile indicated that he felt this situation would work to the mutual benefit of knife buyers and knifemakers alike.

In addition to currently serving on the boards of both the Knifemakers Guild and the American Bladesmiths' Society, Lile also can list a number of other honors, which include being an honorary life member of the Fort Smith, Arkansas, Gun Collectors Association; an honorary colonel in the Alabama State Militia; an honorary colonel in the Arkansas State Police; a life member of the Houston Gun Collectors Association; an honorary life member of the Dallas Arms Collectors Association; and many other achievements. In addition, he has been a life member of the National Rifle Association for more than twenty years.

Perhaps the best indication of a man's true character is

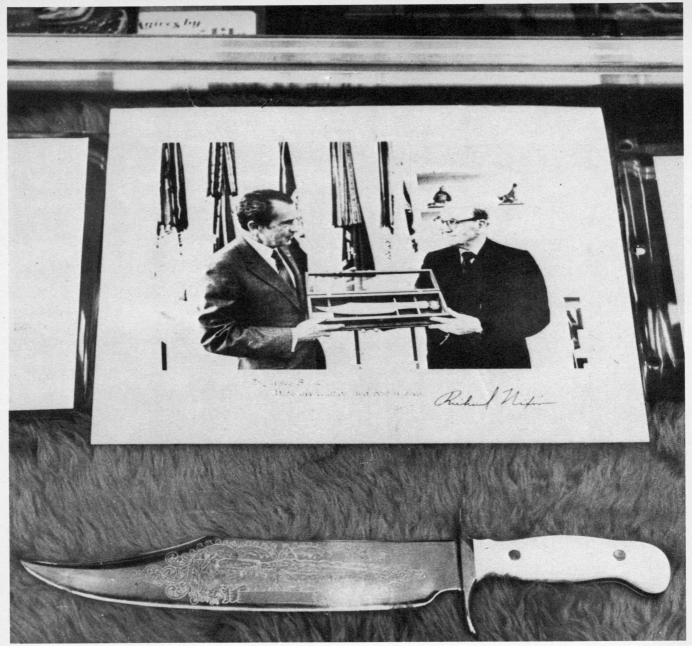

When he was President, Richard Nixon received a Lile Bowie knife similar to the one pictured above. Knife was presented by Arkansas Senator John McClellan in 1971. Duplicates of the Bowie are available to interested collectors.

what the home folks think about him. On February 14, 1973, Dale Bumpers, at that time governor of Arkansas and now a United States senator, proclaimed that day to be "Jimmy Lile Day." Here's the exact wording of the proclamation:

Whereas, Mr. Jimmy Lile, a lifelong resident of Arkansas, is known as "The Arkansas Knifesmith" because of his outstanding ability to hand make knives; and

Whereas, Mr. Lile has gained national recognition through his great skill and craftsmanship in producing the finest quality knives available; and

Whereas, Mr. Lile has brought nationwide recognition not only to himself but to the state of Arkansas by the

production of the Arkansas River Navigation Commemorative Bowie, which was presented to President Nixon; and

Whereas, the excellence of craftsmanship embodied in every Lile knife is unsurpassed anywhere; and

Whereas, Mr. Lile has become an Ambassador of Good Will for the state of Arkansas through his friendship with presidents, senators, congressmen and many other dignitaries; and

Whereas, Mr. Lile, working with his wife Marilyn, represents the American ideal of pride in workmanship;

Now, therefore, I, Dale Bumpers, governor of the state of Arkansas, do hereby proclaim Wednesday, February 14,

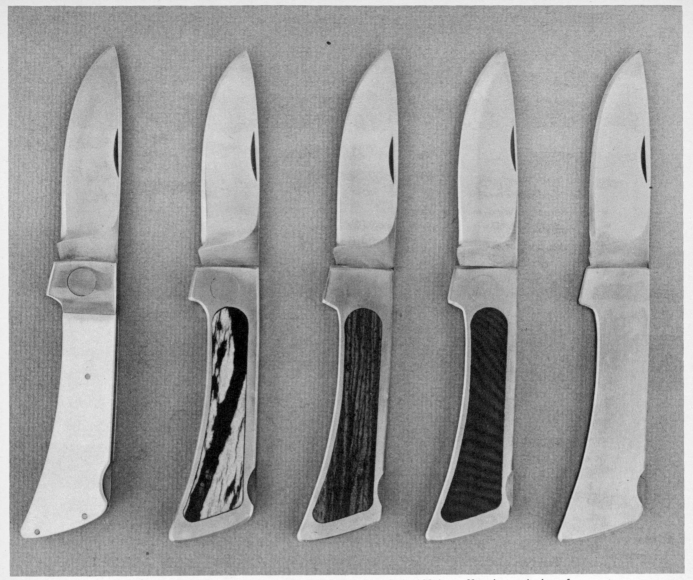

Examples of several of Lile's standard model folders, all with locking blades. Maker offers large choice of handle slab materials and those not of ivory or ebony may be obtained for about $100. Blades are hardened to RC-60.

as "Jimmy Lile Day" in Arkansas in recognition of the *outstanding contributions made to this state by Jimmy Lile and in commendation of his unsurpassed excellence in craftsmanship of the Lile knife."*

Now many knifemakers have been honored in various ways, but, insofar as is known, Lile is the first contemporary American cutler recognized by having a day designated in his honor by the governor of a state.

No question about it. Jimmy Lile is justifiably proud of the plaudits he has earned through his knives, but from talking with this man, it soon becomes evident that his greatest pride comes when a customer stops by his shop to tell him how well one of his knives performed in the field. It's gratifying to know that there are still men who make reasonably priced knives for hunting and carrying, as well as for affluent collectors.

Lile's folding knives may be as fancy as the customer wishes, including tasteful scroll engraving around the handle, scrimshaw work, inlay or special file decoration.

The Custom Craftsmen:

RON LITTLE:

The Acid Test

As A Game Biologist,

He Tests His Own Designs The Hard Way

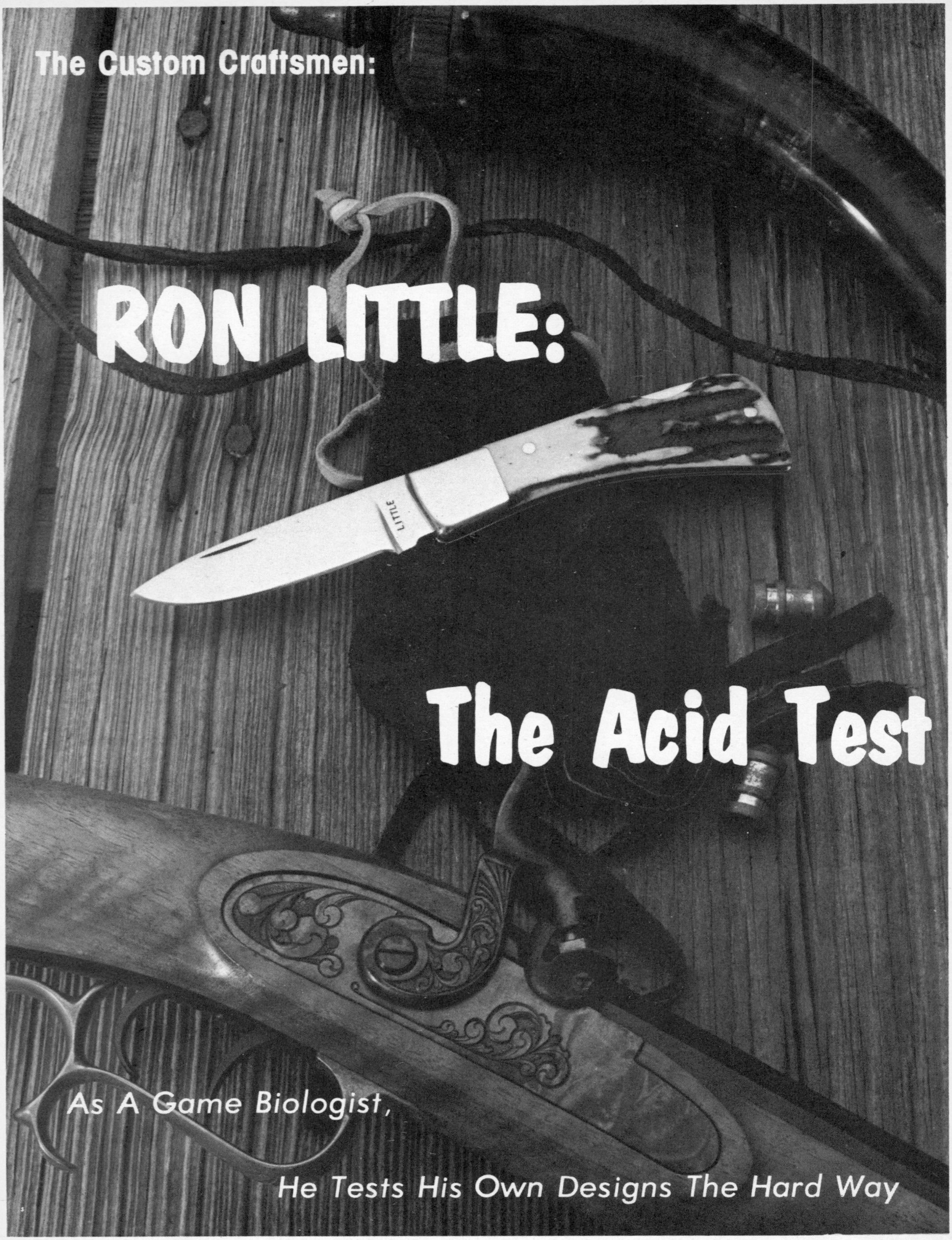

As we were going to press, the authors learned that Ron Little had succumbed to cancer. However, his artistry and craftsmanship will remain for future generations.

This comprises a sampling of the various folding hunting knives now being offered by Ron Little. This craftsman includes both lock blade and nonlockers in his production.

RON LITTLE FIRST came to our attention at the 1976 Knife Exposition held in Dallas.

There were some two hundred knifemakers at that show, give or take a dozen or so, and for a heretofore unknown's work to catch our attention required something special. Little's work was impressive.

Hughes immediately spotted a dropped point folder with the number 357 on it — Little puts a serial number on each of his knives and, obviously, this was his 357th folding model. Since Hughes' favorite Colt single-action revolver is chambered for the .357 caliber cartridge that, combined with the overall beautiful execution and design, was more than the knife scribe could take. He quickly struck a deal with the maker.

Commenting on his purchase after several weeks of use, Hughes mused, "There is more curvature to the handle and blade when the latter is opened on this particular knife than any of my others, but in use it works just fine."

Work it should. We hear a considerable amount about which maker has turned out the most knives, or which cutler has been at it the longest, but in all probability Ron Little has field dressed more big game than any other current maker.

A dedicated outdoorsman who loves hunting and fishing, Little has indeed dressed out his fair share of game that either his muzzleloader or his bow has taken.

"I quit using cartridge guns several years ago," he comments. "I have no argument with those who continue to use and enjoy such guns, but I simply wanted to put more challenge into my hunting." He makes an annual trek to Colorado for either mule deer or elk, but still refuses to use anything other than a front-loading rifle or his bow.

However, the vast amount of game that Ron Little has field dressed has little to do with those that he has dropped.

"While I was doing graduate study in wildlife biology at the University of Georgia, my particular area of specialization was the reproductive physiology of whitetail deer," recalls Little. "Thus, during Georgia's hunting season, I would make it a point to be on hand at the more-popular checking stations. Anytime a hunter would come to the station with a deer that hadn't been dressed out, I would volunteer to do it, no cost, no catches.

"It was," he remembers with a grin, "amazing how many takers I had on my offer. During an average day I would dress from forty to sixty deer. Several weeks of that gives a

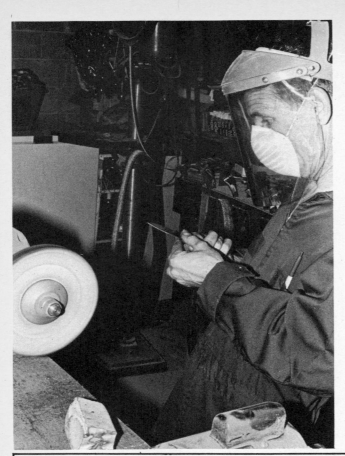

man more experience in dressing big game than a lifetime of actual hunting would."

It was through this experience at the checking stations that Little developed the style that his present knives exhibit: blades approximately three inches long with dropped points, some curve to the handles and a selection of handle materials. "I offer lock-blade and nonlocker types," Little states. "Actually, I can't really see a need for the blade lock, but a lot of folks like it, and I do want to satisfy my customers."

In these days of inflated prices, it is somehow refreshing to note Little's current list price — $60 — which is for a nonlocked blade folder with micarta or hardwood handle slabs. Stag, when available, costs $10 more. Should a lock blade be desired, this costs an additional $30.

Ron Little, born in 1933, in Toombs County, Georgia, "grew up hunting and fishing," to use his own words.

"I turned to making my own knives in 1969, while I was in graduate school. That was when I was working on those deer and I couldn't afford to purchase an expensive knife. I used a couple of cheap knives, but they didn't suit me, so I read an article about handmade knives and it mentioned George Herron of Aiken, South Carolina. That's not too far from my home. I drove up, purchased a blade from him and I've aggravated the life out of him since then," Little recalls with a laugh. "Really, George Herron has been a tremendous help to me, and I can honestly say that he has never failed to answer any of my questions."

That Herron knife proved to Little that a good handmade model was a definite improvement, but he began to

Top: Ron Little wears a face mask to protect himself from steel dust that is plentiful in any knife shop. Center: Except for the rosewood handle slabs, this knife is a duplicate of the one that caught Hughes' eye at the 1976 Knife Expo, held in Dallas, Texas. Right: Little puts the finishing touches on a stag-handled folder produced in his Georgia shop.

get some ideas of his own concerning blade shapes. In those days, he says, he couldn't afford another handmade model — even at $17.50 — and began to make his own.

"I started out using 01 steel, and I had them heat-treated by a commercial firm. Goodness only knows how many hours I had in a finished knife! Somewhere down the line I became interested in folding knives and now I offer only that type."

Ron Little now offers A2, D2 and 154CM for blade materials, although his personal preference is for A2. He feels that a three-inch blade will handle any normal outdoor chore that might confront the outdoorsman.

"If you need more knife than that," he feels, "you'll probably need a hatchet, which you should have in camp."

When asked why he thought a prospective buyer should consider one of his knives instead of the many others available, he pauses, then answers, "I don't really know, unless perhaps mine will feel better in your hand when you're using it. I try to do the best job of which I'm capable, and I never let eye appeal detract from the function of the knife."

The Little techniques vary only slightly from those used by other cutlers offering similar knives, except that the maker uses no jigs or patterns, even for the blades.

"It would be terribly boring to me to have to make the same knife over and over again," he told us. "Each of my knives is really a custom, one-of-a-kind item. It will vary a few hundredths of an inch from any other knife I have ever made, even though it may look identical. This may not work for other makers, but it seems to work for me."

In addition to attending the University of Georgia, Ron Little has received college credit from Georgia Tech and Valdosta State. He received his bachelor's degree from the latter institution. Little met his wife, Carrie, while stationed in South America in the U.S. Army.

Of the many trophies that he has collected hunting and fishing, he is proudest of a couple of fancy mule deer he took in Colorado using a bow.

As for his role as a game biologist, "Every day on a game-management check station is an experience," he relates, "but the most unusual thing that has happened to me to date is being called out to a house to identify a snake that was removed from an elderly lady's toilet. It turned out to be a blind seventy-inch black rat snake that had apparently entered her plumbing through a broken tile. Her husband grabbed the thing by the tail and had kept it in a box until we got there to identify it."

At the present time, Little's knife output is limited by his full-time job of wildlife biologist, but he has no desire to be a full-time cutler.

"I believe my present situation is ideal for me," he explains. "I love working with the wildlife department and I still can spend considerable time on weekends, holidays and during slack periods making knives. For me, this is the best of two worlds."

But it would appear that a lot of folks have taken a liking for this personable Georgian's knives. There is a waiting period of approximately eighteen months for a finished Little knife, and if his home state has a good deer season this Fall, that's likely to be extended quite a bit!

As evidenced by the variations in size, Little also produces smaller knives for either small-game dressing or for everyday pocket use. The middle knife is the one that the custom knifemaker favors for his own use.

The Custom Craftsmen:

HARVEY McBURNETTE:

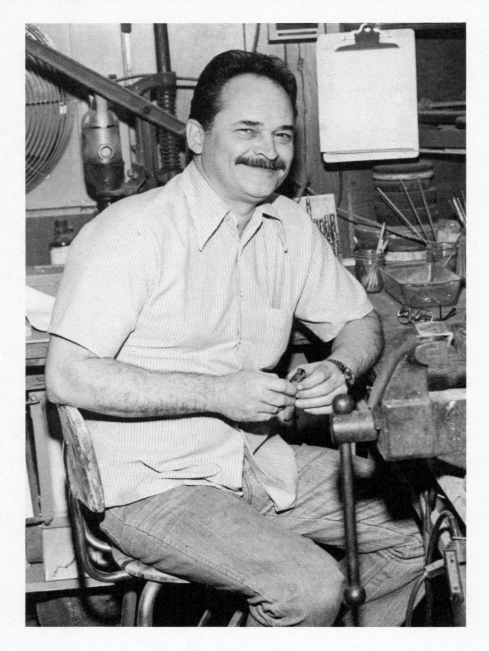

Born Of Boredom

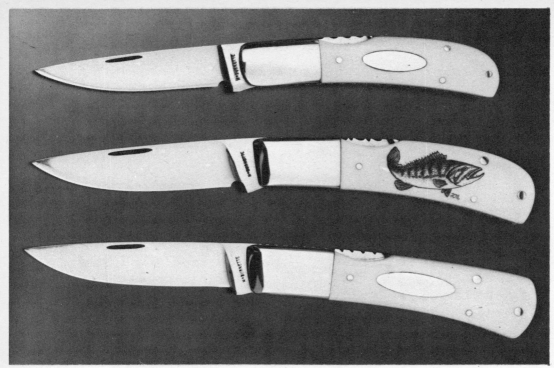

Three McBurnette front locking folders feature natural ivory handles.

He Began Making Knives To Pass The Time In Korea; Today, Time's His Most Precious Commodity!

SHORTLY AFTER the Korean conflict had ended, a young soldier in an ordnance outfit watched a buddy turn out a knife or two, and when the finished products were sold to other soldiers, this particular serviceman got interested to relieve the boredom.

When Harvey McBurnette recalls those days, he gets a twinkle in his eyes. "My friend was from Puerto Rico and when I expressed an interest in knifemaking, he showed me how it was done. The two of us spent a considerable amount of time making knives. I enjoyed it. I still do.

A fine example of McBurnette's engraving skills and blade file work on folder, it sells for $220.

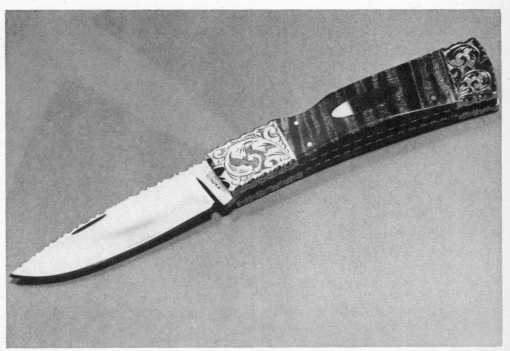

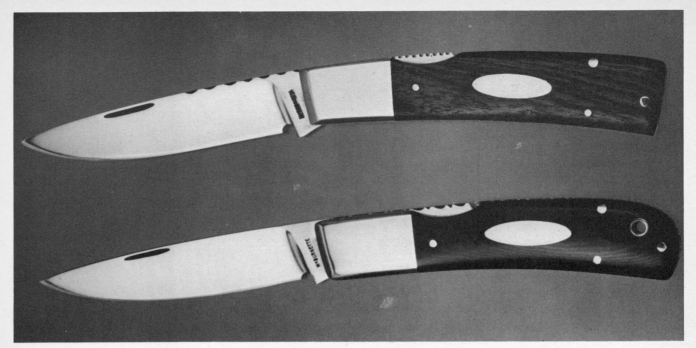

Front locking release system
is well illustrated by these two
knives. Top folder has rosewood
handle, micarta on lower model.

Two-bladed folder sports art
work on ivory handle slabs by
McBurnette. Maker found his
early drafting and painting
experience paid off on knives.

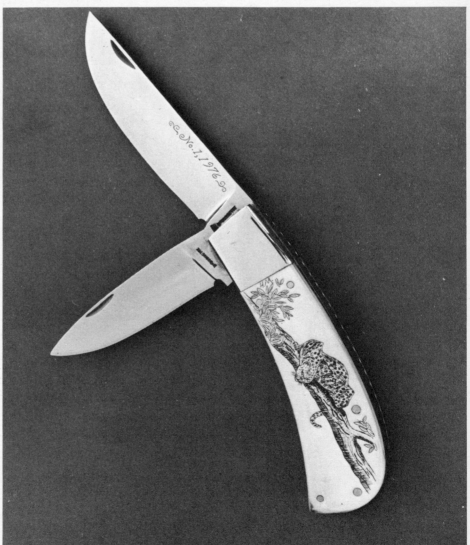

Three folders shown above are examples of fancy file work on springs, liners and bolsters.

McBurnette produced scrimshaw work on these medallions for his wife and daughter.

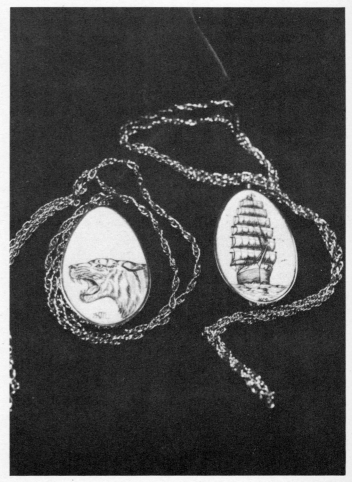

"We made blades from broken jeep springs. All of the knives I made in Korea were forged, since we had no heavy-duty grinders."

According to McBurnette, "It took us maybe five weeks to make one knife, and we would sell them for around $20 or so. I remember trading one of my knives to a Turkish officer for a bush hat. I was pleased that he wanted the knife, because the Turks seemed to appreciate knives more than most people. They used mostly large knives, and some of them were pretty fancy. Most of them were handmade and I seldom saw two that were alike."

That is how Harvey McBurnette got into knifemaking, but there were several sidetracks along the way. Born in 1935 in Lakeland, Florida, he was raised in the rural reaches of Florida, Georgia, Alabama and Tennessee.

"When I was maybe 7 or 8," he recalls, "I used to watch an old man carve sailing ships. That was the first time, as far as I know, that I had ever seen anything made by hand. It fascinated me, so I made myself a boat. Then I carved airplanes, guns and swords. I also spent a lot of time drawing. I'd use anything from notebook paper to boxes. My favorite subjects were cars. I really can't remember when I didn't like to draw."

Raised primarily by aunts, uncles and grandparents, this southerner entered the Army at the age of 18 and served first with the 11th Airborne Division, then with the 702nd. After his discharge, McBurnette entered the Alabama School of Trades where he studied architectural drafting. It was during this period that he first began to paint with oils.

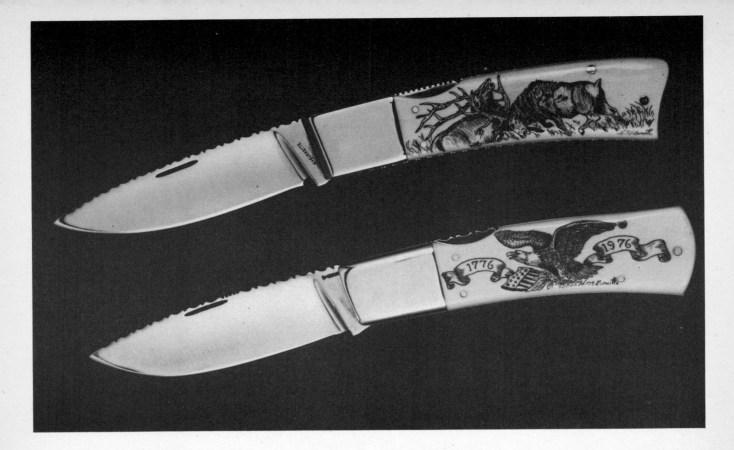

Folding knives with engraving and scrimshaw work on handles have drawn attention at knife shows. McBurnette became full-time knifemaker in 1976.

Following graduation, he went to work at a local steel mill, serving as a maintenance man on freight cars used in the plant.

"My drafting education didn't seem to be of much help in this field," McBurnette adds, "but then my next job, working for a tire manufacturing firm, didn't employ my drafting talents to any greater extent either."

During these years, he continued to paint, but never could completely forget those knives he had made in Korea. So he began to make a few knives, giving most of them to friends. Gradually, he remembers, he began to do more knifemaking than painting, all in his off-the-job spare moments.

His first knife shop was in what McBurnette terms a "mud room." It seems that this is a room in a farmhouse near an outside door where the dirt from the fields could be washed off before entering the house. "That six-by-eight room housed a grinder, band saw, polishing wheels, drill press and numerous other tools. It was, to say the least, crowded."

Obviously, more space was needed, so the craftsman built a shop near his home. By this time → early 1973 — McBurnette was selling quite a few knives and he ventured to Kansas City for the annual meeting of the Knifemakers Guild.

"That was my first knife show," he recalls, "and that is where I saw what I had to do if I hoped to compete in the custom knife market. I sold enough knives to pay expenses, but that was all.

"At that time I was making only fixed-blade hunting knives, and from there, I went to Bowies and collector-type knives. Next, I learned how to acid etch and, later, how to scrimshaw. My interest in art and my training in drafting finally paid off for me.

"I still hadn't made a folding knife, however, and I started giving it a lot of thought. I opened and closed it a hundred times! Next I took it apart, then put it back

together. Finally, I decided I'd give it a try. To be honest, I was pleased with my first attempt. I made a few mistakes and a few miscalculations, but all in all it came out pretty good.

"The one thing that I did discover is that there is virtually no comparison in making a fixed-blade knife and a folder. I learned more about folders from the first one I made than from any other knife I have ever produced, but I also learn something every time I make a folder. Each one seems to have its own personality and I have to work with it until I get it like I think it should be."

McBurnette's folders were first put on exhibition at the 1975 guild show and they went over like pretzels at a beer party!

"Since then," he explains, "I have specialized in folding knives, and at least ninety-eight percent of my current production is for this type of knife."

All of those orders taken at Kansas City, however, meant that McBurnette had a decision to make.

"My regular job and my knifemaking were combining to make an eighteen-hour working day, seven days a week. It was obvious that I either had to give up knifemaking or my job."

History will record that in January 1976, Harvey McBurnette became a full-time knifemaker. At the '76 Knife Expo in Dallas, he had a tremendous show, selling most of what he had brought and taking orders for many more folders.

Although McBurnette does have a handsome brochure, he prefers to work to the customer's specifications. He still does all of his own decorative work, and he has a concept with which we tend to agree:

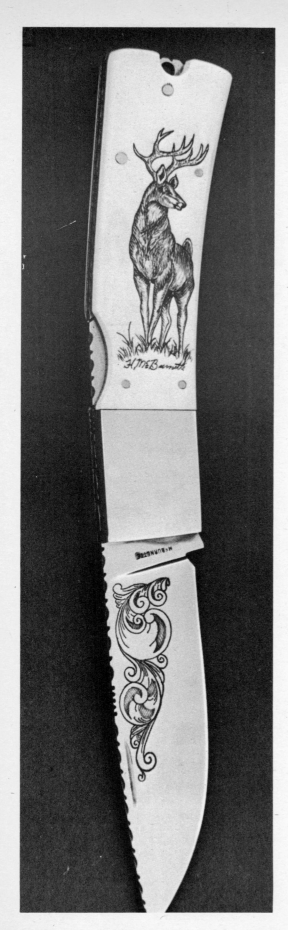

"A folding knife should be opened and closed easily. I've seen some custom folders that you had to have a screwdriver to open! This is poor engineering, and a knife simply should not be sent to a customer in this condition."

A footnote to this comment is in order. At the '76 Dallas Expo, we personally opened perhaps a dozen different McBurnette folders. Each opened and closed as if the blades were mounted on ball bearings.

Harvey McBurnette makes no claims for his steel being any better than that used by other makers. "I've used various types, but I believe that D2 equals anything that I have tried. I keep my D2 blades around the 59 level on the Rockwell C scale and my springs, also made from D2, are tempered to Rockwell C 52. The only lock blades I offer are those with a front lock, which permits the user to close the knife easily with one hand."

When it comes to handle materials, McBurnette will use just about anything desired by the purchaser. His list of materials include stag, elk horn, ivory, whale rib, African blackwood, ebony, cocobolo, rosewood and linen micarta.

"My own favorite," he confesses, "is African blackwood, but the toughest and most durable material I have found to date is micarta. I cannot guarantee natural handle materials against checking or cracking due to various climates and the conditions to which they are exposed. I do, however, guarantee that when the knife is received, there will be no blemishes. Whatever the handle material does after that time is beyond my control."

The base price for a McBurnette folder, at this writing, is $90, with the lock-blade models beginning at $125. If you desire file work, you can add $10 to $15, depending upon the amount of decoration. Some handle materials, such as stag, are extra-cost items. The costs of engraving, scrimshaw and etching depend for the most part upon subject matter and coverage.

"I'm sure," the knifemaker told us, "that there are less-expensive knives on the market, and there also are more-expensive knives available. I simply price my knives in line with the amount of time and cost of materials involved. Hopefully, this will allow me to stay in business and not go bankrupt."

At the present time, a prospective McBurnette customer should be prepared to wait approximately eight months for delivery. "I operate a one-man shop," states McBurnette. "Consequently, I take sole credit or sole blame for every knife that I make. I suspect that the majority of my knives go into collections, but I make them to be used. All knives are made to be used. Even if it is an engraved collector's special-order Bowie, I heat-treat and temper it as painstakingly as I can. Next week or one hundred years from now somebody might have to use it."

McBurnette enjoys deer hunting and bass fishing, but the increasing demand for his knives leaves him little time for his hobbies.

"I don't like another person being in my shop when I work, because I find I cannot concentrate on my knifemaking, but when I'm fishing, absolutely no disturbances of any type will be permitted!"

In coming years, Harvey McBurnette may have even less time for fishing and hunting. He is eight months behind in filling orders as these lines are written. A few months hence, he will probably be two years behind. The demand is overtaking his one inexpandable commodity — time.

The Custom Craftsmen:

BILL MORAN:
Damascus Midwife

This Artisan Figured In The Rebirth Of The Ancient Art Of

Knifemaking From Layered Steel

An historic moment in modern knifemaking circles came at the 1972 meeting of the Knifemakers Guild in Kansas City, when Bill Moran (left) was elected to the post of secretary — now the presidency — succeeding Bob Loveless (right).

THERE IS MUCH discussion among knife buffs as to who is the greatest American cutler at this particular time.

A maker is, if you will recall the definitions from Chapter Seven, a cutler who uses the stock-removal procedure to shape his blades, as opposed to forging.

It would be virtually impossible as well as pointless to list the names of those generally nominated for top maker. Strange to say, however, there is no argument, only general agreement, as to who is America's greatest smith. His name is William F. Moran, Jr.

It may be argued that he is the greatest smith in the history of the forged blade. There is little that can be said to offset such a claim. If ever a man was the absolute, ultimate master of the forge, that man is Bill Moran.

Born at Gayfield Farm, Line Kiln, Maryland, in 1925, Bill Moran began making his first knives at the unlikely age of 10, using the blacksmith shop on his father's dairy farm, located near the Monocacy River.

"I suppose the reason that I started making my own knives was that I had always been possessed of a fascination with steel," Moran says. "History always has fascinated me and I was interested in medieval blades. Naturally, I didn't spend all of my spare time trying to make knives. Like all farm boys, I did a great deal of hunting, canoeing and horseback riding. A hunting knife was an important item to a lad who enjoyed the outdoors, but those early knives were pretty crude."

Although Moran sought assistance, he says, "At that time there was no way that you could obtain information on how to hand-forge blades. I talked to every blacksmith I could find, and today I realize that the men with whom I talked didn't really know anything about bladesmithing. After I had made knives for a few years, people began to contact me. They wanted to buy my knives. It seems that even at that early stage I had learned, mostly by trial and error, how to make a blade that would hold an edge better than most of the commercial knives then available. The demand was small at first, but as the years went by I began making more and more knives. By the time I was 20, I realized that I either had to give up farming or knifemaking. So I became a full-time knifemaker."

At that time — about 1945 — the only full-time cutlers in America were Bill Scagel, Bo Randall and Moran.

The demand for handcrafted knives was relatively small in those early days — early from the standpoint of modern knifemaking — but gradually more and more orders poured into Moran's one-man shop. His reputation grew, until the words "a Moran knife" became a hallmark of excellence among those who appreciated the finest.

What was there about these knives that eventually led to the longest waiting period in American knifemaking history? For the record, a person ordering a Moran knife today is not asked to put up a deposit, nor are deposits accepted, even if offered; but a customer should be prepared to wait from five to seven years for a finished knife. That is not an inflated figure. It is the honest estimate of an honest man who has no desire to mislead his clients. Not so long ago, Moran told us, "I really don't know what to do. If conditions do not change, I will soon have a lifetime back-log of orders, but I refuse to attempt to speed up my procedures or to add hired hands to do my work for me."

Moran uses the same basic principles in making his knives that were employed in the making of fine blades hundreds of years ago. Here, essentially, is how this smith achieves his works of art:

First, a piece of steel is cut from a bar, then is forged to shape. "Great care must be taken not to overheat the steel," comments Moran. "Also, great care is taken not to hammer the steel when it is too cool. The forging heat must be exactly right, neither too hot nor too cold. I use a technique known as hammer hardening or packing. This is an important step that, unfortunately, is understood by few people.

"After the blade is forged almost to the finished shape, the steel is then hammered at a rather low heat with rapid, light blows. This causes the grain to be better aligned and the steel to be far more compact."

After the blade has been forged to shape, it is ground close to the completed size. In Moran's case, all grinding is done freehand. The blade then is heat-treated in the forge.

"This is done in such a manner that the edge will be much harder than the back," explains the Maryland smith.

"The temper can be varied to suit the intended use of the knife. All of my regular steel blades are triple drawn, which gives much the same result as super chilling, and this adds greatly to the quality of the finished blade."

Following tempering, the blade is ground carefully to its final dimensions, with great care exercised not to overheat the metal. Moran then puts the blade through six polishing operations, with the result being a blade that is genuinely mirror-finished. For the handle, the customer may choose from a selection of various hardwoods, stag or ivory.

Moran uses only natural materials for handles and says, "I feel that to use plastics of any kind would be like buying a handmade English shotgun with a plastic stock. Somehow, the two simply do not go together."

For a considerable period of time Moran was the only American cutler to offer classic European-type blades. "For many years it was quite a rare thing that I would sell one," he remembers. "Everyone wanted either a hunting knife or a Bowie. Of course, during the Korean War there was quite a demand for combat models, and after the movie *The Iron Mistress* came out, about the only thing I made for some time were Bowies. I believe I made the first brass-bound tangs that were offered in this country, at least in modern times. As a matter of fact, I was using this method of binding slab-type handle tangs around twenty-five years ago."

It was the reintroduction of Damascus steel that gave Moran his greatest satisfaction. "I think this really gave me

This is a standard steel folding knife with bolsters of silver and a handle of ivory made by Moran in his shop. Moran has long been recognized as a top craftsman at the forge; this was made before he began Damascus work.

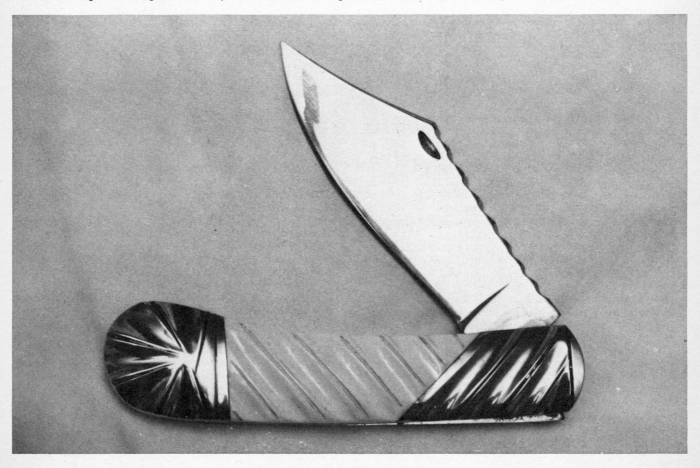

This close-up of a fixed-blade Moran knife fashioned from Damascus steel illustrates his mastery of metal.

the most pleasure of anything I have ever done. I certainly felt more sense of achievement from that than everything else put together!"

Moran introduced Damascus steel blades at the 1973 Knifemakers Guild meeting in Kansas City. Since then, the vast majority of orders that he has received have been for Damascus-bladed knives.

"In all of the years that I have been interested in knives, I have had the opportunity of looking over some of the finest collections in the United States. During the years that I have studied early American knives I never had seen a Damascus-bladed knife that was made in this country. Of course, I have seen Damascus blades from the area of the Saracen Empire and Northern India, but when I first started to work out this process I didn't have the vaguest idea whether there were five layers or five thousand layers. I didn't really know where to start, so I began welding blades with various numbers of layers, from sixteen to over two thousand, and I soon came to the conclusion that somewhere around five hundred was the best number. Such blades closely resembled the originals I'd studied."

A finished Damascus blade, in addition to being most attractive, has a number of excellent qualities. Such blades are extremely flexible, hold an edge in a pleasing fashion and are easy to sharpen. They also are extremely time-consuming to make, and Moran easily can have three to four weeks of work in a completed Damascus-bladed knife. Today, at least five American smiths offer Damascus blades, but Moran blazed the trail for the others.

Bill Moran is adamant in his contention that any properly forged blade is superior to any style of steel currently available. "Today we hear a great deal about new and super steels. In over the thirty years that I have been engaged in knifemaking, I have tried most of the available steels in search of a superior material. It is true that the corrosive-resistant steels of today are far superior to the old stainless steels, but most people do not realize that these steels were designed to hold their hardness at a high degree of heat. This is unnecessary in a knife. Most of the high-alloy steels have twelve to eighteen percent chrome. This is a definite drawback to good edge-holding qualities. Such steels do have some advantages, such as being corrosion resistant, and this can be important to some people.

"I maintain that any steel manufacturer will tell you not

remember that someday you are going to have to sharpen that blade. The high-alloy steels are exceptionally difficult to sharpen, particularly when they are real hard.

"If I ever find a better steel, or better methods of making blades, I will use them, as my interest is in making the finest possible blades. This is more important to me than payment for the knives that I make."

Moran makes a statement in his current brochure that is unique. He poses the question, "Is an expensive handmade knife necessary?" Then answers his question in this manner: "Surprisingly enough, my answer is no. You do not need a fine handmade knife any more than you need a fine handmade shotgun, fly rod or a custom-built car. To skin a deer or other animal, you can buy a commercial knife for a few dollars at the local hardware or sporting goods store that will get the job done.

"The fine handmade knife is bought for two reasons. First, the owner takes great pride in the ownership of a knife of superior quality, workmanship and beauty. For

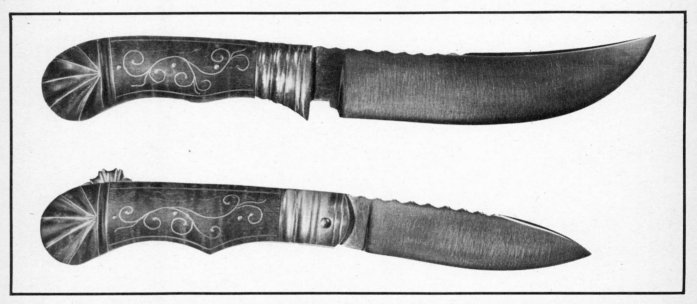

A matched set of Moran-made knives include a fixed-blade style at top, with the similarly designed folder beneath. A technician at more than simply making blades, this East Coast craftsman also did the intricate inlay work.

to use the complex high-alloy steels unless you need tools that allow you to cut under high heat or similar conditions. For most tools and especially knife blades, you should stick to the high-grade carbon steels. I have found, after thirty years of experimentation, that the steel with the best all-around qualities for a blade is in the straight-carbon range. The high-alloy steels have far more drawbacks than advantages.

"The type steel I generally use is high-carbon vanadium. We must remember that the finest blades the world has ever seen were developed hundreds of years ago at a time when one's life depended upon his blades. I have tried to follow the methods and techniques used by the ancient smiths. These methods have worked out quite well for me. In all the years that I have been making knives, I have never had one returned with a broken blade.

"Don't be mislead by the extremely high Rockwell blades. This is comparable to the adage: If a little bit is good, a lot is better. A knife should be tempered to usable hardness. I feel that Rockwell C58 to 60 is the best. Also,

example, I really enjoy fly fishing, however, using a fine handmade rod gives me as much pleasure as the actual fishing itself. Second, is that a few knifemakers are offering knives that are truly art blades. True art blades were not made for quite some time. Once again today a few of us are offering blades that are being bought by art collectors."

If, by this time, you are getting the idea that Bill Moran is a talented, well-spoken, industrious man who is quite capable of doing his own thinking, you are definitely on the right track!

For example, Moran is chairman of the American Blade-smith Society; a past secretary — the title would be president today — of the Knifemakers Guild; he wrote a chapter on Damascus blades for the book, "Collecting Edged Weapons of the Third Reich"; he is a past vice-president of the Frederick County Chamber of Commerce; and he is a staunch conservative.

In the August 21, 1970 *Congressional Record,* Senator C.M. Mathias stated, "Mr. Moran embodies all the qualities of the free enterprise system, of which he is a strong advocate. He is the type of man Thomas Jefferson would have called the 'salt of the earth.' He is a businessman, individualist, patriot, but above all, a master craftsman."

"I can't imagine why he said the kind things about me that he did," muses the object of those glowing remarks. "I supported everyone who ever ran against him."

While Moran's folding knives have not received the recognition that his Bowies and hunting models have attracted, it would be a safe statement to say that no other contemporary maker or smith offers folders with the instant resell value of a Moran folder. One of his all-out creations with a Damascus blade and bolsters, and handle slabs of ivory and silver will currently cost well over $1500 purchased directly from Moran. Bought from a third party the tag on this knife would probably be $2000 to $2500!

Moran moved to Braddock Heights, Maryland, in 1960, where he lives today. Frequently, he is approached by historical societies to present seminars on the art of the smith, and he is generous with his time. Certainly no living person is better qualified to speak on this subject.

An average day will find Bill Moran in his shop for at least eight hours, working with patience, skill and dedication, attempting to make his next masterpiece just a bit better than his last effort. As mentioned earlier, he still makes every part of every knife that bears his name in his small shop, and he made most of the tools that he uses.

Bill Moran has worked his way to the pinnacle of his profession, and it is a rare tribute that no one even challenges him for this lofty honor.

He is the master of the forge.

This type of work would be considered impossible by some, but Bill Moran managed to build a folder around a piece of crown stag. He designed the knife so that it was built around the horn rather than shaping material to fit.

Moran (left) discusses his techniques with others of the Knifemakers Guild: Clyde Fischer, Chubby Hueske, Bob Loveless and Bernard Sparks during annual meeting.

The Custom Craftsmen:
ROBERT OGG:
The Usin' Maker

This Custom Cutler Concentrates On Knives
People Can Afford To Use

SOME CUTLERS HAVE made reputations for themselves by offering one-of-a-kind collectors' items, others by catering almost entirely to that type of clientele generally described as the carriage trade. A few, however, have made it by applying themselves to supplying handmade knives for those folks who desire usin' cutlery.

Robert G. Ogg is one of the last group. This should not be construed to mean that his knives are crude or rough. On the contrary, they are slick and well made, but Ogg always has made every possible effort to keep his prices as low as possible and still turn a profit. He subscribes to the theory that knives are primarily cutting instruments, and his cut well indeed.

We first bumped into Ogg at a gun show in Houston in 1970 or thereabouts. At that time, he was selling his folding knives for approximately $30, and there were no more than perhaps five or six men turning out handcrafted folders in those days. Ogg may be considered one of the real pioneers of the current custom-folder rage.

Born in 1922, in Fort Worth, Texas, his family moved

and serial number to report for shore duty in San Diego. After the war, he signed up with the Air Force and retired in April 1963 as a master sergeant.

While in the Navy, Bob Ogg married a WAVE radio operator. "The shore station to which I was exiled was manned by about sixty-five percent WAVE's," he recalls, "and the rest were South Pacific ruffians and survivors such as myself."

After military retirement, he returned to Arkansas and went to work in a gear factory running a lathe. Over a period of time he became first an inspector, then quality control officer. It was during the latter period that he began to think about knives again.

At first, Ogg used old files and saw blades for materials, then gave away the results. "It is an interesting observation on human nature that when you give someone something and he is unable to reciprocate, pretty soon he begins to resent you. Consequently, I began charging from two to four dollars each for my knives, with much happier results."

 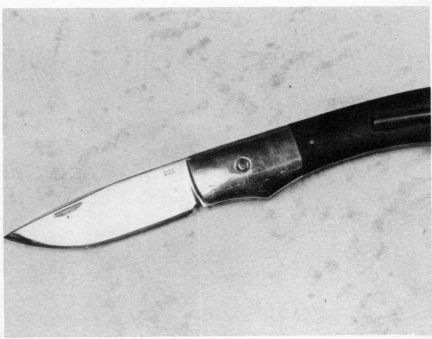

Left (above): If one is looking for a small, compact knife for everyday carrying, this Ogg creation, which is compared to a pack of cigarettes for size, may be just what you want. Right: Ogg's Corporal George model, with a metal match inlaid in the hardwood handle is priced at about $85, in keeping with the maker's price structure.

among such oil field towns as Okmulgee, Wewoka, Seminole and Bowlegs. It was around those oil fields that Ogg, a mere youngster, first became interested in knives.

"I would take those huge spikes they used on the rigs, heat 'em, and flatten 'em out with a hammer. A very crude forging job to be sure," he recalls, adding, "Fortunately, to the best of my knowledge, there are no remaining Ogg knives from this period."

Bob Ogg finished high school in Creston, Iowa, and after his father died in 1939, he and his mother moved to Paris, Arkansas, where Ogg lives today.

"I entered the Navy in October 1940, and after completing radio school, I was assigned to a seagoing tug. We were at Pago Pago, Samoa, when the Japanese hit Pearl Harbor. For the next three years we towed barges all over the South Pacific." Whenever Ogg was offered an opportunity to return to the States, he would pass up the chance, but in December 1944, he was issued orders by name, rank

Those early knives were table and kitchen models for the most part, but sometime around 1967, a man came to Ogg with a broken spring in his pocketknife. "I accepted the job as a challenge and experienced no trouble in making a new spring. Then an idea hit me: Why not start a folding knife from scratch?"

Putting thought to action, Ogg did just that. "I built one and it wasn't much, but it looked like a knife and acted like a knife. Right then and there I decided I was going to have to find something better than hacksaw blades. I spoke to a steel salesman and acquired a batch of 1095 steel. Later, I used 440C and 01. I read everything I could find concerning metallurgy and heat-treating, and I purchased a small electric furnace. With practice, I discovered that heat-treating is about as much art as science. The Japanese sword makers have known this for 2000 years! I get sick when those so-called experts bad-mouth 1095 steel. I use it as my standard blade material, and thus far I have had no complaints — only praise."

Ogg's techniques differ somewhat from those employed by most folding knifemakers. As Ogg himself puts it, "I developed them myself."

Beginning with a 1/8x1½x4½-inch steel blank, he cuts it into two pieces using a cutoff wheel. One piece will become the spring and the other the blade. Ogg then rough-grinds these into shape on a grinding wheel, taking care to see that the heat-treated and tempered spring does not lose its temper. "It doesn't matter so much about the blade," he told us, "because it will be reheat-treated later." He then employs a belt sander to place the bevel on the blade. Next, the blade undergoes additional work on a series of felt wheels with progressively finer grits.

Ogg then turns his attention again to the spring, which is worked to final dimensions and polished. Holes are drilled through the spring and liners, which previously have been cut to size and shape. The spring and liners then are riveted once in the butt area. Now a hole is drilled through the blade and liners.

"I then set the spring in position to create a little tension, clamp and drill through the liners and spring, fit a temporary pin and a main pivot pin. Next comes fitting and buffing to achieve a perfect fit so that the liners, spring and blade are flush in both open and closed positions.

"The bolsters are silver soldered on, sanded down flush with the liners, riveted and further shaped. A permanent rivet is then placed in the tension hole and sanded flat. Handles are fitted and bedded in epoxy and clamped to cure overnight. When cured, the handles are sanded and shaped. Holes are drilled and tapped, two on each handle, and are fitted with optical screws. The blade is annealed, stamped with name and serial number, and heat-treated.

"After this, the blade is reworked on my sander using 220 grit, 400 grit and 500 grit on felt wheels. I then change to a cloth wheel charged with polishing compound for a final mirror polish and the blade is installed using a stainless-steel pivot pin. Afterwards, the entire knife undergoes a final polishing."

When asked for a philosophy of knifemaking, Ogg pondered, then replied, "I want to make my knives as strong as possible, make them as well as I know how and without decoration. Let others do the scrimshaw, etching and engraving. They have their own fields of expertise, and more power to them.

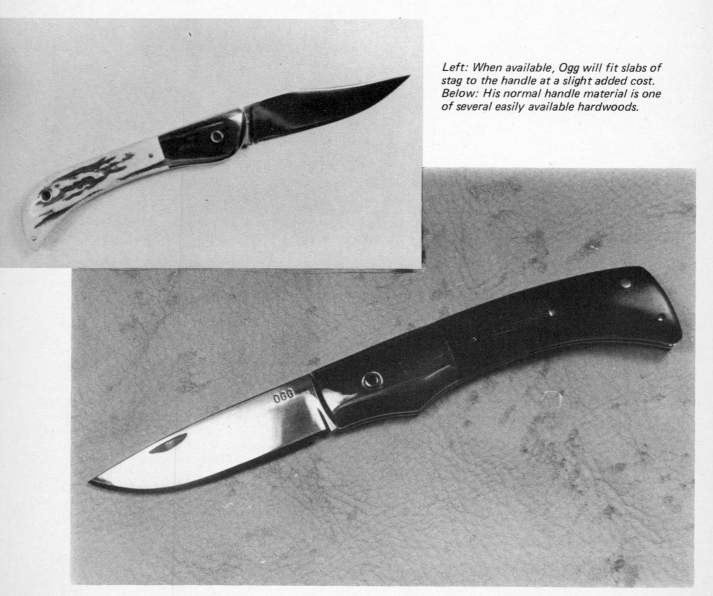

Left: When available, Ogg will fit slabs of stag to the handle at a slight added cost. Below: His normal handle material is one of several easily available hardwoods.

"Whenever a person gets ready to buy a handmade knife, he should select whatever pleases him most, subject to price and availability."

Ogg's current brochure lists only a few models with prices beginning at $70 which includes nickel-silver bolsters and a blade 3¼-inch in length or less, and micarta handle slabs. He also lists a number of options, including longer blades, ivory handles ("not guaranteed against cracking or shrinking"), 01 steel ("frankly, not worth the difference"), and a variety of hardwood handle materials.

When Ogg puts in an appearance at a gun or knife show, it is most unusual for him to have any knives to sell after the first day. Apparently, the Ogg combination of low prices and good quality are just what many folks are searching for today.

Orders will be handled as they are received, as Ogg is currently some eighteen months behind, with no prospects of a shorter delivery period in sight.

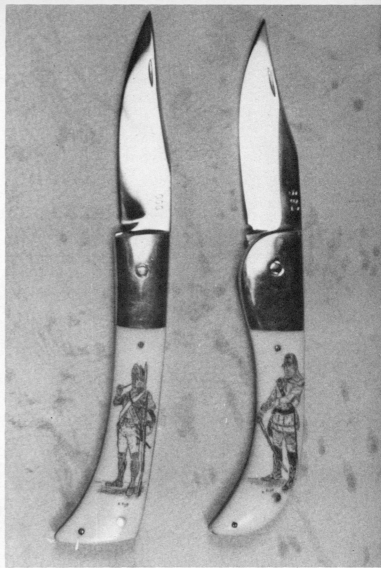

Although Bob Ogg does no decorative work himself, he has no objection if a customer decides to take it upon himself to beautify some of his work. This scrimshaw was done by Richard Frye. Left: Paris, Arkansas, has been Ogg's home for years and it is here he has his shop.

The Custom Craftsmen:

FRED SMITH:

Whose Simple Designs Draw Buyers

FRED L. SMITH of Fair Oaks, California, has a rather common name but produces some uncommon folding knives. He is a man who strives for perfection at whatever he does.

Smith specializes in custom folders and has traveled thousands of miles and devoted hundreds of hours to reach a level of craftsmanship of which he can be proud.

"I've been to a good many custom knife shows around the country and there are some absolutely beautiful examples of seemingly perfect handmade knives being displayed by a number of top-rate makers. I doubt if you could find a flaw in their workmanship. Given the present level of technological development, I don't see how there is much room left for improvement," says the outspoken Smith.

Smith's own knives seem to be examples of what he is

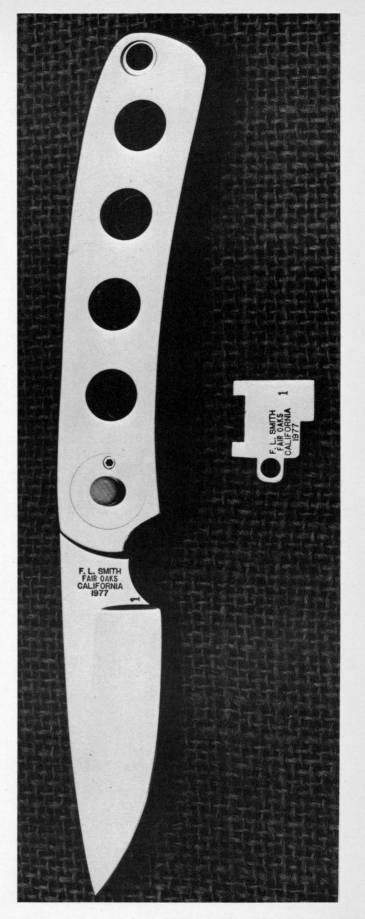

talking about. It would be difficult for the naked eye to detect any flaw in construction, grinding or finish of his knives. He uses what he believes to be the very best materials available, and uses them to their utmost. Perhaps, opines Smith, the only thing left is to work faster and harder to satisfy the demand from collectors and users of the custom makers' output.

Lest we chalk up the previous statements to a brash, impulsive or egotistical young man, perhaps a look at Fred Smith the knifemaker is in order.

The term dynamic personality has been overworked but it would certainly seem to fit Smith. He attacks everything with a gusto that in itself seems to hurdle any obstacles. He is as enthusiastic about his knifemaking as he is about his skin diving, shooting, muzzleloading, gun collecting or his family obligations.

In fact, it was Smith's long-time interest in shooting and gun collecting that led him into knives and knifemaking. Custom knives began to show up at more and more gun collectors shows that Smith and his associates attended, and he was quick to realize the workmanship and skill shown by many of those on display. Smith had done some of his own firearms repair and minor home gunsmithing and the step to a homemade knife seemed logical.

About six or seven years ago, Smith tried his first couple of custom knives. They were sheath knives — hunters — intended for rugged outdoor use. He showed them to some of the better, well-known craftsmen in California — makers such as Bob Loveless and the Coopers — and asked for their frank comments. He got them. They told Smith to go back home and take up some other hobby. "Not up to the standard," was one of the kinder comments.

A remark such as that to Fred Smith had quite the opposite effect of touting him off the knifemaking project. He accepted the comments as constructive criticism — a tough challenge that he was determined to overcome. It was back to the drawing board and the workbench. He remarked sometime later that he was determined to produce a custom knife worthy of the name and of a quality matching the best craftsmen he knew.

Fred Smith decided that part of the problem was that he was not familiar enough with the custom knifemakers and their products. So he and his wife spent their vacations traveling around the United States attending gun, knife and collector shows and talking to any knifemaker who had the time to spare. Smith visited and talked with dozens of cutlers and visited commercial knifemaking factories whenever he could. He traveled thousands of miles in the quest for knowledge.

"Everyone we talked to was just terrific. I don't know of any other business or craft that has so many people in it that give so freely of their time," says Smith. "Once we established our interest and sincerity, every maker we talked to gave generously of his time and information. It was a great help."

One of the things that soon became apparent was the large demand for folding knives — pocket, hunting, skinning

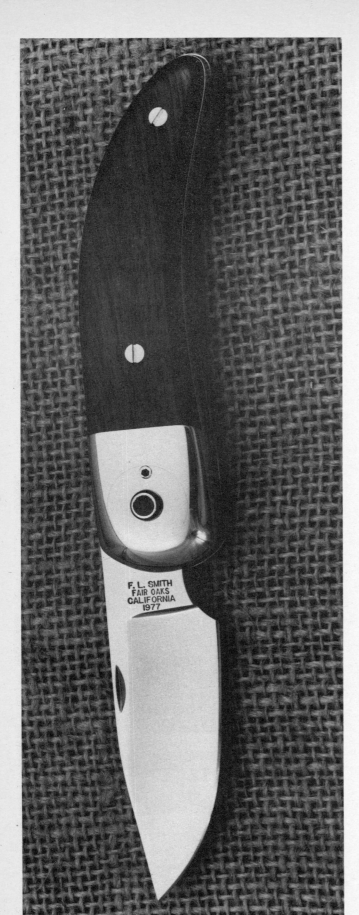

or collector models. Folding knives seemed to be about five years behind the boom in custom knife popularity.

Smith determined there was more than one drawback to a fine folding knife. The most obvious was that a folder is more complicated and thus more time-consuming and expensive to produce; there are more components and moving parts to a folder. Nothing moves on a good sheath knife. Design and construction of a locking system, if there is to be one, requires considerable engineering. Smith believes that a folding blade must not touch the inside case as it moves in and out. It must be reasonably easy to open and close, but must be positively locked open and shut to avoid possible accidents.

The major advantage of a folder over a sheath knife is the lighter weight, smaller profile and ease of carrying. Smith feels it is simply a smaller, lighter package.

The other major disadvantage is lack of easy and rapid availability for use. According to Smith, this is the area where the design of folding hunters or skinning knives was the weakest. True, the folder might be carried in a pocket or handy sheath on the belt while hunting, but often, in the midst of skinning or cleaning fish and game, the user's hands may be cold, wet and slippery. It normally takes two hands to open the blade. In other words, comments Smith, a folding knife may not be as convenient nor as immediately available for use as a sheath knife at a critical moment. One-handed switch blades and pushbutton knives are generally illegal and carry an unsavory reputation.

The problem was placed on Smith's workbench when a friend asked him if he would make a hunting folder. Trouble was, the potential customer had but one hand. There was the kind of challenge Smith likes — design and make a folding hunting knife that could be opened and closed easily with one hand. Period.

So Smith did make a folder that could be opened and closed with one hand. Furthermore, it locked the blade in the open or the closed position. The knife also is unique in that it may be taken apart completely for easy cleaning and repair, should it become necessary. The folder is taken apart with a simple little tool that Smith includes with his knives. The tool is made of steel, shaped not unlike an anvil, and is serial numbered the same as the knife it accompanies.

The folder unlocks, opens, and locks open with one hand. The force required to operate the mechanism is adjustable to satisfy the individual user. One merely presses down with the thumb onto a small projection extending out slightly from between the bolsters. The projection acts as a lever on the opposite end of the blade and the blade pivots out of the case and into its locked position. Reverse the procedure to close.

Smith relates that it's a helluva lot easier to operate than it was to design and build. He finds people at shows where he displays his knives fascinated by the folder's operation. Buyers and nonbuyers stand for hours opening and closing the folder with one hand.

After typical Smith thoroughness in testing and investigation of the steel types available, he settled on either D-2

Operation of a Smith folding knife may be by one hand. Button in pivot pin unlocks blade from open or closed position. Blade is then rotated into place — open or closed — by levering with thumb on protrusion to right of blade.

or 154CM steel for the blades, which are hollow ground and heat-treated to a Rockwell hardness testing of 58 to 60C. The blade thickness measures one-eighth-inch when finished. He uses 303 stainless steel for the folder cases and offers a choice of ivory, natural woods, stag or a number of the micartas for handle material.

One of his designs is especially for backpackers, hunters or hikers who desire to cut their pack weight to the bare minimum. The handle is of stainless steel, no inlay material and no bolsters, finished to a silvery luster. The handle

profile then is drilled out with four lightening holes to bring the weight to an absolute low limit without jeopardizing strength. Smith finds this knife, in 2½ to 2¾-inch blade length, in considerable demand.

From the feedback he gets, Smith believes most of his knives are going to tough users, rather than collectors. Several of his customers have written saying how well the knives have performed on hunting or fishing trips. They especially appreciate the disassembly feature after cleaning a large catch of fish or field dressing big game. Smith has

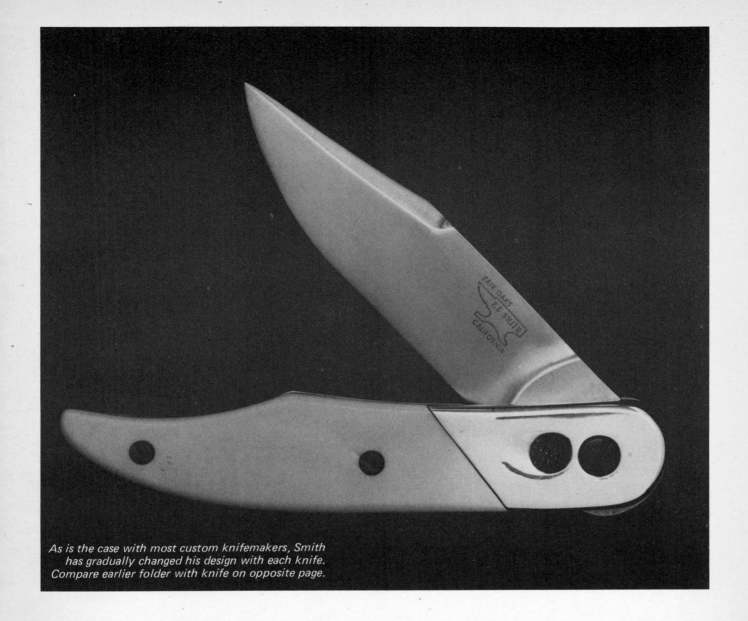

As is the case with most custom knifemakers, Smith has gradually changed his design with each knife. Compare earlier folder with knife on opposite page.

detected a rather interesting situation regarding the East and West Coast. Western custom knifemakers, says Smith, "enjoy a sort of mystique in the East." The terms California knifemaker or Western custom knife produces an almost automatic demand for the product in the East. Smith doesn't explain it, he merely notes it.

Fred Smith spends two to four hours a day and most weekends at his part-time avocation in his well-equipped home shop in a Sacramento suburb. He likes to work hard on a knife to get it out as rapidly as possible without endangering quality. Orders are accepted and completed on a first-come, first-served basis. At present, Smith is quoting a delivery time of three to four months for a folder. He specializes in folding knives, although he has been known to produce a sheath knife on custom order.

Fred Smith folding knives start at $295. Options such as scrimshaw work, ivory handle materials, inlays, worked backs, engraved initials or special bolsters will add to that price. For a dollar, he offers an illustrated information package which may be obtained by writing F.L. Smith, Dept. GW, P.O. Box 817, Fair Oaks, California 95628. Smith guarantees satisfaction.

What about the future? Will Fred Smith become a full-time custom knifemaker? "Probably not," he says. Smith has been involved in mechanical engineering work for the past several years and loves it. He sees no reason to change his life style at present.

"As long as I'm happy doing what I'm doing, why should I change?" he asks. "I'm able to keep up with the knife orders working part-time on them — although sometimes I wonder if twenty or thirty hours a week is part-time — and as long as I can enjoy the work and feel comfortable with my customers, I'll just keep on as I am," he declares. Perhaps a bigger challenge to the status quo will cause a change.

Is Smith offering perfection? He definitely is offering a unique design with no detectable flaws. His knives are made of the finest materials obtainable. The folders operate without a hitch. The question must be answered by each beholder.

Chapter 23

How To:

BUILD YOUR OWN FOLDER

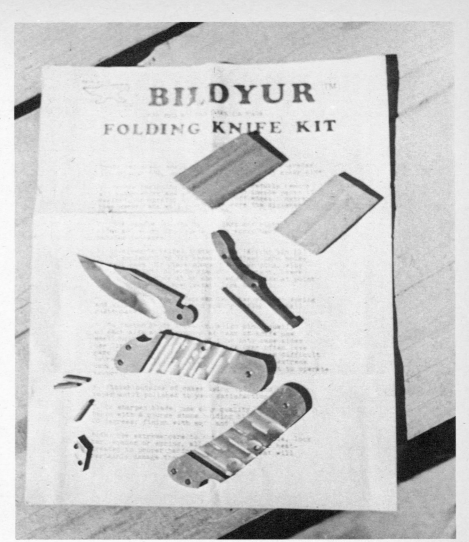

Components of the Bildyur folding knife kit include instructions, two American walnut handle slabs, two steel cases, blade, spring and steel pins.

There Is Plenty Of Room To Customize As This Folding Knife Kit Is Assembled!

THERE IS AN alternative between the factory folding knife that is of good quality, reasonably priced, but mass-produced, and the beautifully crafted and unique, but rather expensive, custom-built folder — the Bildyur Folding Knife Kit from Fred L. Smith of Fair Oaks, California.

For the knife collector, user, do-it-yourselfer, the curious and for those who enjoy a challenge, the Bildyur lock-blade folding knife kit offers plenty of gratification.

Statements about "the biggest," "the smallest," "the oldest" or "the only" seem always able to be disputed by someone somewhere, but as nearly as we can determine, Smith is the only supplier offering a folding knife kit to the public. There are a number of fixed-blade knife kits on the market that the builder may purchase and produce a fine sheath knife. But folding knives have moving parts, precision fittings, locking systems and other highly sophisticated mechanical operations that would seem to

frustrate the beginner or the unskilled handyman attempting to produce a folder. The Bildyur Knife Kit has solved most of these mechanical problems but has left enough assembly and fitting work to satisfy the average home workman.

The kit itself is being marketed through a number of retail sporting goods outlets around the country but they may be difficult to locate. It also is available through mail order from F.L. Smith, at the address listed in the directory of custom knifemakers in this publication. The price is $52, plus sales tax for those who live in California. Not what you might call a cheap knife, but the quality of the finished folder will be considered by most to be somewhat higher than the initial cost.

The kit may be finished with the use of standard power tools or, as Smith contends and as we did, with the use of nothing more than a small hammer, a couple of files, several

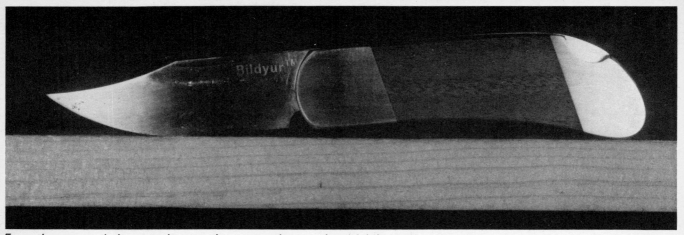

From the parts and pieces on the opposite page to the completed folding knife as it appears above may require 20 to 30 hours of work, several sheets of sandpaper and perhaps some frustration. Results, however, are worth effort.

grades of sandpaper and the home sharpening stone. A bench vise and/or a C clamp or two are helpful tools to add to the list. A small amount of two-part epoxy cement also is required.

Assembly sounds rather simple, and it is. The kit comes with each metal part completely precision made and finished. All interior parts, blade, lock bar, spacer and spring are vacuum heat-treated, leaving the builder with no additional finishing or expensive treating to do. The case sides are surface ground, contoured and relieved for the handle inserts, precision drilled, reamed and countersunk for the pins.

The parts are checked for tolerance after manufacture and Smith guarantees that they will fit and operate correctly as received. Smith goes to the quality control point of personally hand fitting together the metal parts of

each kit to ensure that every piece fits and operates as it is supposed to. The only minor adjustment that may be required is in the locking spring as explained in the instructions shipped with the kit.

The major cut-and-fit work required of the builder is in the final fitting and forming of the walnut handle inserts, also explained in easy-to-follow instructions. Replacement parts are available if needed and a price list comes with the kit.

The knife blade is of D-2 steel, hardened to a Rockwell C reading of 58-60. That kind of hardness would be considered rather high for the average factory knife, but is on a par with most of the custom jobs available. It does present a challenge on the sharpening stone but once honed, the knife will hold an edge nicely. The blade is an eighth of an inch thick, 2½ inches long and hollow ground,

After familiarization with the instructions and an inventory of the parts, the first step, below left, is marking and cutting the handle inserts. Extreme care must be exercised in measuring, marking and cutting the walnut slabs. Bearing surface of lock spring may need polishing with increasingly fine sandpaper to ensure smooth operation.

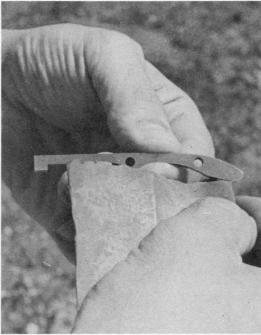

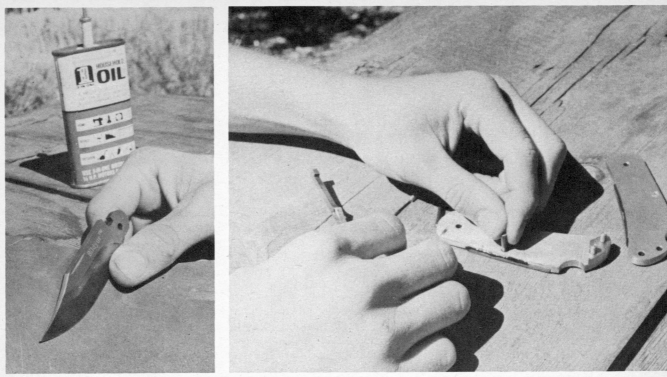

A judicious amount of machine lubricating oil may be used with fine sandpaper as edges, knicks and machining marks are removed. Components of folder may be assembled to test operation and fit of Bildyur, as shown in instructions.

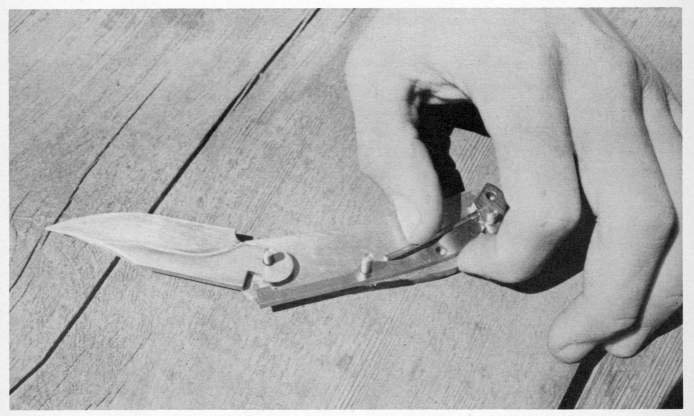

Operation of locking system is tested with parts assembled on one case side. Blade is unlocked by depressing rear of lock bar against opposite force of bar spring as it protrudes from spacer. Note how bar pivots out of blade notch.

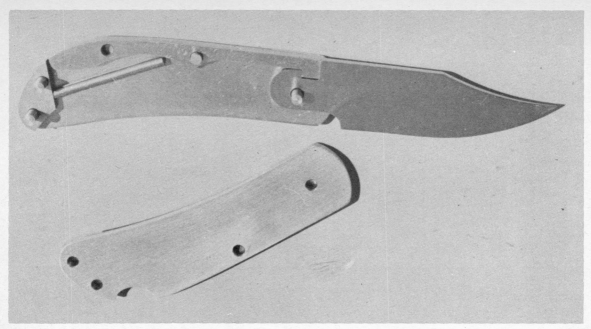

Case and internal parts as they would appear with blade in lock-open mode. Accidental unlocking and folding is impossible as long as lock spring maintains pressure against lock bar. Factory fit of steel parts is precise.

with a black or gray coating that will be removed by the craftsman with fine sandpaper or belt sander and buffing wheel.

The lock bar and case spacer also are made of D-2 steel, while the case itself is made of white tombasil of which Smith thinks most highly. The material has a tensile strength of 90,000, a yield strength of 45,000 and is hardened to Rockwell 90B. It is highly resistant to corrosion and stains. As it is delivered to the builder, the case has a polished luster finish that may be left untouched or highly polished as desired.

The handles are of a fine grain American walnut that lends itself to a variety of shapes and finishes. Ours, as we worked it down, revealed an interesting little swirl pattern in one of the slabs that didn't show at first.

As with any other sort of kit, the first step in construction would seem to be an inventory of the parts as they are received. The kit includes a parts listing as well as a clearly drawn diagram showing the parts in their relative position. This facilitates identification and inventory of the right and left case sides, the three case pins and one pivot pin — the four pins actually are identical and interchangeable. There are four one-eighth-inch diameter steel pins, one lock bar, one spacer, one spring, one blade and two handle slabs. An easy technique is to lay them out on the enlarged instruction drawing. Needless to say, caution must be exercised as some of the listed parts are relatively small and subject to loss or misplacement. Some sort of plastic containers might be in order during the construction steps.

Prior to actual assembly, feel and closely examine each part. The rough edges should be removed using care not to round off any of the machined angles. Spending extra time here will result in an improved finished product.

Using the printed diagram, it would seem wise and prudent to assemble the working parts to familiarize oneself with the folding and locking mechanism of the Bildyur knife. It is easy to do and takes but a few minutes.

Start with the so-called left case side, as shown in the drawing. Place it on the workbench surface with the two drilled pin holes on the right. Lay the spacer down on the case on the right over the appropriate holes. Next, simply press the two one-eighth-inch pins through as far as they will go. Carefully insert the spring into the hole that is drilled into the spacer. The opposite end of the spring must reach or extend slightly past the edge of the case side. Ours did extend past the side edge by slightly less than a sixteenth of an inch and no adjustment was necessary. With Smith's inspection and attention to fit, it seems unlikely that the springs wouldn't meet the criteria outlined, although conceivably, some slight rework of the spring may be required at this point.

Slip the lock pivot pin and blade pivot pin into their appropriate holes in the side. Slide the lock bar down on the lock pivot pin ensuring that the rounded end of the bar is to the right. Now slide the blade on its pin in what will be the open position. The lock bar may have to be depressed against the spring to allow the blade to drop completely down into position.

With the parts in place, the next check is to slide the right case side down over the four pins. At this point, the knife actually should be functioning as a folder and, except for appearance, gives the builder a preview of the finished knife's heft and feel.

This procedure is the exact assembly method that is used to complete the knife after the handle materials have been fitted and finished. The kit is engineered to a degree that it seems likely that the average craftsman could build it even without instructions.

Walnut slabs fitted and partly shaped prior to epoxy cementing to case.

Good grade of epoxy cement may be mixed in any convenient vessel before being carefully applied.

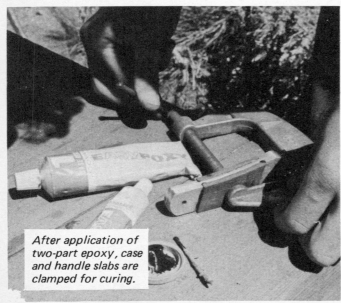

After application of two-part epoxy, case and handle slabs are clamped for curing.

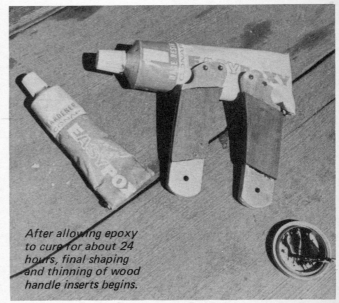

After allowing epoxy to cure for about 24 hours, final shaping and thinning of wood handle inserts begins.

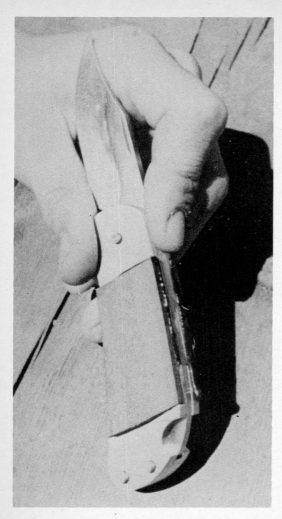

Now disassemble all components and begin work on the handle slabs.

One of the first things we wanted to get done was the fitting of the handle slabs to the steel case sides. Once this is done, they can be epoxied and clamped to cure while other work is being done.

The walnut handles are manufactured somewhat larger than the space into which they must fit. This allows the builder plenty of time and opportunity to exercise his creative abilities for final shape and finish. We first sandpapered the handles down to dimension with rough paper until they fit fairly tight in the cases. We tried some thinning at this point but found that because of the rather small size they were difficult to hang onto and decided to wait until they had been attached to the steel cases to bring the wood slabs down to finished thickness. The assembly was easier to hold and work with after the parts were glued together.

Here we should insert a word of caution. After mixing up the two-part epoxy cement, we found we had to work rather rapidly, because of the 90 degree heat of the day, and the epoxy wanted to harden almost too fast. Furthermore, if the builder uses one clamp for both slabs as we did, care must be exercised so that no glue squeezes through the drilled pin holes or gets in-between the steel case sides. Otherwise, the result may be that the two sides end up being cemented together, something to be avoided.

Once clamped, we put the assembled handles and cases aside to cure for twenty-four hours. We've found that trying to rush at this stage results in gummed-up files and clogged sandpaper from the still-uncured epoxy cement.

We were unable to use this curing time profitably. Plenty of elbow grease, fine sandpaper and a bit of machine oil, at times, began the smoothing and finishing process of the blade and the lock bar. A good many man-hours were spent at this step as power tools were not part of our plan.

Excess wood and extruded epoxy cement (above) must be filed and sanded to match steel case contour. An important aspect to be double-checked before final assembly is insurance that lock spring reaches or extends past edge of case. If not, careful adjustment may be made by slightly bending rod-shaped spring in the required direction.

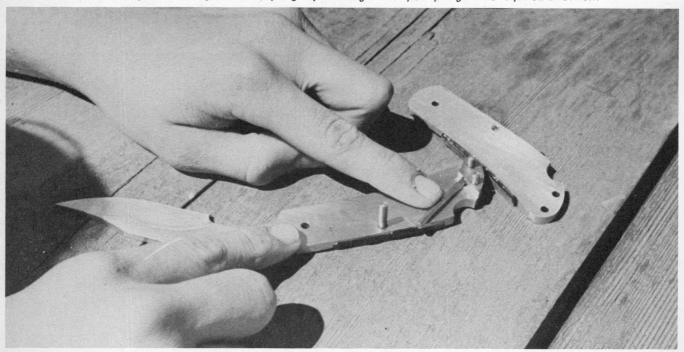

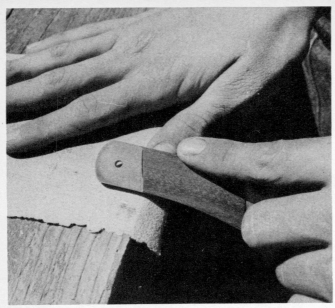

Bringing the wood handle inserts down to the desired thickness required several hours of sandpaper work.

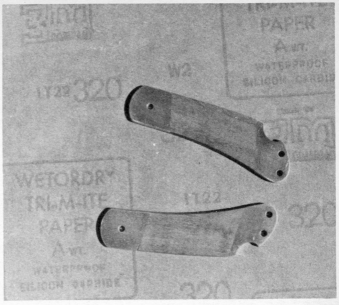

Final finish is left up to the individual builder. Sandpaper grades of 150 through 600 are recommended.

When knife blade is closed, edge should not contact spacer.

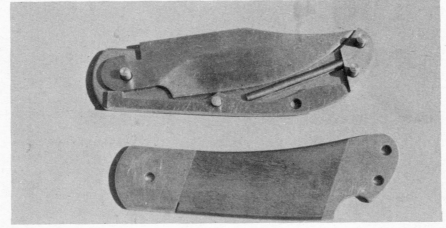

Last operational check is advisable before both case sides are joined and case pins are peened.

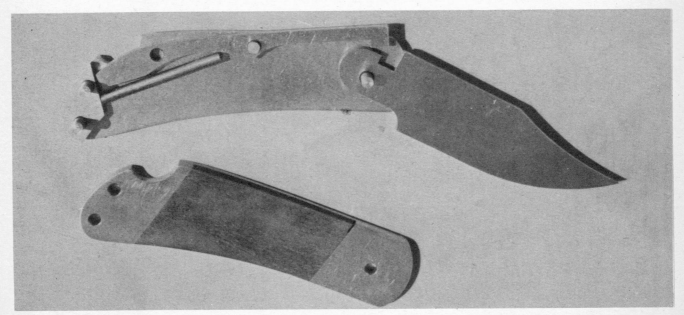

After the epoxy has cured, begin sanding down the walnut slabs to their final shape and thickness. We took ours down to the exact thickness of the metal case, although the builder may leave a slight bulge or remove even more wood for a slightly concave configuration. Here, the builder's imagination may invent a number of possibilities. The walnut may be left in its sanded, relatively raw state, or may be oil finished. One might even consider some sort of waterproof polyurethane finish for the wood. It would depend on the ultimate use and conditions for the finished product. The hours devoted to the handle, more than any other part, will determine the final appearance of your knife.

The walnut slabs and steel case sides do not have to be completely and finally finished to proceed on with assembly, however. Once the general configuration of the handle is completed, return to the metal parts and the assembly instructions. Reassemble the sides, pins, spacer and locking mechanism as was done when first inventorying the parts. Press the pins through the case so that they extend equally out each side. This is another point at which the builder may use his own creativity. The lock bar pivot pin is produced the same length as the case pins; they will extend through the entire knife. The builder may drill through the walnut and allow the lock pivot pin to show through or he may cut it shorter so it is about three-sixteenths of an inch long. The pin will be long enough to extend through the pivot bar and case sides but not through the handle slabs.

With all parts in place, preferably on a solid metal or wood surface, the pins are ready to be peened. Extreme care is advised here so that accidental dents are not hammered into the wood handle or steel sides. Peen the two pins passing through the spacer first. Peen lightly and carefully, turning the knife over often so that each end of the pin is peened equally. Light, even plows produce the best results. The blade pin is peened last and with even more care than the first two. Too much hammering on the blade pivot pin will cause it to expand to the point where the blade will become too tight on the pin and the folder will not operate properly. Test the action with each blow.

After the pins have been worked and peened to the builder's satisfaction, the whole assembled knife may be filed and sanded down to the point where the pins almost disappear, leaving a smooth solid appearance.

A buffing wheel or belt sander may be used at this point to produce a mirror finish to the knife. However, the builder is well-advised to not overheat the blade, case or spacer, as each has been precision heat-treated and excessive heat will damage the metal by altering the steel hardness.

Final step for the Bildyur folding knife — which now may be called a custom folder — is sharpening the blade. As mentioned, the blade is hardened to RC 58-60, which will require considerable honing to bring out the best edge possible with this knife. Use a good, soft Arkansas oil stone and honing oil. Hold the blade at an approximate 20 degree angle with the stone, working one stroke on each side of the blade. Stroke the blade edge with considerable pressure as if trying to cut into the sharpening stone itself and work until a sharp edge has been reached. Chapter 5 of this book provides more detailed instructions on knife sharpening.

And there you have it. Your own custom finished folding knife. There will be no other exactly like it, no matter how many you build. Some builders have been offered sums several times the original price for their completed Bildyurs. The knife may be put together in as little as a couple of evenings or the builder may take considerably more time to create a special work of art. If completion of such a kit does nothing else, it will definitely increase one's appreciation of the custom knifemakers' skills and abilities.

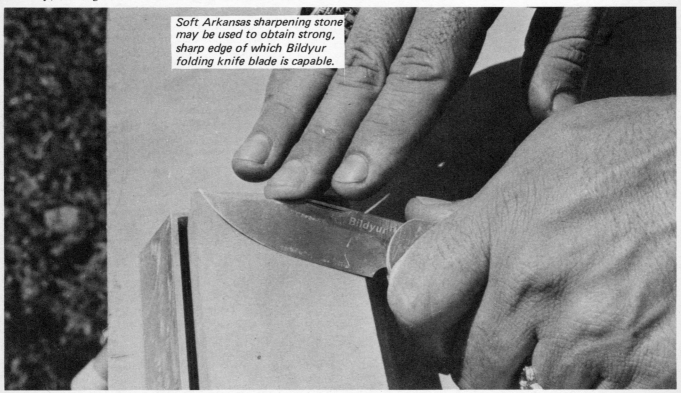

Soft Arkansas sharpening stone may be used to obtain strong, sharp edge of which Bildyur folding knife blade is capable.

Chapter 24

THE COMMEMORATIVE SCENE

*Whether Such Creations
In Cutlery Will
Increase In Value
Appears To Be
A Question
Of Numbers*

A CENTURY ago, there were a few fancy knives being produced by masters of the craft that boasted etched blades and handles of ivory, often inlaid with silver or gold. Usually, these were one-of-a-kind items intended as special gifts or presentation items, often going to royalty or political powers.

There also were a few expensive gimmick knives built in Sheffield, England, a century ago for the express purpose of showing what could be done by a cutler. There are examples of such knives that have more than sixty blades — in the broad term, as they included such implements as scissors, metal toothpicks, ad infinitum.

It has been only within the last few years that anything that could be called a commemorative knife actually has appeared on the market on a commercial basis. By this, we mean a commercial run of knives designed specifically to call attention to or commemorate a famous person, place or event. Incidentally, the American Heritage Dictionary defines *commemorative* as *to serve as a memorial to.*

There have been numerous commemorative firearms in recent years, with the crescendo of manufacturing as well as interest being reached during the recently concluded Bicentennial observances. In a land that will turn out a red, white and blue coffin or cesspool in a Bicentennial year, it's not surprising that a number of knives featuring the dates 1776-1976 would appear.

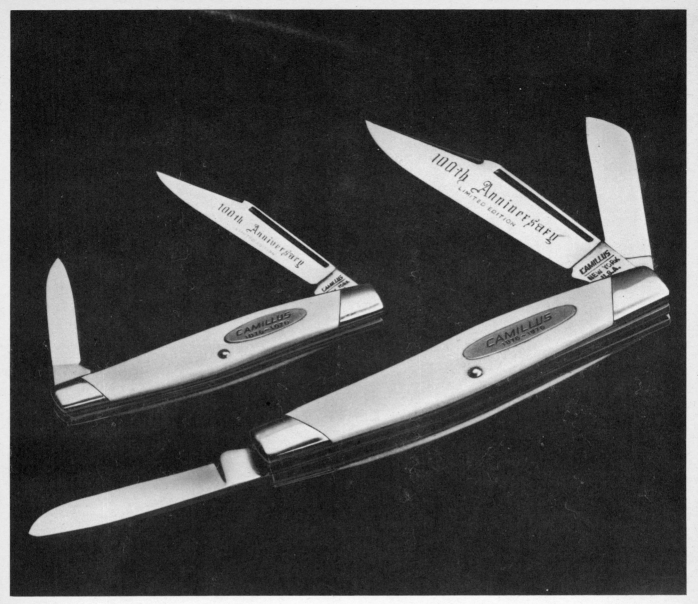

The Camillus Cutlery Company offered a couple of commemorative models that noted not only the 200th anniversary of the United States but also the 100th of the company itself. Each folder is serial numbered.

There are varying schools of thought on the value of commemoratives. Edward Y. Breese, a writer and collector down Florida way, tends to have a somewhat jaundiced view.

"Knives got into the commemorative act about the time that knives, in general, became popular as collector items and that has been relatively recently," he contends. "When the only collectors were men who used knives in their daily lives and the trading was at general stores and turkey shoots, the knife with the fancy handle and the motto or inscription wasn't in the picture at all.

"Today, all that has changed. Thousands have discovered the joy of collecting. Collector's dealers abound. There are knife dealer tables at the antique shows, the gun shows, sporting goods shows and at a thousand flea markets," Breese points out. "Knives are popular, they're selling and the really good, old ones are becoming rare and expensive."

Breese feels that nothing was more natural "than for someone to want to sweeten the pot. The scoundrels did it by forging and feloniously 'restoring' old knives. Some of these jobs are done well enough to fool even an expert at times. Others were as laughable as the Case XXX, a nonexistent model offered at a flea market I visited."

The cutlers came up with a better idea: "Take one of their stock numbers, dress it up with some fancy work and a name, call it a commemorative and increase the retail price.

"In the beginning, this wasn't a bad idea. To some extent, everyone benefited. The knifemaker and his wholesale and retail outlets made money. A lot of fellows who couldn't otherwise have bought a knife at all were attracted by the fancy-up job. They got a pretty knife for not too bad a price. Then they bought another — and another — then branched out into picking up used knives. A

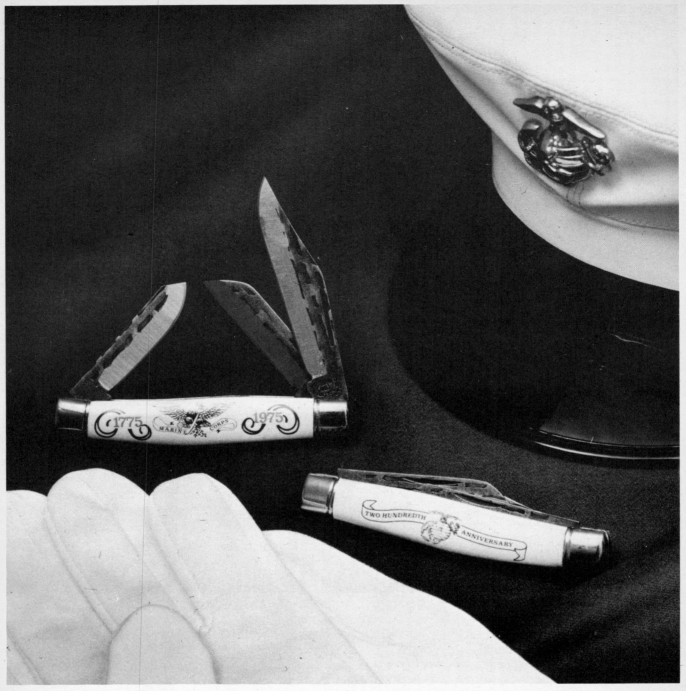

Schrade Cutlery produced folding commemoratives that honored the Bicentennials of each of the older Armed Forces. The model above commemorates the founding of the United States Marine Corps, November 10, 1775.

great many new collectors were born that way and it was good for them and for all the rest of us, too," Breese says.

"That's how it started. Then it began to get crowded. By now, I've seen at least fifty of these run-of-the-mill commemorative knives advertised. With a few lamentable exceptions, they were pretty good knives and not too overpriced.

"The trouble is that there now are so many of them! If fifty were the top — which I strongly doubt — and if the average price were $25, this would mean a collector trying to build a complete set would have to put out at least $1250, plus another hundred for postage and handling. For

the average guy in a time of inflation and recession, that's a lot of money and the price suggested is more than conservative!"

Breese contends that "contrary to the impression most guys have when they put the money down, these are not investor's items. Most of them aren't even limited editions — unless you limit by the number that can be sold.

"They are pretty," Breese admits, "and most of them

*Founding of the U.S. Army and Navy is commemorated
by Schrade with these three-bladed folders.
About one thousand of these knives were produced.*

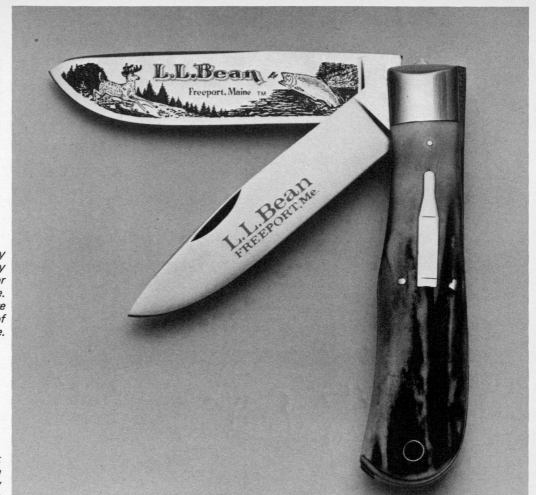

The Bowen Knife Company makes faithful copy of Remington knife for L.L. Bean of Maine. Reproductions have become part of commemorative scene.

This Johnston lock-back folding hunter is in extremely limited supply as produced by custom knifemaker R.W. Trabbic.

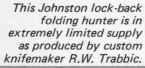

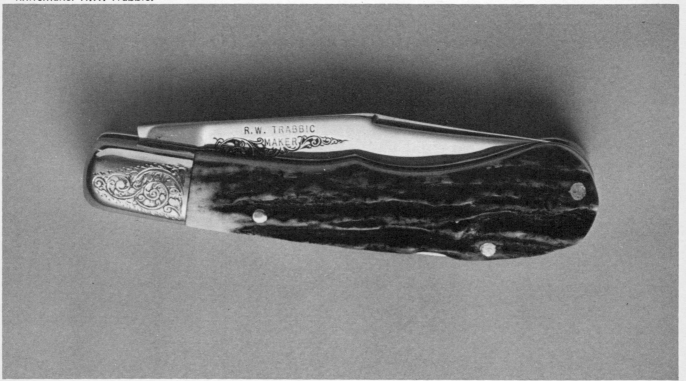

Jimmy Lile of Arkansas produces the folder and R.E. Skaggs adds the special wildlife scenes, offered in limited numbers for collectors.

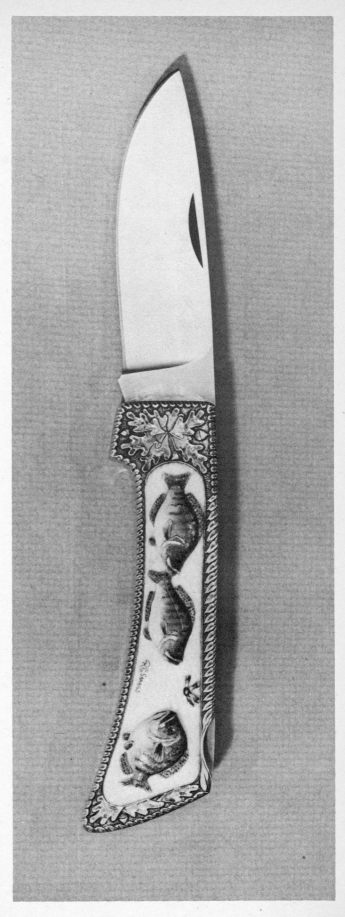

would make a fairly good pocketknife, as they tend to come in the whittler and small stockman patterns. But they aren't going to shoot up and up in value. There may be a small rise in keeping with general inflation, but that's about all you can expect."

Breese also foresaw the flood of Bicentennial commemoratives, saying, "The temptation to put a fancy shield on a model already in production and try to tie it in with the national Bicentennial will be too much for a lot of people to resist. Look for some sort of knife to commemorate every battle and probably every general of the 1776 Revolution. Some will be worth buying. Some won't."

Manufacturers did turn out a number of commemorative models and styles, but the models were not nearly so broadspread as Breese expected perhaps. There still are many of these knives around and according to this collector, "the criteria the smart knife collector will use in making up his mind which of these knives to buy should be the same he applies to the assembly of the rest of his collection."

In putting together any collection of commemoratives, Bicentennial or otherwise, Breese suggests that the buyer "first of all, look for quality and craftsmanship. Some of the offers have both. Look for fine steel in the blades, brass liners, brass or nickel silver bolsters and ornaments on the handles. Look for handles of sambar stag, quality bone, ivory or rosewood instead of plastic. Look for a big knife and one of such quality that you wouldn't hesitate to carry and use even under difficult conditions.

"After quality," he says, "look for rarity. A limited edition that is limited only by the number of knives that can be sold adds nothing to the value of a knife.

"On the other hand, an edition limited to 3000 or so knives, as some of them are, will be sure to have a scarcity value in a few years."

In the best of these, the knives usually are individually stamped with consecutive serial numbers from 1 to 3000 or whatever number signifies the end of the run. Collectors, of course, go for the low numbers — 1 to 100 or 1 to 500 mostly. Usually these lower numbers are sold at a premium price to begin with and the resale value goes up rapidly.

As an example, Ka-Bar Knives put out a Bicentennial folder in a limited edition. Each knife was handcrafted and individually serialized. The master blade carries an etched commemorative Bicentennial banner, along with a deep-struck original Ka-Bar trademark. The individual serial numbers, 0001 through 7500 were struck deep on the reverse side. An early Ka-Bar marking, the dog's head

Limited edition Heirloom Special is by talented cutler Gary Kelley of Oregon. Prices start at $200. There are a number of custom makers producing replica commemoratives which may be profitable investments.

shield, was inlaid into the red, white and blue handle.

The Olean, New York, firm included a white leather sheath with each of these folders, as well as a certificate confirming that it was a limited edition.

During the Bicentennial, Schrade Cutlery was another maker that issued a limited run, combining three knives in a set to commemorate the two hundredth anniversaries of the founding of the Marine Corps, the Army and the Navy. Each of these was based upon Schrade's standard stock knife design. As we understand it, the entire run was turned over to one dealer for sale and was gobbled up quite quickly by collectors, since only 1000 or so sets were made. Some of the knives also were sold on an individual basis.

There were a number of custom cutlers who also put out special commemorative knives during the Bicentennial. Due to the outstanding workmanship and the fact that each knifemaker turned out only a few — some of them even one-of-a-kind — these are certain to increase in value. These

individually made knives incorporated such scarce materials as ivory and real India stag. Most became collector specials the day they came out of the maker's shop.

"I have one of this sort which cost me thirty-five bucks a couple of years ago," Edward Breese recounts. "You couldn't buy it from me today for $200!"

After quality and rarity, look for beauty in the commemorative knife. It costs more — sometimes a lot more — but usually is worth the outlay, if you can afford it.

"In this connection," Breese reports, "the special knives put out for purchase by members of the Knife Collector's Club, starting with the beautiful, ivory-handled Kentucky Rifle Commemorative, usually have been put out in three grades. The best and most expensive premium grade of each knife is magnificently engraved and ornamented. Knives put out by the better known collector groups and clubs can be depended upon as collector and investment items.

"That doesn't mean you can't find the three essentials of quality, rarity and beauty in other knives. Rarity is the hardest to find. After all, the business of the big cutlery firms is to sell knives. When one of their models catches the public's fancy, they are equipped to turn out that model by the tens of thousands, and it's only natural that they do just that.

"Another source of limited edition pocketknives is in the reproduction field," Breese adds. "By this, I mean

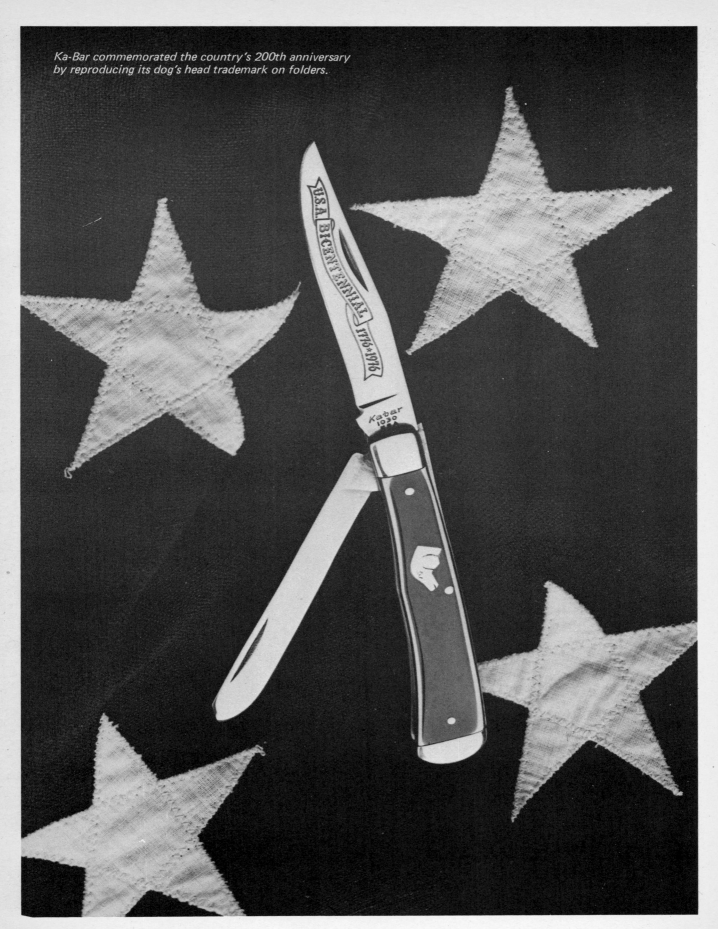

Ka-Bar commemorated the country's 200th anniversary by reproducing its dog's head trademark on folders.

legitimate copies of famous early models or knives that were put out by firms that no longer are in business at all."

As an example, Breese points to a beautiful five-inch copy of an early Winchester Trapper model. The two blades are of top-quality steel and the workmanship is beautiful.

This particular knife was crafted in Germany and is clearly marked as a reproduction. It is not a forgery or a rebuilt job; it doesn't pretend to be anything more than a faithful copy. However, it is from a limited edition of slightly over 1200 specimens.

"I bought my specimen of this Winchester reproduction from a known and reputable dealer and paid $45 for it," Breese recalls. "Since then, I've been offered knives from the same run at shows and from other dealers at prices ranging from $75 to $90. The knife is a prize in my own collection and I'm not selling it.

A.G. Russell (right) shows some of his Morseth knives to collector George Miller. Russell operates knife collectors club from Springdale, Arkansas, headquarters.

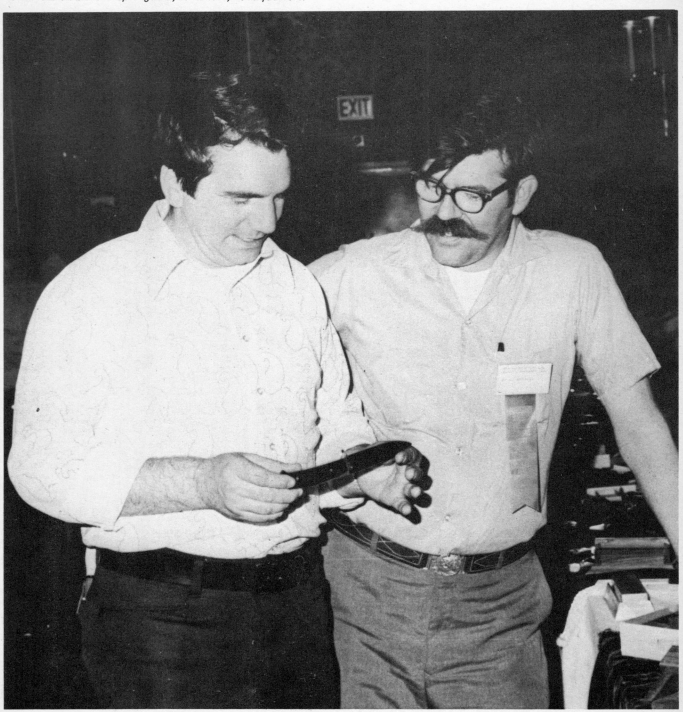

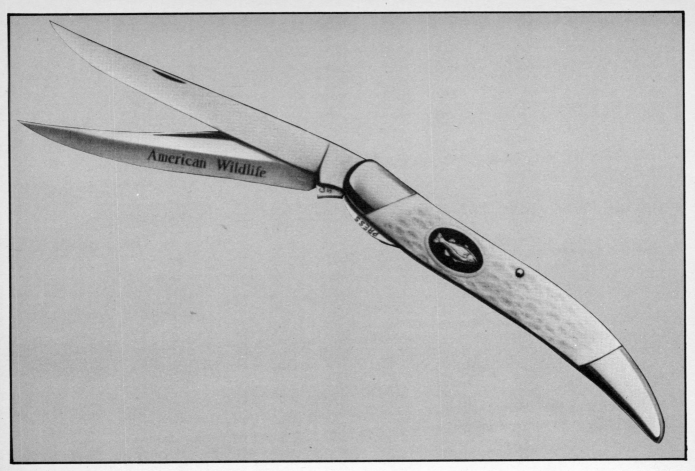

Part of Camillus Cutlery's American Wildlife series, is this functional fillet knife featuring fish inlay.

"Yet I have friends who wouldn't touch that knife with a ten-foot pole. They collect only Barlows, only pearl-handled styles or the finely crafted and delicate small knives called gentlemen's pens. It's a matter of individual taste."

An individual who is making a career of limited editions, many of them faithful reproductions of the knives of the past, is A.G. Russell, one of the founders of the Knifemakers' Guild.

Working out of Springdale, Arkansas, where he also operates Morseth Knives, Russell charges a fee for membership in the aforementioned Knife Collectors Club. If one buys a knife, which Russell advertises widely, he becomes a member automatically and receives all of the club's literature, as well as the monthly knife offering.

Russell is recreating many old classics, as well as creating some of his own. He is putting them out in limited editions, numbering each of them. The numbers ranging in the first fifty, of course, cost more than the rest of the numbered run.

He says that some of the club members have purchased all of the knives that have been put out by his organization, thus building a select collection. In the beginning, virtually all of the styles such as the Luger commemorative were variations on Schrade's standard stock knife pattern; more recently, new styles have been introduced along with the faithful reproductions of the old favorites.

Just where it all will end is open to question of course, but Russell and others may be taking a tip from the firearms manufacturers. Winchester was in the commemorative rifle business in a big way a few years ago, but made the mistake of overproducing some items. These have failed to increase in value, while those that were produced in strictly limited numbers have shown a notable increase. All of these commemoratives have been based upon the familiar Model 94 styling and have been in .30-30 caliber. Only the cosmetics have changed.

Colt has followed a similar program, producing differing commemorative versions of their famed Single Action Army revolver each year. The number has been strictly limited and these have been sought after by collectors. The value tends to increase each year.

In short, they have been creating a market. Russell and others are doing the same thing with knives, using the limited edition idea to give them value.

It will be years before the results are known; whether they tend to increase in value. It will be interesting to watch.

The 50th anniversary of Charles Lindberg's solo flight across the Atlantic in May 1927 is the objective of the Spirit of St. Louis commemorative folder.

A.G. Russell put the folding Kentucky Rifle commemorative (below) on the market.

Recent collectors' replica of famous folding hunting knife is Grandaddy Barlow, right.

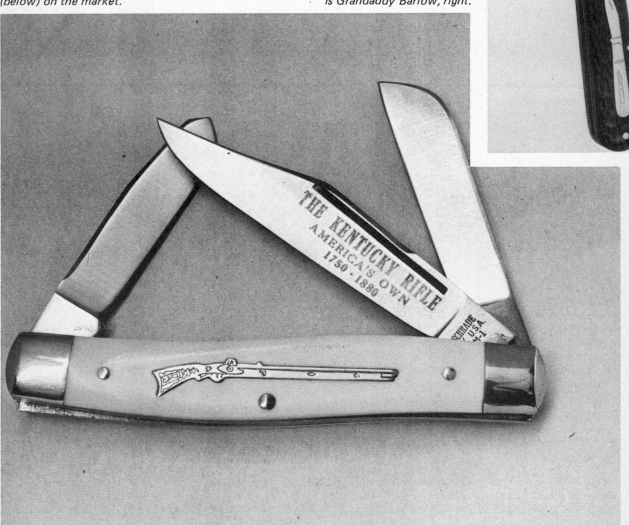

Commemoratives may come in various shapes and sizes, such as this tiny boot knife, by A.G. Russell.

Folders noting the 75th anniversary of the Luger pistol and Luger bullet are available in several grades and serial numbers. Production was limited.

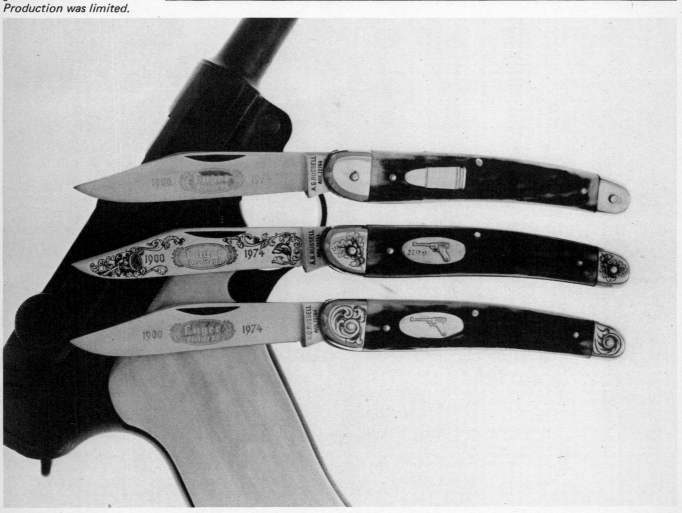

TODAY'S KNIFEMAKERS

Not all of the knifemakers listed below are makers, manufacturers or importers of folding knives. However, with the popularity being enjoyed by this type of cutlery, chances are all — or nearly all — of them will be turning out such models in the near future. Therefore, we are offering a complete list.

DIRECTORY OF CUSTOM KNIFEMAKERS

ALABAMA

Amick, Lendell, R., 753 Pinewood Avenue, Hueytown, Ala. 35020
Amick, Ronnie, 1445-B Rollingwood, Sylacauga, Ala. 35150
Bullard, Bill, Rt. 5, Box 33-D, Andalusia, Ala. 36420
Day, Phillip, Rt. 1, Box 464-T, Bay Minette, Ala. 36507
Dorough, R.A. Dick, (DD Knives), Rt. 1, Box 130, Gadsden, Ala. 35901
Fuller, W.T., 400 S. 8th Street, Gadsden, Ala. 35903
Fuller, Burt (F&H Knives), Box 734, Livingston, Ala. 35470
Hall, Allan (F&H Knives), Box 734, Livingston, Ala. 35470
Levine, Norman (Dragon Knives), 915 Tascosa Drive, Huntsville, Ala. 35802
Lovett, Michael S., 334 Taylor Street, Scottboro, Ala. 35768
McBurnette, Harvey, Rt. 4, Box 337, Piedmont, Ala. 36272
McFarland, Lester E. Jr., Box 2732, Opelika, Ala. 36801
Sonneville, W.J., 1050 Chalet Drive, West Mobile, Ala. 36608

ALASKA

Amoureux, A.W., 2300 Barrow, Anchorage, Ak. 99503
Dykes, Leonard (L&L Knives), One Mile, Old Nenana Road, SR Box 10682, Fairbanks, Ak. 99701
England, Virgil, Box 10197 Klatt Station, Anchorage, Ak. 99502
Isaacs, Dan, 3701 Eureka, SP 59-A, Anchorage, Ak. 99503
Isaacs, Ron, 3701 Eureka, SP 59-A, Anchorage, Ak. 99503

ARIZONA

Weiler, D.E., Box 1576, Yuma, Az. 85364
Weiss, Charles L., 18847 No. 13th Ave., Phoenix, Az. 85008
Cheatham, Bill, 2930 W. Marlette, Phoenix, Az. 85017
Clark, Rodger, 2624 W. Belmont, Phoenix, Az. 85021
Hendricks, L.R., 9919 E. Apache Trail, Mesa, Az. 85207
Holder, D'Alton, 6808 N. 30th Drive, Phoenix, Az. 85017
Lofgreen, Bob, (LOF Knives), Box LOF, Lakeside, Az. 85929
Parrish, F.D., 2528 E. McKellips, 174, Mesa, Az. 85203
Poletis, Jerry, Box 1582, Scottsdale, Az. 85252

ARKANSAS

Crabtree, H.W., Rt. 1, Alama, Ar. 72921
Crawford, Pat, 205 N. Center, West Memphis, Ar. 72301
Dickey, Charles E., 803 N.E. A Street, Bentonville, Ar. 72712
Dodson, Frank C. Jr., 29 Flintwood, Little Rock, Ar.
Hale, Lloyd, 609 Henryetta Street, Springdale, Ar. 72764
Hicks, Vernon W., Rt. 1, Box 387, Bauxile, Ar. 72001
Kirk, Jon, 800 N. Olive Street, Fayetteville, Ar. 72701
Lile, James B., Rt. 1, Box 79, Russellville, Ar. 72801
Ogg, R.G., Rt. 1, Box 230, Paris, Ar. 72855
Price, Jerry L., Box 782, Springdale, Ar. 72764
Morseth Knives, Springdale, Ar. 72764
Wiman, Art, Box 92, Plummerville, Ar. 72127

CALIFORNIA

Anselmo, Victor, 6109 Clyboune, Apt. B, North Hollywood, Ca. 91606
Baylis, R. Brian, 1390 Orpheus Avenue, Leucadia, Ca. 92024
Berryman, Les, 7122 Calais Place, Newark, Ca. 94560
Biggs, H.L., 3816 Via Selva, Palos Verde, Ca. 92266
Boye, David, Box 187, Davenport, Ca. 95017
Boyd, Francis, c/o Buxton, 1730 Kern Street, San Francisco, Ca. 94133
Cockrell, Dan, 19845 E. Cienega Avenue, Covina, Ca. 91724
Cooper, John Nelson, Box 1423, Burbank, Ca. 91507
Cosby, Dave, 1016 Cliff Drive, Apt. 111, Santa Barbara, Ca. 93109
Dachtler, Orville, 35182 Cabral Drive, Fremont, Ca. 94536

Davis Custom Knives, 1464 E. Lexington, El Cajon, Ca. 92021
Duff, Bill, (Duff Custom Knives), Box 217, El Cajon, Ca. 92022
Engnath, Bob, 1019 E. Palmer, Glendale, Ca. 91205
Ferry, Thomas L., 4208 Canoga Drive, Woodland Hills, Ca. 91364
Finley, C.H., 4176 St. Patrick Avenue, Redding, Ca. 96001
Filburn, Robert, 3843 Beckwith Road, Modesto, Ca. 95351
Francek, Edward, 634 N. Kingsley Drive, Los Angeles, Ca. 90004
Funderburg, Joe, Box 582, Arcadia, Ca. 91006
Goldenberg, Ted, Box 3101, Walnut Creek, Ca. 94598
Hayes, Robert E., Box 141, Railroad Flat, Ca. 95248
Henry, D.E., Star Route, Mountain Ranch, Ca. 95246
Hoffmann, Donald B., Box 174, San Miguel, Ca. 93451
Horn, J.L. Jr., Box 1274, Redding, Ca. 96001
Holguin, Paul, 2015 Lees Avenue, Long Beach, Ca. 90815
Jones, Fred, 858 E. "I" Street, Ontario, Ca. 91762
Jones, Jolly, 1240 Abbot Avenue, Campbell, Ca. 95008
Kvitka, Dan, 17600 Superior Street, Northridge, Ca. 91324
Leppert, A.R., 17718 Rhoda Street, Encino, Ca. 91316
Loveless, Robert W., Box 7836, Riverside, Ca. 92503
McEvers, Ron, 3110 G Street, Oxnard, Ca. 93030
Moser, James W., 17432 Marken Lane, Huntington Beach, CA. 92647
Mulholland, Gary, Box 93, Davenport, Ca. 95017
Nativo, George, 15011 Florwood Avenue, Hawthorne, Ca. 90250
Oda, Kuzon, Box 7836, Riverside, Ca. 92503
Oleson, Robert, 800 Keokuk St., Petaluma, Ca. 94952
Pitt, David, (Bear Paw Knives), 36601 Leone Street, Newark, Ca. 94560
Planas, Richard J., (Huk Knives), 516 Double Street, Carson, Ca. 90745
Poehlman, Paul W., Box 445, Stinson Beach, Ca. 94970
Richards, Don T., 170 23rd Street, Costa Mesa, Ca. 92627
Rodriques, Joe, (Teco Knives), 10606 San Gabriel Avenue, South Gate, Ca. 90280
Samson, Jody J.C., Box 1423, Burbank, Ca. 91507
Schneider, H.J., 24296 Via Aquara, Laguna Niguel, Ca. 92677
Schmier, Jack, 16787 Mulberry Circle, Fountain Valley, Ca. 92708
Shirley, Dave, 39723 Plumas Way, Fremont, Ca. 94538
Smith, F.L., 8072 Dorian Way, Fair Oaks, Ca. 95628
Stranahan, D.L., Box 2812, Oxnard, Ca. 93030
Thayer, Leroy, 15600 Pinto Way, Chino, Ca. 91710
Tinker, Carolyn, 1699 N. Marengo Avenue, Pasadena, Ca. 91103
Tye, Virgil Dee, 901 S. Chester Avenue, Bakersfield, Ca. 93304
Vairag Knives, 111 Marine Street, Davenport, Ca. 95017
Wesolowski, Mike, 902 Lohrman Lane, Petaluma, Ca. 94952
Wood, Barry B., 38 South Venice Boulevard, Venice, Ca. 90291
Wyman, Gary, 6047 Pitcairn Street, Cypress, Ca. 90630

COLORADO

Campbell, R.C., 1136 South Taos Way, Denver, Co. 80223
Dennehy, Dan, (Dan-D Knives), Box 2F, Del Norte, Co. 81131
Giovannetti, M. Jim, Rt. 2, Box 102, Ignacio, Co. 81137
Mumford, Peter, (Red Canyon Knives), Box 3, Farisita, Co. 81037
Sasser, Jim, 1811½ Santa Fe Drive, Pueblo, Co. 81006
Yancey, T.J., Box 943, Estes Park, Co. 80517

CONNECTICUT

Anderson Knives, RD 4, Shepard Hill Road, Newton, Ct. 06470
Romano, Richard, 31 Arlington Road, Windsor, Ct. 06096
Janiak, J., RFD 2 Park Road, Colchester, Ct. 06415
Jean, Gerry, 633-D Center Street, Manchester, Ct. 06096
Jean, Mary, 633-D Center Street, Manchester, Ct. 06096
Pankiewicz, Phillip, RFD 1, Waterman Road, Lebanon, Ct. 06249
Zaleski, William, 97 Evans Avenue, East Hartford, Ct. 06118

DELAWARE

Willey, Gerald, Rt. 1, Greenwood, De. 19950

FLORIDA

Brown, Floyd E., 1940 SW 83rd Avenue, Miami, Fl. 33155
Centofante, Frank, Box 17587, Tampa, Fl. 33612
Combs, Ralph Jr., Box 1371, Naples, Fl. 33940
Ek, John, 1543 NW 119th Street, North Miami, Fl. 33167
Enos, T.M. III, Rt. 1, Box 66, Winter Garden, Fl. 32787
Lyle, E. III, 4501 Meadowbrook Avenue, Orlando, Fl. 32808
Manley, Clinton J. Jr., Rt. 1, Box 28, Zolfo Springs, Fl. 33890
Owens, John, 8755 SW 96th Street, Miami, Fl. 33156
Palmer, Howard, 2031 Tronjo Road, Pensacola, Fl. 32952
Pass, W.C., 1455 Phillips Drive, Merritt Island, Fl. 32952
Powell, Wesley R., 7211 Tropicana Street, Miramar, Fl. 33023
Pardue, Melvin, M., 2402 Parkland Blvd., Tampa, Fl. 33609
Randall, W.D., Box 1988, Orlando, Fl. 33476
Zaccagino, Don, Box ZACK, Pahokee, Fl. 33476

GEORGIA

Barrett, Jack, 2133 Peach Orchard Road, Augusta, Ga. 30947
Cassaberry, Bill, Box 2005, Castle Park, Valdosta, Ga. 31601
Collins, Michael, Rt. 4, Battlesville Road, Woodstock, Ga. 30188
Dickson, Jim, 2349 Eastway Road, Decatur, Ga. 30033
Hawkins, Rade, (Hawkins Custom Knives), Box H, Red Oak, Ga. 30272
Kelly, Lance, Box 115, Avondale Estates, Ga. 30002
Little, Ronald H., 160 Marion Drive, Ringgold, Ga. 30736
Pittman, Leon, Rt. 1, Box 46, Pendergrass, Ga. 30567
Small, Jim, 474 Foster Street, Madison, Ga. 30650
Schulenberg, E.W., Box 563, Carleton, Ga. 30117
Thomason, Bill, 167 Lower Dawnville Road N.E., Dalton, Ga. 30720
Walters, A.F., 604 E. 20th, Tifton, Ga. 31794

IDAHO

Carlson, Randy, Rt. Box 163, Moscow, Id. 83843
Davis, Larry, 411 Cedar Drive, Pierce, Id. 83456
Lane, Donald C., (Lane Knife Co.), Rt. 4, Box 287-B, Blackfoot, Id. 83221
Mead, Herbert A., Star Rt. 2, Box 171, Bonners Ferry, Id. 83805
Schenek, Clifton, Box 1017, Bonners Ferry, Id. 83805
Sparks, Bernard, Box 32, Dingle, Id. 83233
Towell, Dwight, Rt. 1, Midvale, Id. 83645
Tracy, Bud B., 3913 Rose Hill Street, Boise, Id. 83705

ILLINOIS

Baker Forged Knives, Box 504-B, Hinsdale, Il. 60521
Breeze, Oran E., 11 Oak Park Lane, Buford, Il. 62814
Foreman, William P., 1200 Catherine Street, Metropolis, Il. 62960
Lake, Ron, 38 Illini Drive, Taylorville, Il. 62568
Lane, Jerry I., (Lane Custom Knives), Rt. 5, Carbondale, Il. 62901
Meier, Daryal, 700 W. Walnut, Carbondale, Il. 62901
Wright, Tim, 5831 S. Blackstone, Chicago, Il. 60637

INDIANA

Birt, Sid, (Birt Custom Knives), Box 544, Bunker Hill, In. 46914
Cronk, W.N., 511 Boyd Avenue, Greenfield, In. 46140
WHW Knives, Box 7017, Fort Wayne, In. 46807

KANSAS

Smith, Jim, 1608 Joann, Wichita, Ks. 67203

KENTUCKY

Bugden, John W., 106 S. 13th Street, Murray, Ky. 42071
Root, George R., Box 6, Manchester, Ky. 40962
Clay, J.D., 4A Grayranch Road, Lloyd, Ky. 41156
Sanders, 2358 Taylor Lane, Louisville, Ky. 40205

LOUISIANA

Bagwell, Bill, Box 869, Vivian, La. 71082
Busch, Raymond A. Jr., 418 Depre Street, Mandeville, La. 70448
Callan, Peter Jr., 7813 River Road, Wagerman, La. 70094
Culpepper, John, (Pepper Crafts), 2102 Spencer Avenue, Monroe, La. 71201
Decker, G.W., 2207 Greenwell, Baton Rouge, La. 70552
Dozier, Bob, Box 58, Palmetto, La. 71358
Faucheaux, Howard, Box 206, Lereauville, La. 70552
Fitch, C.S., 1755 Laurel Street, Baton Rouge, La. 70802
Kellogg, Robert L., P.O. Box 2006, West Monroe, La. 71291
Keyes, Roger C., 8951 Jefferson Highway 128, Baton Rouge, La. 70809
LeBlanc, John, Box 81, Sulphar, La. 70001
Lenaze Emmett, 4449 Metaire, Metaire, La. 71052
Smith, Gary, (Gary's Custom Knives), 804 Carnation Avenue, Metaire, La. 70001
Vought, Frank Jr., Box 62, Plattenville, La. 70393
Wiggins, Horace, Box 152, Mansfield, La. 71502

MARYLAND

Freiling, A.J., 4082 Adams Court, Wheaton, Md. 20902
Moran, W.F., Rt. 5, Fredrick, Md. 21701

MICHIGAN

Ankrom, W.E., Box 308, Highland, Mi. 48031
Leach, Milo J., 5377 W. Grand Blanc Road, Swartz Creek, Mi. 48473
McEvoy, Harry, (Tru-Balance Knives), 2155 Tremont Boulevard, Grand Rapids, Mi.

MISSISSIPPI

Pou, Ed., 322 Cleveland Street, New Albany, Ms. 38652
Smith, John T., 6048 Ceder Drive, Southhaven, Ms. 38671

MISSOURI

Andrews, E.R. II, Box 16007, St. Louis, Mo. 63136
Barnhart, Carl, 3726 Nottingham Drive, St. Charles, Mo. 63301
Davis, W.C., R-2 S. Madison, Raymore, Mo. 64083
Graham, C.W., Box 11, Eolia, Mo. 63344
Selvey, N.H., 108 S. 11th Street, Blue Springs, Mo. 64015

MONTANA

Frank, H.H., 1 Mountain Medow Road, Whitefish, Mt. 59937
Lienenmann, L.B., 625 Grand Avenue, Billings, Mt.
Pursley, Arron, Bear Paw Rt. 6A, Big Sandy, Mt. 59520
Ruana, R.H., Box 527, Bonner, Mt. 59823

NEBRASKA

Fisher, Mike, RFD 3, Beatrice, Nb. 63810
Masek, R.L., Rt. 2, Box 180, David City, Nb. 68632

NEVADA

Hanson, Burt, 440 N. 21st, Las Vegas, Nv. 89901

NEW JERSEY

Booth, Lou, 16 Cypress Terrace, Boonton, NJ 07005
Viele, Howard J., 88 Lexington Avenue, Westwood, NJ 07645
Weber, F.E., 401 W. Clinton Street, Haledon, NJ 07508

NEW MEXICO

Backward, B.J., Box 903, Farmington, NM
Cordova, Joseph G., Rt. 1, Box 1636A, Albuquerque, NM 87105
Couchman, Don, Star Route, La Mesa, NM 88044
Karlin, Don, Box 668, Aztec, NM 87410

NEW YORK

D'Elia, Frank, 2050 Hillside Avenue, New Hyde Park, NY 11040
Kegler, Ray, (Heritage Knives), 8532 Main Street, Eden, NY 14057
Lemery, Howard, Box 98, Knoxboro, NY 13362
Marx, D.F., 40 Erie Street, Tonawanda, NY 14150
Staudinger, C.R. II, 37 Beverly Place, Utica, NY 13501

NORTH CAROLINA

Britton, G.M., Rt. 2, Box 271-B, Kinston, NC 28501
Craddock, Mike, Rt. 1, Box 202-C, Burlington, NC 27215
Fox, Paul, (Fox Knife), Box 2130, Hickory, NC 28601
Howie, David M., Box 32, Lilesville, NC 28091

OHIO

Brown, D.L., 1803 Birdie Drive, Toledo, Oh. 43615
Dagget, Dan, Rt. 1, Stewart, Oh. 45778
Flint Custom Knives, Box 9343, Olstead Falls, Oh. 44138
Franklin, Mike, Box 88, Aberdeen, Oh. 45101
Johnston, Ladow, 2322 W. Country Club Parkway, Toledo, Oh. 43614
Kovals Knives & Tomahawks, Box 14130, Columbus, Oh. 43214
Kneubuhler, Walter, (WK Knives), Box 327, Pioneer, Oh. 43554
Tice, Robert, (Star Custom Knives), 219 Park Avenue, Franklin, Oh. 45005
Tice, Ronald, (Star Custom Knives), 5958 US 22, New Holland, Oh. 43145

OKLAHOMA

Bamford, Larry, 1712 Carlisle Road, Oklahoma City, Ok. 73120
Faulconer, Ralph, Rt. 3, Frederick, Ok. 73542
Grow, Jim, 1712 Carlisle Road, Oklahoma City, Ok. 73120
Landers, Steve, 3817 NW 125th Street, Oklahoma City, Ok. 73120
Naifeh, Woody, Rt. 13, Box 380, Tulsa, Ok. 74107
Sanders, Sandy, 211 Klondike, Yukon, Ok. 73099

OREGON

Dowell, T.M., (TMD Knives), 138 St. Helens Place, Bend, Or. 97701
Drew, Frank, 729 Main Street, Klamath Falls, Or. 97601
Goddard, Wayne, 473 Durham Avenue, Eugene, Or. 97402
Fleming, Jim, Rt. 1, Box 784, Bonanza, Or. 97683
Kelly, Gary, 11485 SW Pheasant Lane, Aloha, Or. 97005
Madison, Wes, 390 Crest Drive, Eugene, Or. 97405
Maxwell, Lindsay, 2787 Olympic Warehouse Plaza 8, Springfield, Or. 97477
Overholser, W.C., 235 NE 11th Street, Newport, Or. 97365
Prouty, Ralph, 5240 SW 49th Drive, Portland, Or. 97365
Pugsley, Bill, (Gemini Knives), 1255½ W. 12th Street, Eugene, Or. 97402
Rocha, Gay, (Tinker & Rocha), General Delivery, Glide, Or. 97433
Roy, John, (JR Custom Knives), Box 191, Veneta, Or. 97487
Tinker & Rocha, General Delivery, Glide, Or. 97433
Wrench, Bob, Rt. 5, Box 768, Eugene, Or. 97402

SOUTH CAROLINA

Collins, Walter, Box 10311, Rockhill, SC 29730
Davis, Jerry, (Davis Bros. Knives), Box 793, Camden, SC 29020
Davis, John, (Davis Bros. Knives), Box 793, Camden, SC 29020
Herron, George, 920 Murrah Avenue, Aiken, SC 29801
Lee, Tommy, Rt. 2, Box 463, Gaffney, SC
Thornton, Danny, Box 334, Fort Mill, SC 29715
Wilber, W.C., 400 Lucerne Drive, Spartanburg, SC 29020

TENNESSEE

Bennett, William N., 431 W. King Street, Jackson, Tn. 38301
Corby, Harold, 1714 Branonwood Drive, Johnson City, Tn. 37601
Hales, Joe R., (Hales Knives), 1745 Dellwood, Memphis, Tn. 38127
Harwood, Oscar, 903 S. Cooper Street, Memphis, Tn. 38104
Maxwell, Gipsy, 219 Leore, Jackson, Tn. 38301
Taylor, Gary C., 137 Lana View, Kingsport, Tn. 37664
York, David C., 213 Ben Lomand Drive, McMinnville, Tn. 37110
Whitaker, Bob, 4633 Bertha Road, Memphis, Tn. 38109

TEXAS

Adair, Earl, (Silver Fox), 4714 44th Street, Dickenson, Tx. 77539
Barbee, James L., (Bar-Bee Knives), Box 1702, Fort Stockton, Tx. 97935
Bernhart, John, Box 28066, Dallas, Tx. 75228
Black, John C., 1225 Evergreen, Richardson, Tx. 75080
Blalock, Keith W. Jr., Box 18541 Serna Station, San Antonio, Tx. 78218
Bone, Ralph, 806 Avenue "J", Lubbock, Tx. 79401
Carter, Fred, 2303 Dorothy, Wichita Falls, Tx. 76306
Davenport, Steve, (Steve's Custom Knives), 301 Meyer, Alvin, Tx. 77511
Dew, Norman, 742 Nobhollow, Channelview, Tx. 77530
Dumatrait, Gene, Box 3071, Beaumont, Tx. 77704
Elder, Ray, 121 E. 11th Street, Colorado City, Tx. 79512
Fisher, Clyde, Rt. 1, Box 170-M, Victoria, Tx. 77901
Gault, Clay R., Rt. One, Box 184, Lexington, Tx. 78947
Hajovsky, Robert J. (Bob-Sky Knives), Box 21, Scotland, Tx. 76379
Harrison & Son, Box 42, Edom, Tx. 75756
Harrigan, Mike, (Silver Fox), 4717 44th Street, Dickinson, Tx. 77539
Hastings, Don, (Red River Knives), 725 S. Magnolia, Palestine, Tx. 75801
Heller, Henry, 4107 Keeler Court, Pasadena, Tx. 77503
Hueske, Chubby, 4808 Tamarisk, Bellaire, Tx. 77401
Hundley, John, 531 Grabo, San Antonio, Tx. 78215
Hunt, Jerry, 4606 Princeton, Garland, Tx. 75040
Johnson, Ruffin, 215 La Fonda, Houston, Tx. 77060
Johnson, G.W., 5426 Sweetbriar, Houston, Tx. 77034
Ludwig, Robert, 1028 Pecos Avenue, Port Arthur, Tx. 77640
Martin, Joe, Box 6552, Lubbock, Tx. 79413
Meyers, Max, 418 Jolee, Richardson, Tx. 75080
Mitchell, Bob, 511 Avenue "B", South Houston, Tx. 77587
McAlphin, Jerry, Box 7, Bullard, Tx. 75757
Nolen, J.V., (Nolen Bros. Knives), 302 Meldo Park Drive, Corpus Christi, Tx. 78411
Nolen, R.D., (Nolen Bros. Knives), Rebel Field, Mercedes, Tx. 78570
Phillips, Ken, Box 593, Brackettville, Tx. 78830
Pugh, Jim, 917 Carpenter Street, Azle, Tx. 76020
Richardson, Charles, Box 38329, Dallas, Tx. 75238
Stone, G.W., 259 Arapaho Central Park, Richardson, Tx. 75050
Vaughn, Eddie W., 1905 Virginia Drive, Grand Prairie, Tx. 75050
Weather, Ron, 4775 Memphis Street, Dallas, Tx. 75207
Weatherford, Bill, 4775 Memphis Street, Dallas, Tx. 75207
Williams, W.C., (WCW Knives), Rt. 2, Box 452, Atlanta, Tx. 75551

UTAH

Draper, H.E., Box 94, Ephriam, Ut. 84627
Johnson, Steve, 202 E. 2nd, North Manti, Ut. 84642
Shaw, David, 2009 N. 450, East Ogden, Ut. 84407
Warenski, Buster, Box 214, Richfield, Ut. 84701

VIRGINIA

Agee, Taylor, Rt. 1, Farmville, Va. 23901
Shelor, Ben A., 24 N. Battery Street, Highland Springs, Va. 23075
Tomes, R.J., 41 Greenbeiar Avenue, Hampton, Va. 23661

WASHINGTON

Chappel, Rod, (Davis Custom Knives), N. 1405 Ash, Spokane, Wa. 99201

WEST VIRGINIA

Manley, Louis W., (Manley Blade), 186 River Street, Glenville, WV 26351
Manley, Cliff, (Manley Blade), 186 River Street, Glenville, WV 26351
Schwartz, John J., 41 15th Street, Wellsburg, WV 26070
Sigman, Robert, Rt. 1, Box 212A, Liberty, WV 25124
Wilson, R.W., Box 2012, Weirton, WV 26062

WISCONSIN

Alexander, John, Jamiska Road 72, Maple, Wi. 54854
Hein, L.T., 3515 4 Mile Road, Racine, Wi. 53404
Heath, C.M., 113 Grant Street, Winnieconne, Wi. 54986

WYOMING

Grant, Larry, Box 404, Auburn, Wy. 83111

MANUFACTURERS & IMPORTERS

AAA Engineering & Mfg., P.O. Box 273, Arcadia, CA 91006
American Colonial Armament, P.O. Box F, Chicago Ridge, IL 60415
Atlanta Cutlery Corp., Box 33266 GA, Decatur, GA 30033
L.L. Bean, Inc., 215 Main St., Freeport, ME 04033
Ballard Cutlery, P.O. Box 97, Golf, IL 60092
Bosch Cutlery, P.O. Box 22064, Dallas, TX 75222
Buck Knives, Box 1267, El Cajon, CA 92022
Buckle & Blade, 150 Nassau St., New York, NY 10038
Camillus Cutlery, Main Street, Camillus, NY 13031
W.R. Case & Sons, 20 Russell Blvd., Bradford, PA 16701
Classic Arms International, 547 Merrick Rd., Lynbrook, NY 11563
Crown-Castle Ltd., 51 Bank St., Stamford, CT 06901
Custom Knifemakers Supply, P.O. Box 308, Emory, TX 75440
Duff Custommade Knives, P.O. Box 217, El Cajon, CA 92022
Ensign Company, Gunnison, UT 84634
Executek, 777 S. Central Expwy., Richardson, TX 75080
Firearms Import & Export, P.O. Box 520691, Miami, FL 33152
Gerber Legendary Blades, 14200 SW 72nd Ave., Portland, OR 97223
Gurkha Knives, 4535 Huntington Dr. South, Los Angeles, CA 90032
Gutmann Cutlery, 900 S. Columbus Ave., Mt. Vernon, NY 10550
Herder's Cutlery, Inc., 32 W. King St., Malvern, PA 19355
Heritage Custom Knives, 2895 Seneca St., Buffalo, NY 14224
Herter's, Inc., Waseca, MN 56093
Imperial Knife Co., 1776 Broadway, New York, NY 10019
Indian Ridge Traders, P.O. Box X-50, Ferndale, MI 48220
IPCO, 331 Lake Hazeltine Dr., Caska, MN 55318

Ithaca Gun Co., Terrace Hill, Ithaca, NY 14850
Jet-Aer Corp., 100 Sixth Ave., Patterson, NJ 07524
Ka-Bar Cutlery, 5777 Grant Ave., Cleveland, OH 44105
Kershaw Cutlery, 100 Foothills Rd., Lake Oswego, OR 97034
Jay Luttrull Enterprises, 26255 Walker Rd., Bend, OR 97701
Lake Knives, 904 W. England, Taylorville, IL 62568
Marble Arms Co., P.O. Box 111, Gladstone, MI 49837
Markwell Arms Co., 2414 W. Devon Ave., Chicago, IL 60645
Midwest Knife Co., 9043 S. Western, Chicago, IL 60620
Nolen Knives, Box 6216, Corpus Christi, TX 78411
Precise, 3 Chestnut St., Suffern, NY 10901
Rigid Knives, P.O. Box 460, Santee, CA 92071
A.G. Russell Co., 1705 Hiway 71 N, Springdale, AR 72764
Russell Harrington Cutlery, 44 River St., Southbridge, MA 01550
Schrade Cutlery, Coral St., Ellenville, NY 12428
Seven Seas Trading Co., P.O. Box 4284, Portland, OR 97208
Shaw-Leibowitz, Rt. 1, Box 421, New Cumberland, WV 26047
Smith & Wesson, P.O. Box 2208, Springfield, MA 01101
Throwing Knives, 4535 Huntington Dr., Los Angeles, CA 90032
Texas Tools, Brownsboro, TX 75756
Tru-Balance Knife Co., 2155 Tremont Blvd., NW, Grand Rapids, MI 49504
Unique Imports, Inc., 610 Franklin St., Alexandria, VA 22314
S. Weckman, 2711 Taylor Blvd., Louisville, KY 40208
Westbury Sales Co., 373 Maple Ave., Westbury, NY 11590
Western Cutlery, 5311 Western Ave., Boulder, CO 80301
W.C. Wilbur, 400 Lucerne Dr., Spartanburg, SC 29302
R.W. Wilson, P.O. Box 2012, Weirton, WV 26062
Wyoming Knife Corp., 115 Valley Dr., Casper, WY 82601
Utica Duxback Corp., Utica, NY 13502